POPE FRANCIS
His words during the coronavirus pandemic

STRONG IN THE FACE OF TRIBULATION

The Church in Communion:
A Sure Support in Time of Trial

Cover image
Exultet iam angelica turba caelorum, Ms Vat. Lat. 3784, f. 1r
© Vatican Apostolic Library

Photo on page 310
© Vatican News

00120 Città del Vaticano
Tel. 06.698.45780 - Fax 06.698.84716
E-mail: commerciale.lev@spc.va

Printed edition
ISBN 978-88-266-0441-1

Digital edition
ISBN 978-88-266-0420-6

www.vatican.va
www.libreriaeditricevaticana.va

Table of Contents

Appendix I

What if I can't participate in the sacraments?
How to receive the grace of the Lord when unable to participate physically in liturgical celebrations

Appendix II

The prayer of the Church in difficult times
The universality of intercession

Introduction

The grave situation in which many countries throughout the world have plunged, due to the very rapid spread of Covid-19, puts us all to the test. Unfortunately, we know that this crisis will not be resolved quickly, and that the pandemic is spreading. We are facing a state of affairs that until just a few weeks ago would have seemed unimaginable, like the premise of a science fiction film.

Everything has suddenly changed. What we previously took for granted seems to be uncertain: the way we relate with others at work; how we manage our emotions, study, recreation, prayer; even the possibility of attending Mass.

In any case, the most serious aspect is that this epidemic - like every epidemic - is not only a threat to habits formed over time. It is, above all, the cause of many deaths, of great pain, and great suffering. Thousands of people are gravely ill, thousands have died. Many families mourn their loved ones, to whom they were unable to stay close, to whom they were unable to say farewell, and who were cremated without the possibility of a funeral.

A characteristic of death in the time of Covid-19 is indeed solitude, the impossibility of having one's loved ones close by, the impossibility of receiving the Sacraments, of going to confession, of being accompanied in one's last breath by a friendly voice other than that of doctors or nurses working in hospital wards and pushed to their limits. We all owe a debt of gratitude to them, as they fight on the front line for people's lives every day. Alongside them, we must remember civil servants, those who provide strategic activities, the many volunteers who continue to help those most in need, the elderly who are alone, and the poor. Also to be remembered are the many priests, and men and women religious who share the sufferings of their people. Many of them have sacrificed their lives.

For many members of the faithful, the impossibility of participating in the liturgy and partaking of the Sacraments aggravates this condition of uncertainty, discomfort and confusion, even though the Church invites us to renew our faith in the Risen Christ, who conquered death, and made it the place of the sure encounter with the loving face of the Father. The present difficulties have stimulated the creativity and inventiveness of many priests, who by using the new means of communication, make themselves present in the life of their communities and families confined to their homes in semi-deserted cities.

The evidence of what is happening demands that we to live this time for the benefit of all, especially for those most at risk, in the solitude of our homes, hospitals and nursing homes. Of course, the questions of faith remain, for not even as believers have we been educated recently to live through such crises, to experience ecclesial communion in spite of separation and distance, without yielding to the temptation of an entirely personal devotion.

It is useful to remember that it is certainly not the first time that humanity, and Christians, have found themselves facing these types of events. Christian faith, lived daily in its essential elements, generates an outlook on reality. It provides the possibility of glimpsing the hand of a God Who is a good Father and Who has loved us so much that He sacrificed His Son for us. The Church thus bears in the treasury of her living tradition, a treasury of wisdom, of hope, the opportunity to continue to experience - in solitude or even in isolation - that we are truly "one" thanks to the action of the Holy Spirit.

This book is intended to be a little help offered to all, so as to know how to discern and experience God's closeness and tenderness in pain, in suffering, in solitude and in fear. Of course, faith does not eliminate pain; ecclesial communion does not eliminate anguish. Rather, it does illuminate reality and reveal that it is pervaded by the love and hope based not on our abilities, but on the One Who is faithful and never abandons us.

This edition is divided into three sections.

First we find the words that Pope Francis pronounced from 9 March - 18 May 2020 as he sustained the entire ecclesial community in this time of trial. They are, more or less, the daily homilies during Mass at the Casa Santa Marta and the *Angelus* and *Regina Coeli* texts and a few other messages. Listening to his words helps us reflect and hope, it makes us feel in communion with and united to Peter.

Then there is the first appendix which gathers together the indications given by the Church to continue to live and to receive the grace of the Lord, the gift of forgiveness and the Eucharist, the power of the Easter liturgies when we cannot participate physically in the Sacraments.

Finally, the second appendix, where we find the prayers and supplications for difficult moments. They are texts that originate from various ecclesial contexts and diverse historical epochs. Thus they can be a further source of sharing for the universal Church. There are prayers for the sick, for the liberation from evil, to entrust ourselves confidently to the action of the Holy Spirit.

On the cover there is an image of the Archangel Michael, who protects the Church against evil and sustains us in this difficult trial, so that this evil may not prejudice our trust in the Father and the solidarity among us, but rather become an opportunity to look at what is truly essential for our lives and to share the love received from God among us all, and in a special way with those who are most in need today.*

Andrea Tornielli

---

* This book that the Holy See's Dicastery for Communication prepared so as to be put at everyone's disposal was thought of from the beginning as having a fundamental characteristic: that it would be constantly updated in view of new discourses given by Pope Francis, and to the "rediscovery" of other treasures of our ecclesial tradition. It was therefore published daily on the site of the Vatican publishing house, Libreria Editrice Vaticana, as a free .pdf download. Now, at the end of the time in which Pope Francis presided over the live daily broadcast of the celebration of the Eucharist, many readers have suggested that it be made available in print so as to be able to keep this booklet which accompanied them as they lived through faith the first phase of the coronavirus pandemic.

Pope Francis's words*

Homilies, *Angelus, Regina Coeli* and Messages, beginning with March 9, 2020

* Collected here in chronological order are the homilies, the *Angelus* and *Regina Coeli* messages and other messages given between March 9 and May 18, 2020. These Papal discourses can be viewed on the Vatican News YouTube channel.

Monday, March 9, 2020

Holy Mass[1]

Introduction

In these days, I will offer the Mass for those who are sick as a result of this coronavirus epidemic, for the doctors, the nurses, the volunteers who help so much, the relatives, the elderly in rest homes, detainees who are locked up. Let us pray together, this week, this powerful prayer to the Lord: "Redeem me, O Lord, and have mercy on me. My foot stands on level ground" (Entrance Antiphon, *Ps* 25).

Homily - The grace of shame

The first Reading, from the Prophet Daniel (9:4-10), is a confession of sins. The people recognize that they have sinned. They acknowledge that the Lord has been faithful to us, but that "we have sinned, we have done wrong, we have acted wickedly,and have betrayed your commandments and your ordinances. We have not listened to your servants the prophets, who spoke in your name to our kings, our princes, our ancestors, and to all the people of the land" (vv. 5-6). There is a *confession* of sins, a recognition that we have sinned.

And when we prepare to receive the sacrament of Reconciliation, we must do what is called an "examination of conscience" and see what I have done before God: I

[1] Liturgy of the Word: *Dn* 9:4-10; *Psalm* 78(79); *Lk* 6:36-38.

have sinned. Recognize the sin. But this acknowledgment of sin cannot merely be an intellectual list of sins, saying "I have sinned", then I will say it to the priest and the priest will forgive me. This is not necessary, it is not the right thing to do. This would be like making a list of the things I need to do, or need to have, or that I have done badly, but which stays in the head. A *true* confession of sins must remain in the heart. To go to confession is not just saying this list to the priest, "I did this, this, this and this ...", and then I go away, I am forgiven. No, it is not this. It takes a step, a further step, which is the confession of our miseries, but from the heart; that is, that the list I have made of bad things comes down to the heart.

And this is what Daniel, the Prophet, does. "Justice, Lord, is yours; ours the look of shame" (see v. 7). When I recognize that I have sinned, that I have not prayed well, and I feel this in my heart, a sense of shame comes to us: "I am ashamed of having done this. I ask your pardon with shame". And shame for our sins is a grace; we must ask for it: "Lord, may I be ashamed". A person who has lost his shame loses his moral judgment, and loses respect for others. He is shameless. The same happens with God: "Shame belongs to us, righteousness belongs to you". Shame belongs to us. "Ours the look of shame we wear today", he. [Daniel] continues, " to our kings, our princes, our ancestors,, because we have sinned against you" (v. 8). "To the Lord our God" first he had said "justice", now he says mercy" (v. 9). When we have not only the recollection, the memory of the sins we have committed, but also the sense of shame, this touches God's heart and He responds with mercy. The journey that leads towards God's mercy consists of shame for the bad, for the evil things we have done. In this way, when I go to confession, I will say not only the list of sins, but also the feelings of confusion, of shame for having done this to a God so good, so merciful, so just.

Let us ask today for the grace of shame: to be ashamed of our sins. May the Lord grant this grace to all of us.

Tuesday, March 10, 2020

Holy Mass[2]

Introduction

Let us continue to pray together for the sick, medical personnel, all those suffering from the epidemic. Let us pray to the Lord also for our priests, so that they may have the courage to go out to the sick, bringing the power of the Word of God and the Eucharist, and accompany medical personnel, volunteers, in the work they are performing.

Homily - Sinners, but in dialogue with God

Yesterday, the Word of God taught us how to recognize our sins and to confess them, but not only with the mind, also with the heart, with a spirit of shame; shame for our sins as a most noble attitude before God. And today the Lord calls all of us sinners to dialogue with Him (see *Is* 1:10.16-20). Because sin closes us up in ourselves, it makes us hide, or hide our truth, inside. It is what happened to Adam and Eve: after sinning they hid themselves because they were ashamed; they were naked (see *Gn* 3:8-10). And the sinner, when he or she feels shame, is then tempted to hide. And the Lord calls: " 'Come now, let us talk this over, says the Lord' (*Is* 1:18); let us talk about your sin, let us talk about your situation. Do not be afraid". And He continues: "Though your sins are like scarlet, they shall

---

[2] Liturgy of the Word: *Is* 1:10, 16-20; *Psalm* 49(50); *Mt* 23:1-12.

be as white as snow; though they are red as crimson, they shall be like wool" (v. 18). "Come, because I am able to change everything", the Lord tells us. "Do not be afraid to come and speak. Be courageous even with your misery".

I am reminded of that saint who was so penitent: he prayed so much. And he always tried to give the Lord everything the Lord asked of him. But the Lord was not pleased. And one day he got a little angry with the Lord, because the saint had quite a character. And he said to the Lord, "But, Lord, I don't understand you. I give you everything, everything, and you're always dissatisfied, as if something were missing. What's missing?" "Give me your sins: that's what's missing". Have the courage to go with our misery and speak to the Lord: "Come, come, let's talk about it! Do not be afraid". "Though your sins are like scarlet, they shall be as white as snow; though they are red as crimson, they shall be like wool" (v. 18).

This is the Lord's invitation. But there is always a deception: instead of going to talk with the Lord, to pretend not to be sinners. That is why the Lord rebuked the doctors of the law (see *Mt* 23:1-12). These people do deeds "for people to see: Wearing broader phylacteries and longer tassels, like wanting to take the place of honor at banquets and the front seats in the synagogues, being greeted obsequiously in the market squares and having people call them Rabbi" (vv. 5-6). Appearance, vanity. Covering the truth of our heart with vanity. Vanity never heals! Vanity never heals. Rather, it is poisonous, and continues till it makes the heart ill, leading you to that hardness of heart that says to you: "No, do not go to the Lord, do not go. Remain alone...".

Vanity is precisely the place where we close ourselves off from the Lord's call. Instead, the invitation of the Lord is that of a father, a brother: "Come! Let's talk, let's talk. In the end I can change your life from red to white".

May this Word of the Lord encourage us. May our prayer be a true prayer: about our reality, about our sins, about our misery. He knows, He knows what we are. We know it, but our vanity always invites us to cover it up. May the Lord help us.

WEDNESDAY, MARCH 11, 2020

Holy Mass[3]

Introduction

Let us continue to pray for the sick because of this epidemic. And today, in a special way, I would like to pray for prisoners, for our brothers and our sisters who are detained in prisons. They suffer, and we must be near to them with our prayer, so that the Lord might help them, might console them in this difficult moment.

Homily - Vanity distances us from Christ's Cross

The First Reading, a passage from the prophet Jeremiah (18:18-20), is truly a prophecy of the Passion of the Lord. What do the enemies say? "Come, let us destroy him by his own tongue; let us carefully note his every word", "Let's contrive a plot against him". It does not say, "Let's conquer him, let's get rid of him", no. To make his life difficult, to torment him. It is the suffering of the prophet, but there is a prophecy of Jesus. In the Gospel (*Mt* 20:17-28), Jesus Himself talks to us about this: "We are going up to Jerusalem, and the Son of Man is about to be handed over to the chief priests and scribes. They will condemn him to death and will hand him over to the pagans to be mocked and scourged and crucified" (vv. 18-19). It is not only a death sentence: there is more than that. There is humil-

[3] Liturgy of the Word: *Jer* 18:18-20; *Psalm* 30(31); *Mt* 20:17-28.

iation, hounding. When there is the dogged persecution of a Christian, of a person, the devil is there. The devil has two styles: seduction, with worldly promises, as he wanted to do with Jesus in the desert, to seduce him, and with seduction to make him change the plan of redemption; and, if this does not work, doggedness. The devil has no half measures. His pride is so great that he tries to destroy. He destroys enjoying the destruction with dogged fury. Let us think of the persecution of so many saints, of so many Christians: their persecutors do not kill them at once, but make them suffer and try to humiliate them in all sorts of ways, to the end. We must not confuse a simple social, political and religious persecution with the dogged fury of the devil. The devil hounds in order to destroy. Let us think of Revelation: he wanted to devour the woman's child who is about to be born (see 12:4).

The two thieves who were crucified with Jesus were condemned, crucified and left to die in peace. Nobody insulted them: no one was interested. The insult was only for Jesus, against Jesus. Jesus tells the apostles that He will be condemned to death, but He will be "mocked and scourged and crucified"... They mock him.

And the way out of the devil's fury, out of this destruction, is the worldly spirit, what the mother asks for her children, the children of Zebedee (see *Mt* 20:20-21). Jesus speaks of humiliation, which is His own destiny, and right then and there they ask Him for visibility, for power. Vanity, the worldly spirit, is precisely the way the devil offers to distance onself from Christ's Cross. One's own fulfilment, careerism, worldly success: they are all non-Christian roads, they are all roads for obscuring the Cross of Jesus.

May the Lord give us the grace to know how to discern when the spirit that wants to destroy us with doggedness is present, and when the same spirit wants to console us with the appearances of the world, with vanity. But let us not forget: when there is dogged fury, there is hatred, the vengeance of the defeated devil. This is how it is until today, in the Church. Think of so many Christians, how cruelly persecuted they are. In recent days the newspapers have been talking about Asia Bibi: nine years in prison, suffering. It is the devil's dogged fury.

May the Lord give us the grace to discern the Lord's way, which is the Cross, from the way of the world, which is vanity, appearance, *maquillage*.

Thursday, March 12, 2020

Holy Mass[4]

Introduction

Let us continue to pray together in this moment of pandemic: for the sick, for family members, for parents with children at home... But above all I would like to ask you to pray for those who govern: they must make decisions, and very often decide on measures that people do not like. But it is for our own good. And very often those in authority feel lonely and misunderstood. Let us pray for our government leaders who must make decisions on these measures: may they feel accompanied by the prayer of the people.

Homily - Do not fall prey to indifference

This account of Jesus (see *Lk* 16:19-31) is very clear; it may even seem like a child's story. It is very simple. Jesus wants to bring to our attention not only a story, but the possibility that all humanity might be living like this. That we too, all of us, might be living this way.

Two men, one satisfied, who knew how to dress well, who perhaps sought out the best fashion designers of the time to dress well. He wore purple and fine linen clothes. And then, he enjoyed himself, throwing lavish banquets himself for every day. He was happy like this. He was

[4] Liturgy of the Word: *Jer* 17:5-10; *Psalm* 1; *Lk* 16:19-31.

not worried. He took some precautions, maybe some cholesterol pills because of the banquets. His life was going along well like this. He was content.

There was a poor man at his door: Lazarus was his name. The rich man knew the poor man was there, he knew it, but it seemed natural to him: "I am getting along well and this man… well, that's life, you make do". At most- the Gospel does not say it - perhaps he at times sent maybe a few crumbs. And so, the life of these two men went on. And both submitted to the law that applies to us all: to die. The rich man died, and Lazarus died. The Gospel says that Lazarus was taken to Heaven, with Abraham, into the bosom of Abraham. Of the rich man, it tells us, "He was buried". Period. And there it ended (see v. 22).

There are two things that are striking: the fact that the rich man knew that there was this poor man and that he knew his name, Lazarus. But he didn't care, it seemed natural to him. The rich man probably even carried out his business, which in the end was against the poor. He knew very clearly, he was informed of this fact. And the second thing that touches me greatly is the phrase "great abyss" (v. 26), which Abraham says to the rich man. "Between us and you there is a great abyss: we cannot communicate, we cannot pass from one side to the other" (see v. 26). It is the same abyss that was present in life between the rich man and Lazarus: the abyss did not begin there, the abyss began here.

I have thought about what this man's problem was: the problem of being very, very informed, but with a closed heart. This rich man's information did not reach his heart, he could not be moved by the tragedy of others.

He was not even able to call one of the boys who served in the kitchen and say: "Take him this, that, or the other...". The tragedy of information that doesn't penetrate the heart. This happens to us too. We all know, because we have heard it on the television news or seen it in the newspapers: how many children suffer from hunger in the world today; how many children do not have the necessary medicines; how many children cannot go to school. We know of continents affected by this tragedy: we know. "Eh, poor things...". And on we go. This information does not penetrate our heart. And many of us, many groups of men and women live in this detachment between what they think, what they know, and what they feel: the heart is detached from the mind. They are indifferent. Just as the rich man was indifferent to Lazarus's pain. There is the abyss of indifference.

On Lampedusa, when I went for the first time, this word came to mind: the globalisation of indifference. Perhaps we today, here, in Rome, are worried because it appears that the shops are closed. We have to go and buy this and that, and it seems that we can't go for a walk every day, and it seems that this...". We are worried about *our own* problems. And we forget about starving children, we forget about the poor people who are at the borders of countries, in search of freedom; these forced migrants who flee from hunger and war, and find only a wall, a wall made of iron, a wall of barbed wire, a wall that does not let them pass through. We know that this exists, but the heart does not go there, it does not penetrate. We live in indifference: indifference is the tragedy of being well-informed but not *feeling* the reality of others. This is the chasm: the chasm of indifference.

Then there is another thing that strikes us. Here we know the name of the poor man, we know it: Lazarus. Even the rich man knew it, because when he was in the underworld he asked Abraham to send Lazarus, he recognized him there: "Send Lazarus". (see v. 24). But we do not know the name of the rich man. The Gospel does not tell us what the name of this "Sir" was. He had no name. He had lost his name. He had only the adjectives of his life: rich, powerful... so many adjectives.

This is what selfishness does to us: it makes us lose our real identity, our name, and leads us to evaluate ourselves and others only in terms of adjectives. Worldliness contributes to this. We have fallen into the culture of adjectives, in which your value is what you have, what you can do, but not your name: you have lost your name. Indifference leads to this. Losing your name. We are only "the rich", we are this, we are that. We are the adjectives.

We ask the Lord today for the grace of not falling into indifference, the grace that all the information we have about human suffering might penetrate our hearts and move us to do something for others.

Friday, March 13, 2020

Holy Mass[5]

Introduction

These days we are united with the sick, the families, who are suffering as a result of this pandemic. I would also like to pray today for pastors who need to accompany the people of God during this crisis. May the Lord grant them the strength and the ability to choose the best ways to help. Drastic measures are not always good. Therefore, we pray that the Holy Spirit might grant pastoral discernment to pastors so that they perceive measures that might not leave the holy, faithful people of God alone, and so that people of God might feel accompanied by their pastors, and by the comfort of the Word of God, the Sacraments and prayer.

Homily - Let us not forget the gratuitousness of revelation

Both of the readings are a prophecy of the Passion of the Lord. Joseph is sold as a slave for twenty silver pieces, and delivered to the Gentiles (see *Gn* 37:3-4, 12-13, 17-28). And Jesus's parable which clearly speaks in symbols of the killing of the Son (see *Mt* 21:33-43, 45). This story tells of a landowner "who planted a vineyard" - the care with which he did so - "he fenced it round, dug a winepress in it and built a tower" - he did it well. "Then he leased it

[5] Liturgy of the Word: *Gn* 37:3-4, 12-13, 17-28; *Psalm* 104(105); *Mt* 21:33-43, 45.

to tenants and went abroad" (v. 33). This is God's people. The Lord chose those people; there is an election of the people. They are the chosen people. There is also a promise: "Go forth. You are my people" - a promise made to Abraham. And there is also the covenant made with the people at Sinai. The people must always keep that election in their memory - that they are a chosen people; the promise - so they always look ahead in hope; and the covenant in order to live daily in fidelity.

But what happens in this parable is that when the time came to reap the fruits, these people had forgotten that they were not the masters: "The tenants seized his servants, thrashed one, killed another, and stoned a third. Next he sent more servants to them, this time a larger number, and they dealt with them in the same way" (vv. 35-36). Jesus clearly shows here - He is speaking to the doctors of the law - how the doctors of the law treated the prophets. "Finally, he sent his son to them. 'They will respect my son,' he said. But when the tenants saw the son, they said to each other, 'This is the heir. Come on, let's kill him and take over his inheritance'" (vv. 37-38). They stole the inheritance, which belonged to another. A story of infidelity, of infidelity to their election, of infidelity to the promise, of infidelity to the covenant, which is a gift. The election, the promise and the covenant are a gift from God. Disloyalty to God's gift. Not understanding that it was a gift and taking it as though it were their possession. These people appropriated the gift. They took away the aspect as gift to turn it into their property. And the gift that is wealth, openness, blessing, was closed up, caged in a doctrine of so many laws. It was "ideologized". And so the gift lost its nature as a gift, and ended up as part of an ideology. In particular, as part of a moralistic ideology full of precepts, and indeed ridiculous as it lowers itself to sophisticated arguments for everything. They appropriated the gift.

This is the great sin. It is the sin of forgetting that God made a gift of Himself to us, that God gave us this as a gift. and, forgetting this, becoming owners. And the promise is no longer a promise, the election is no longer election, and the covenant comes to be interpreted according to "my" opinion, becoming an ideology.

Here, in this attitude, I see in the Gospel perhaps the beginning , of clericalism, which is a perversion, which always denies God's gratuitous election, God's gratuitous covenant, God's gratuitous promise. It forgets the gratuitous nature of revelation; it forgets that God manifested Himself as a gift, He made Himself a gift for us and we must give this, make others see this as a gift, not as our possession. Clericalism is not something that belongs only to these times. Rigidity is not something of these days. It already existed at Jesus's time. And then, Jesus goes ahead in explaining the parable - this is chapter 21 - He goes ahead up to chapter 23 with the condemnation, where we see God's wrath against those who take the gift as if it were a possession and reduce its richness to the ideological whims of their own mind.

Let us ask the Lord today for the grace to receive the gift as a gift, and of transmitting the gift as a gift, not as a possession, not in a sectarian way, in a rigid way, or in a clericalist way.

Saturday, March 14, 2020

Holy Mass[6]

Introduction

Let us continue to pray for those who are sick as a result of this pandemic. Today, I would like to ask for a special prayer for families, families who from one day to the next find themselves at home with their children because schools are closed for safety reasons, and have to manage a difficult situation and manage it well, with peace and also with joy. I think especially of families with members with disabilities. Welcome centers for people with disabilities are closed and the people remain in their families. Let us pray for families so that they don't lose peace at this time and that they might succeed to carry the whole family forward with strength and joy.

Homily – Living at home, but not feeling at home

We have often heard this passage from the Gospel (see *Lk* 15:1-3, 11-32). Jesus tells this parable in a special context: "The tax collectors and the sinners were all seeking the company of Jesus to hear what He had to say, and the Pharisees and the scribes complained. 'This man,' they said, 'welcomes sinners and eats with them'" (vv. 1-2). And Jesus answers them with this parable.

---

[6] Liturgy of the Word: *Mi* 7:14-15, 18-20; *Psalm* 102(103); *Lk* 15:1-3, 11-32.

What do they say? The people, the sinners, approach in silence. They do not know what to say, but their presence says many things. They wanted to listen. The doctors of the law, what do they say? They criticize. They "complained", the Gospel says, trying to eradicate the authority Jesus had with the people. This is the great accusation: "He eats with sinners, He is impure".

The parable is in part an explanation of this situation, of this problem. What do they feel? The people feel in need of salvation. The people do not know how to distinguish well, intellectually: "I need to find my Lord, who fills me". They need a guide, a shepherd. And the people approach Jesus because they see in Him a shepherd. They need to be helped to walk in life. They feel this need. The others, the doctors, feel self-sufficient: "We went to university", "I have a doctorate, no, two doctorates. I know very, very well what the law says. Actually, I know every single explanation of the law in detail". And they feel self-sufficient and they despise the people, they despise sinners: disdain for sinners.

In the parable, the same one, what do they say? The son says to the Father: "Give me the money and I'll be on my way" (see v. 12). The Father gives, but says nothing, because he is a father. Perhaps he remembered some boyish pranks he did when young, but he says nothing. A father knows how to suffer in silence. A father bides his time. He lets the bad moments pass. At times the attitude of a father is to "play the fool" in the face of his children's shortcomings. The other son rebukes the father: "You have been unjust".

And what do those in the parable feel? The boy feels the desire to "eat the world", to go beyond, to get out of the house, which perhaps he experiences as a jail. And he also has the front to say to his father, "Give me what is mine". He feels he has courage, power. What does the father feel? The father feels pain, tenderness and great love. Then when the son says those other words: "I will leave this place and go to my father" (v. 18) he finds the father who awaits him, who sees him from afar (see v. 20). A father who knows how to bide his time for his children. And what does the elder brother feel? The Gospel says: "He became angry" (v. 28), he feels this indignation. And at times being indignant is the only way these people can feel deserving.

These are the things that *are said* in this passage of the Gospel, and the things that *are felt.*

But what is the problem? The problem - let's begin with the elder brother - the problem is that he was at home, but he never understood what it meant to live at home. He did his duties, he did his work, but he did not understand what a relationship of love with his father was. That son "became angry and refused to go in" (v. 28). "But is this not my home?" he thought. The same as the doctors of the law. "There is no order, this sinner has come here and they throw a party for him. What about me?" The father tells him clearly: "My son," the father said, "you are always with me, and everything I have is yours" (v. 31). And this son did not realize this. he lived at home as if it were a hotel, without feeling that fatherliness... Many "guests" in the house of the Church feel that they are the owners! It is interesting: the father does not say a word to the son who returns from sin. He simply kisses him, embraces him and celebrates his return (see v. 20). Instead, to this [the elder] one he has to explain to enter into his heart.

His heart was protecting itself beacuse of his concepts of fatherhood, sonship, of the way to live.

I remember once a wise elderly priest - a great confessor, a missionary, a man who greatly loved the Church. He spoke of a young priest - very sure of himself, a great believer - who thought he was worth something and that he had rights in the Church. He said: "This is what I pray for: that the Lord might put a banana peel in front of him to make him slip. That would do him good". It was as if he had said - it seems like blasphemy - "It would be good for him to sin because he will need to ask for forgiveness and find the Father".

This parable tells us many things about the Lord. It is the answer to those who criticized Him because He kept the company of sinners. But even today too there are many, people of the Church, who criticize those who approach people in need, humble people, who work, even those who work for us. May the Lord give us the grace to understand what the problem is. The problem is living at home but not feeling at home, because there is no paternal or fraternal relationship; there is merely the relationship of companions at work.

Sunday, March 15, 2020

Third Sunday of Lent (A)

Holy Mass[7]

Introduction

This Lenten Sunday let us all pray together for the sick, for people who suffer. And today I would like to pray with all of you a special prayer for the people who, through their work, guarantee the functioning of society: those working in pharmacies, supermarkets, transport, policemen... We pray for all those who are working so that at this moment social life, civil life, can keep going ahead.

Homily - Addressing the Lord with our truth

The Gospel (see *Jn* 4:5-42) tells us about a dialogue, a historical dialogue. - it is not a parable, it happened - of Jesus's encounter with a woman, with a sinner.

It is the first time in the Gospel that Jesus declares His identity. And He declares it to a sinner who had the courage to tell Him the truth: "These men were not my husbands" (see vv. 16-18). And then with the same argument, she went to proclaim Jesus: "Come, see a man who told me everything I ever did. Could this be the Messiah?" (see v. 29). She did not go with theological arguments - as she perhaps wanted in the dialogue with Jesus: "On this

---

[7] Liturgy of the Word: *Ex* 17:3-7; *Psalm* 94(95); *Rm* 5:1-2, 5-8; *Jn* 4:5-42.

mountain, on the other mountain..." (see v. 20). She goes with her truth. And her truth is what sanctifies her, it justifies her. It is her truth that the Lord uses to proclaim the Gospel.

We cannot be Jesus's disciples without our own truth, that which we are. One cannot be disciple of Jesus with arguments alone: "On this mountain, on the other one...". This woman had the courage to dialogue with Jesus - because these two peoples did not dialogue with each other (see v.9); she had the courage to take interest in Jesus's proposal, in that water, because she knew she was thirsty. She had the courage to confess her weaknesses, her sins. Rather, she had the courage to use her history as a guarantee that He was a prophet. He "told me everything I ever did" (v. 29).

The Lord always wants transparent dialogue, without hiding things, without dual intentions: "I am like this". I can speak with the Lord this way, just as I am, with my own truth. Thus, from my own truth, by the power of the Holy Spirit, I find the truth: that the Lord is the Saviour, He Who came to save me and to save us.

This transparent dialogue between Jesus and the woman ends with that confession of the Messianic reality of Jesus, and with the conversion of those people [of Samaria], with that field that the Lord saw was flowering, that came to Him because it was ripe for harvest (see v. 35).

May the Lord grant us the grace to pray always with the truth, to turn to the Lord with our own truth, not with others' truth, not with truths distilled in debates: "It is true, I had five husbands. This is my truth" (see vv. 17-18).

Angelus

Dear Brothers and Sisters, Good Morning!

At this moment the Mass for the sick, doctors, nurses and volunteers, that is being celebrated by the Archbishop [Mario Delpini] in Milan's *Policlinico* (hospital) is coming to an end. The Archbishop is close to his people and also close to God in prayer. Last week's photograph of him alone on the roof of the Duomo, praying to Our Lady comes to mind. I would also like to thank all the priests, the creativity of priests. A lot of news of this creativity has been reaching me from the Region of Lombardy. It is true that Lombardy has been highly affected. There are priests who think of thousands of ways to be close to the people, so that the people do not feel abandoned; priests with apostolic zeal, who have fully understood that during this time of pandemic, one must not be like "Don Abbondio" (character from *The Betrothed*). Many thanks to you priests.

The Gospel passage from today, the Third Sunday of Lent, tells us of Jesus's meeting with a Samaritan woman (cf. *Jn* 4:5-42). He is on a journey with his disciples and takes a break near a well in Samaria. The Samaritans were considered heretics by the Jews, and were very much despised as second-class citizens. Jesus is tired, thirsty. A woman arrives to draw water and He says to her: "Give me a drink" (v. 7). Breaking every barrier, He begins a dialogue in which He reveals to the woman *the mystery of living water,* that is, of the Holy Spirit, God's gift. Indeed, in response to the woman's surprized reaction, Jesus says: "If you knew the gift of God and who is saying to you, 'Give me a drink', you would have asked him and he would have given you living water" (v. 10).

Water is the focus of this dialogue. On the one hand, water is an essential element that slakes the body's thirst and sustains life. On the other, water is a symbol of divine grace that gives eternal life. In the biblical tradition God is the source of living water: as it says in Psalms and in the Prophets: distancing oneself from God, the source of living water, and from His Law, leads to the worst drought. This is the experience of the People of Israel in the desert. During their long journey to freedom, as they were dying of thirst, they cried out against Moses and against God because there was no water. Thus, God willed Moses to make water flow from a rock, as a sign of the Providence of God, accompanying His people and giving them life (cf. *Ex* 17:1-7).

The Apostle Paul, too, interprets that rock as a symbol of Christ. He says: "And that rock was Christ" (cf. 1 *Cor* 10:4). It is the mysterious figure of His presence in the midst of the People of God on their journey. Christ, in fact, is the Temple from which, according to the prophets, flows the Holy Spirit, the living water which purifies and gives life. Whoever thirsts for salvation can draw freely from Jesus, and the Spirit will become a wellspring of full and eternal life in him/her. The promise of living water that Jesus made to the Samaritan woman becomes a reality in His Passion: from His pierced side flowed "blood and water" (*Jn* 19:34). Christ, the Lamb, immolated and risen, is the wellspring from which flows the Holy Spirit who remits sins and regenerates new life.

This gift is also the source of witness. Like the Samaritan woman, whoever personally encounters the living Jesus feels the need to talk about him to others, so that everyone might reach the point of proclaiming that Jesus "is truly the savior of the world" (*Jn* 4:42), as the woman's fellow townspeople later said. Generated to new life through Baptism, we too are called to witness the life and hope that are within us. If our quest and our thirst are thoroughly quenched in Christ, we will manifest that salvation is not found in the "things" of this world, which ultimately produce drought, but in Him who has loved us and will always love us: Jesus, our Savior, in the living water, that He offers us.

May Mary, Most Holy, help us nourish a desire for Christ, font of living water, the only one who can satisfy the thirst for life and love that we bear in our hearts.

After the Angelus

Dear brothers and sisters, Saint Peter's Square is closed during these days. Therefore, my greetings go directly to you who are connected through the means of communications. In this time of pandemic in which we find ourselves living more or less isolated, we are invited to rediscover and deepen the value of communion that unites all members of the Church. United to Christ we are never alone, but rather, we form one sole Body, with Him as the head. It is a union that is nourished by prayer and by spiritual communion in the Eucharist, a practice that is highly recommended when it is not possible to receive the Sacrament. I say this to everyone, especially to those who live alone.

I renew my closeness to all the sick and those caring for them. This extends to all the caregivers and volunteers who help those who cannot leave their homes, and those who are meeting the needs of the poorest and the homeless.

Thank you so much for all the effort that each of you is making to help during this difficult time. May the Lord bless you. May Our Lady keep you; and please do not forget to pray for me. Have a nice Sunday. Enjoy your lunch! Thank you.

Monday, March 16, 2020

Holy Mass[8]

Introduction

Let us continue to pray for the sick. I am thinking of families, who are cooped up, children who do not go to school, perhaps parents who cannot go out; some will be in quarantine. May the Lord help them to discover new ways, new expressions of love, of living together in this new situation. It is a beautiful opportunity to creatively rediscover true affection in the family. Let us pray for the family, that relationships within the family at this time may always flourish for good.

Homily - God always acts in simplicity

In both texts that today's Liturgy has us meditate on (see 2 *Kgs* 5:1-15; *Lk* 4:24-30) there is an attitude that attracts attention, a human attitude, but not a good spirit: indignation. The people of Nazareth began to listen to Jesus, they liked how He spoke, but then someone asked: "Which university did this man study at? This is the son of Mary and Joseph! This man is a carpenter! What could He possibly have to tell us?" And the people are indignant. They enter into this indignation (see *Lk* 4:28). This indignation then leads them to violence. And that Jesus, whom they admired at the beginning of the sermon, is cast out, to be thrown down from the mountain (see v. 29).

---

[8] Liturgy of the Word: 2 *Kgs* 5:1-15; *Psalm* 41(42); *Lk* 4:24-30.

Naaman too – this man Naaman, was a good man, open to faith – when the prophet sends a messenger to tell him to bathe seven times in the Jordan he is outraged. But why is that?

"'I was thinking he would be sure to come out to me, and stand there, and call on the name of the Lord his God, and wave his hand over the spot and cure the leprous part. Surely Abana and Pharpar, the rivers of Damascus, are better than any water in Israel? Could I not bathe in them and become clean?' And he turned round and went off in a rage" (2 *Kgs* 5:11-12). With indignation.

There were good people too in Nazareth. But what is there behind these good people that leads them to react indignantly? And in Nazareth, worse: violence. Both the people in the synagogue of Nazareth and Naaman thought that God manifested Himself only in the extraordinary, in things that were out of the ordinary; that God could not act through the commonalities of life, in simplicity. They despised the simple. They became indignant, they despised simple things. And our God makes us understand that He always acts in simplicity: in the simplicity of the house of Nazareth, in the simplicity of everyday work, in the simplicity of prayer... Simple things. Instead, the worldly spirit moves us towards vanity, towards appearances…

Both end in violence. Naaman, who was very educated, slams the door in the prophet's face and takes off – violence, a violent action. The people in the synagogue begin to become agitated, they get angrier and angrier. They make the decision to kill Jesus, however unconsciously, and they drive Him out to throw Him down. Indignation is an ugly temptation that leads to violence.

A few days ago, I was shown a short film, a video, from the door of a building that was in quarantine. There was a person, a young man, who wanted to go out. And the guard told him he couldn't. And he started to punch him indignantly, contemptuously. "And who are you, 'Negro', to stop me from going out?" Indignation is the attitude of the arrogant, but of the arrogant with a nasty poverty of spirit, the arrogant who live only with the illusion of being more than they really are. It is a spiritual "class", those who become indignant. Indeed, very often these people need to become indignant, to feel outraged to feel they are a someone.

This can happen to us too - "the Pharisaic scandal", theologians call it - that is, being scandalized by the simple things of God, the simplicity of the poor, the simplicity of Christians, as if to say: "But this is not God. No, no. Our God is more cultivated, wiser, more important. God cannot act in this simplicity". Outrage always leads to violence; either to physical violence or verbal violence, which kills just like the physical form.

Let us think about these two passages: the indignation of the people in the synagogue of Nazareth and Naaman's outrage, because they did not understand the simplicity of our God.

Tuesday, March 17, 2020

Holy Mass[9]

Introduction

Today I would like us to pray for the elderly who are suffering in a particular way at this moment: with great inner solitude, many times with a lot of fear. Let us pray to the Lord that He might be near our grandparents and all the elderly, that He might give strength to those who have given us wisdom, life, our story. May we also be near them with our prayer.

Homily – Asking for forgiveness implies forgiving

Jesus has just given a catechesis on the unity of brothers and sisters, and concluded it with beautiful words: "Truly I tell you that if two of you, two or three, agree about anything they ask for, it will be done for them" (see *Mt* 18:19). Unity, friendship, peace between brothers and sisters attracts God's benevolence. And Peter asks the question: "Yes, but what are we to do to the people who offend us?" "Lord, if my brother sins against me, how often must I forgive him? As many as seven times?" (v. 21). And Jesus answered with that word which means, in their language, "always": "Seventy times seven" (v. 22). One must always forgive.

---

[9] Liturgy of the Word: *Dn* 3:25, 34-43; *Psalm* 24(25); *Mt* 18:21-35.

It is not easy to forgive because our self-centered hearts are always attached to hatred, to revenge, to resentment.

We have all seen families destroyed by family hatred that is passed down from one generation to the next. Siblings who, in front of a parent's coffin do not greet each other because they are still carrying past resentments. It seems that attachment to hatred is stronger than that of love- This is precisely - let's say - the devil's "treasure". He always lurks among our grudges, among our hatreds, and makes them grow. He keeps them like that to destroy, to destroy everything. He often destroys over small things.

It is what destroyed this God who came not to condemn but to forgive. This God who is able to throw a feast for a sinner who draws near to Him and forget everything. When God forgives us, He forgets all the evil we've done. Someone has said "it's God's sickness". He doesn't have a memory. He can lose His memory in these cases. God loses his memory regarding the ugly story of so many sinners, of our sins. He forgives us and goes on. He only asks us to do the same: to learn to forgive, not to continue to bear this fruitless cross of hatred, of resentment, of "You're going to pay for this".

This teaching is neither Christian nor human. Jesus's generosity teaches us that to enter into heaven, we must forgive. Moreover, He says: "You, do you go to Mass?" "Yes." " 'But if when you go to Mass, you remember that your brother or sister has something against you, be reconciled first' (see *Mt* 5:23-4). Do not come to me with love for me in one hand and hatred for your brother or sister in the other". Consistency in love. Forgiving. Forgiving from the heart.

There are people who live by condemning people, speaking ill of people, continually harming their co-workers' reputations, and that of their neighbors, their relatives... Because they do not pardon something that was done to them, or they do not forgive something that they did not like. It seems that the wealth of the devil is this: sowing the love of non-forgiveness, living attached to non-forgiveness. Indeed, forgiveness is a condition for going to heaven.

The parable that Jesus tells us (see *Mt* 18:23-25) is very clear: forgive. May the Lord teach us this wisdom of forgiving, which is not easy. And let us do something: when we go to receive the Sacrament of Reconciliation, let us first ask ourselves: "Do I forgive?". If I feel that I do not forgive, I cannot make believe that I am asking forgiveness because I will not be forgiven. Asking forgiveness means forgiving. Both go together. They cannot be separated. Moreover, those who ask for forgiveness for themselves, like that man whose master forgives everything, but do not forgive others, end up like that man (see vv. 32-34). "So will my heavenly Father do to you, unless each of you forgives your brother from your heart" (v. 35).

May the Lord help us understand this, to lower our heads so as not to be proud but magnanimous in forgiving. At least to forgive "out of interest". Why? Yes, to forgive, because if I do not forgive, I will not be forgiven. At least this. But always forgiveness.

Wednesday, March 18, 2020

Holy Mass[10]

Introduction

Today let us pray for the deceased, for those who have died because of the virus. In particular, I would like us to pray for the medical personnel who have died in these days. They have given their lives in service to the sick.

Homily - Our God is close and asks us to be close to each other

The theme of both of today's readings is the law (see *Dt* 4:1, 5-9; *Mt* 5:17-19): the law that God gives to His people, the Law that the Lord wanted to give to us and that Jesus wished to bring to its ultimate perfection. But there is something that attracts attention: the *way* in which God gives the law. Moses says: "What great nation is there that has its gods so near as the Lord our God is to us whenever we call to him?" (*Dt* 4:7). The Lord gives the law to His people with an attitude of *closeness*. They are not the prescriptions of a governor, who may be far-off, or of a dictator... No. There is closeness. And we know through revelation that there is a paternal nearness of a father accompanying His people, giving them the gift of the law. A God who is near. Indeed, "What great nation is there that has its gods so near as the Lord our God is to us whenever we call to him?"

---

[10] Liturgy of the Word: *Dt* 4:1, 5-9; *Psalm* 147; *Mt* 5:17-19.

Our God is the God of closeness. He is a God who is near, who walks with His people. That image of the desert, in Exodus: the cloud and the column of fire to protect the people. He walks with His people. He is not a God who leaves the prescriptions of the law in writing and then goes His own way. He writes the prescriptions with His own hand on the rock. Then He gives them, hands them over to Moses. He doesn't give them and then go on His own way. He walks, He is close. "What great nation is there that has its gods so near?" It is closeness. Our God is a God of closeness.

And the first response of man, in the first pages of the Bible, consists of two attitudes of non-closeness. Our response is always to distance ourselves. We distance ourselves from God. He comes close to us and we pull away. Those first two pages. The first reaction of Adam with his wife is to hide. They hide themselves from God's closeness. They are ashamed, because they have sinned. Sin leads us to hide ourselves, to not want nearness. (see *Gn* 3:8-10). So many times we adopt a theology thinking of a God who is a judge. And so I hide myself, I am afraid. The second human reaction before this proposal of God's closeness, is to kill. To kill one's brother. "I am not my brother's keeper" (see *Gn* 4:9).

Two types of reaction that inhibit every type of nearness. Man rejects God's nearness. He wants to be in control of relationships. And relationships always bring with them some type of vulnerability. God draws near making Himself weak. And the closer He comes, the weaker He seems to be. When He comes to live among us, He makes Himself man, one of us. He makes Himself weak. He bears that weakness even unto death, the most cruel death, the death at the hands of murderers, the death of the worst sinners. God humbles Himself when He draws near. He humbles Himself to be with us, to walk with us, to help us.

The "God who is near" speaks to us of humility. He is not a "great God", no. He is nearby. He is at home. We see this in Jesus, God made man, close to us even unto death. His disciples accompany Him, He teaches them, He lovingly corrects them ... Let us think, for example, of Jesus's closeness to the anguished disciples of Emmaus: they were anguished, defeated, and He drew close to them slowly, to allow them to understand the message of life, of the resurrection (see *Lk* 24:13-32).

Our God is close and asks us to be close to each other, not to distance ourselves from one another. In this moment of crisis because of the pandemic we are experiencing, this nearness begs to be manifested more, to be seen more. Perhaps we cannot draw near physically to others because of the fear of contagion, but we can reawaken in ourselves a habit of drawing near to others through prayer, through help. There are many ways of drawing near. And why must be close to each other? Because our God is near. He wished to accompany us in life. He is the God of closeness. For this reason we are not persons in isolation. We are near to each other, because the inheritance we have received from the Lord is closeness, that is, the gesture of closeness.

Let us ask the Lord for the grace of being near to each other; *not to hide ourselves from each other*, not to wash our hands of others' problems as Cain did, no. Closeness. Proximity. Nearness. Indeed, "What great nation is there that has its gods so near as the Lord our God is to us whenever we call to him?" (*Dt* 4:7).

Thursday, March 19, 2020

Solemnity of Saint Joseph

Holy Mass[11]

Introduction

Today let us pray for our brothers and sisters who are in prison. They suffer a lot because of the uncertainty of what is happening inside the prison, They are also thinking of their families and how they are doing, if some of them are sick, wondering if they need anything... Let us be near those in prison today. They are suffering a lot during this uncertain and painful moment.

Homily - Living in the tangibility of daily life and of mystery

The Gospel (*Mt* 1:16, 18-21, 24) tells us that Joseph was a "just man", that is, a man of faith, who lived the faith. A man who could be included in the list of all those people of faith we remembered today in the Office of Readings (see *Hb* 11); those people who lived faith as the "foundation of what one hopes, as a guarantee of what cannot be seen, and the proof that cannot be seen". Joseph was a man of faith: for this reason he was "just". Not only because he believed but also because he lived this faith. He was a "just" man. He was chosen to educate a man who was true man, but who was also God. Only a

---

[11] Liturgy of the Word: *2 Sam* 7:4-5, 12-14, 16; *Psalm* 88(89); *Rm* 4:13, 16-18, 22; *Mt* 1:16, 18-21, 24.

man-God could have educated such a person, but there wasn't someone like that. The Lord chose a just man, a man of faith, a man who was capable of being a man, and also capable of speaking with God, of entering into God's mystery. This was Joseph's life: living his profession, his life as a man and entering into the mystery. A man capable of dialoguing with mystery, of interacting with the mystery of God. He was not a dreamer. He entered into the mystery with the same naturalness with which he pursued his craft, with the precision of his craft. He was able to adjust a wooden angle within a millimeter, he knew how to do it. He was able to sand down, to reduce a wooden surface by a millimeter. He was precise, but also able to enter into the mystery that he could not control.

This was Joseph's holiness: going through life, being just and professional at his job, and at the right moment, entering into the mystery. When the Gospel talks about Joseph's dreams, it enables us to understand this: he enters into the mystery.

I think of the Church, today, on this Solemnity of Saint Joseph. The members of the faithful, our bishops, our priests, our consecrated men and women, popes: Are they capable of entering into the mystery, or do they need to be in control through rules and regulations which defend them against what they cannot control? When the Church loses the possibility of entering into the mystery, she loses the ability to adore. The prayer of adoration happens only when one enters into God's mystery. Let us ask the Lord for the grace that the Church may live in the concreteness of everyday life and also in that "concreteness" of the mystery. If she cannot do so, she will be just half a Church, a pious association, going ahead by prescriptions but without a sense of adoration. Entering into the mystery is not about dreaming. Entering into the mystery is precisely this: to adore. Entering into the mystery is doing today what we will do in the future. When we will have arrived in God's presence: adore.

May the Lord grant His Church this grace.

Video message of the holy father Francis to mark the moment of prayer promoted for the whole Country by the Italian Bishops' Conference (CEI), on the feast of Saint Joseph

Dear Brothers and Sisters,

I join in this moment of prayer that the Episcopal Conference [of Italy] is promoting, as a sign of unity for the whole country.

In this unprecedented situation, in which everything seems to be uncertain, let us help each other to remain steadfast to what really matters. This is the advice I have received in so many letters from your Pastors who, in sharing such a dramatic moment, seek to sustain your hope and your faith with their word.

The Rosary is the prayer of the humble and of the saints. In its mysteries, they contemplate, along with Mary, the life of Jesus, the merciful face of the Father. O, how much we all need to be truly comforted, to feel embraced by his loving presence!

The truth of this experience is measured in our relationship with others, who at this moment, are our closest relatives. Let us be close to one another, being charitable, understanding, patient and forgiving.

Though you may be confined to your own homes, allow your hearts to expand so that it may be available and welcoming to all.

This evening we are praying together, entrusting ourselves to the intercession of St Joseph, Guardian of the Holy Family, Guardian of all our families. The carpenter of Nazareth too, experienced precariousness and bitterness. Though he worried about the future, he knew how to walk in the darkness of certain moments, always letting himself be guided by God's will without reservation.

Protect, O Holy Guardian, this our nation.

Enlighten those responsible for the common good, so that they might know – like you do – how to care for those entrusted to their responsibility.

Grant intelligence of knowledge to those seeking adequate means for the health and physical well-being of their brothers and sisters.

Sustain those who are spending themselves for those in need, even at the cost of their own safety: volunteers, nurses, doctors who are on the front lines in curing the sick.

Bless, St Joseph, the Church: beginning with her ministers, make her the sign and instrument of your light and your goodness.

Accompany, O St Joseph, our families: with your prayerful silence, create harmony between parents and their children, in a special way with the youngest.

Preserve the elderly from loneliness: grant that no one might be left in desperation from abandonment and discouragement.

Comfort those who are the most frail, *encourage* those who falter, *intercede* for the poor.

With the Virgin Mother, beg the Lord to liberate the world from every form of pandemic.

Amen.

Friday, March 20, 2020

Holy Mass[12]

Introduction

Yesterday, I received a message from a priest from Bergamo, who asks that we pray for the doctors of Bergamo, Treviglio, Brescia, Cremona, who are working at the end of their strength; they are giving their lives to help those who are ill, to save others' lives. And let us pray also for those in positions of responsibility. It is not easy for them to manage this moment and very often they suffer from being misunderstood. Whether they are doctors, hospital staff, health care volunteers or civil authorities. Right now they are pillars helping us to move forward and defend us in this crisis. Let us pray for them.

Homily - Return to God and return to the embrace of the Father

When I read or listen to this passage from the prophet Hosea, which we heard in the First Reading (see 14:2-10), which says "Return Israel, to the Lord, your God" (v. 2), "return"... When I hear it, I remember a song that Carlo Buti sang 75 years ago. The Italian families in Buenos Aires used to listen to it. They liked it a lot. "Return to your daddy. He will still sing you a lullaby". "Return." It is your daddy who tells you to return. God is your Daddy, not a judge. He is your Daddy. "Come home, listen,

[12] Liturgy of the Word: *Hos* 14:2-10; *Psalm* 80(81); *Mk* 12:28-34.

come". And that memory - I was still just a boy - leads me straight away to the father in Chapter 15 of Luke, that that father who, it says, "while he was still a long way off, ... saw him" (see v. 20), that son who had gone away with all his money and squandered it (vv. 13-14). If he sees him from a distance, it's because He was waiting for him. How many times He went up the terrace day after day, month after month, perhaps years even. He waited for His son. He saw him from afar (see v. 20). Return to your Daddy, return to your Father. He is waiting for you. It is God's tenderness that speaks to us, especially during Lent. It is the time to enter into ourselves and to remember the Father, to return to our Daddy.

"No, father, I am ashamed to return because... You know, father, I have done many things, I have done so many things wrong...". What does the Lord say? "Return, I heal their disloyalty, I will love them with all my heart, for my anger has turned from them. I will fall like dew on Israel. He shall bloom like the lily, and thrust out roots like the poplar" (see *Hos* 14:5-6). Return to your father who awaits you. The God of tenderness will heal us. He will heal us from so many of life's wounds, of the many bad things we have done. Everyone has their own!

Let us think of this: Going back to God is going back to an embrace, the Father's embrace. And let us think of that other promise that Isaiah makes: "Though your sins are like scarlet, they shall be as white as snow" (see 1:18). He is capable of transforming us, He is capable of changing our hearts, but we must make the first step: to return. It is not going to God, no. It is going back home.

And Lent always focuses on this conversion of the heart that, in the Christian way of life, takes form in the sacrament of Confession. It is the moment to... I don't know whether to say "settle accounts", I don't like that – to let God "whiten" us, to let God "purify" us, to let God embrace us.

I know that many of you go to confession before Easter so you can be right with God again. But many will say to me today: "But, Father, where can I find a priest, a confessor, when I can't leave the house? And I want to make peace with the Lord. I want Him to embrace me. I want my Daddy to embrace me... How can I do it if I can't find a priest?" Do what the Catechism says.

It is very clear. If you don't find a priest to go to confession, speak to God. He is your Father. Tell Him the truth: 'Lord. I did this and this and this. Pardon me.' Ask His forgiveness with all your heart with an Act of Contrition, and promise Him, 'afterward I will go to confession, but forgive me now.' You will return to God's grace immediately. You yourself can draw near to God's forgiveness, as the Catechism teaches us, without having a priest at hand. Think about it: this is the moment! This is the right moment, the appropriate moment. An Act of Contrition, made well. In this way our souls will become as white as snow.

It would be good if today this "Return" could echo in our ears, this "Return to your Daddy, return to your Father". He is waiting for you and will throw a feast for you.

Saturday, March 21, 2020

Holy Mass[13]

Introduction

Today I would like to remember the families who cannot leave their homes. Perhaps the only horizon they have is the balcony. And inside, the family, with the children, teenagers, parents… May they find the way to communicate well with each other, to build loving relationships in the family, and may they succeed in vanquishing the anguish of this time, together, as a family. Let us pray for the peace of families today, in this crisis, and for creativity.

Homily - With a "naked heart"

The Word of the Lord that we heard yesterday: "Return, come home" (see *Hos* 14:2); in the same book of the prophet Hosea we also find the answer: "Come, let us return to the Lord" (*Hos* 6:1). It is the answer when that "return home" touches the heart: "Let us return to the Lord: He has torn us to pieces but He will heal us. He has injured us but He will bind up our wounds … Let us acknowledge the Lord; let us press on to acknowledge Him. As surely as the sun rises, He will appear" (*Hos* 6:1, 3). The trust in the Lord is sure: "He will come to us like the winter rains, like the spring rains that water the earth" (v. 3). And with this hope, the people commence their journey to rediscover the Lord. And one of the ways, one of the methods for

[13] Liturgy of the Word: *Hos* 6:1-6; *Psalm* 50(51); *Lk* 18:9-14.

finding the Lord is prayer. Let us pray to the Lord, let us return to Him.

In the Gospel (see *Lk* 18:9, 14), Jesus teaches us *how to pray*. There are two men, a presumptuous one who goes to pray, but in order to say that he is good, like saying to God: "Look at me, I am so good: if you need anything, tell me, and I will solve your problem". He addresses God in this way. Presumptuously. Perhaps he did all the things that the Law said, he says: "I fast twice a week and give a tenth of all I get" (v. 12) ... "I am good". This reminds us also of the other two men. It reminds us of the older son in the parable of the prodigal son, when he says to the father : "I have been so good but you never throw a party for me, but he is a wretch and you celebrate for him..." Presumptuous (see *Lk* 15:29-30). The other, whose story we have heard in these days, is that rich man, the man without a name, but who was rich; incapable of making a name for himself but rich, and the misery of others did not matter to him (see *Lk* 16:19-21). These are the ones who are sure of themselves or of their money or their power.

Then there is the other, the publican. He does not go to the altar but stays at a distance. "The tax collector stood off at a distance and would not even raise his eyes to heaven, but beat his breast and prayed, 'O God be merciful to me a sinner'" (*Lk* 18:13). This also leads us to the memory of the prodigal son: he is aware of the sins he has committed, of the bad things he has done; he too beat his breast: "I shall ... go to my father and I shall say to him, 'Father, I have sinned'". Humiliation (*Lk* 15:17-19). It reminds us of the other, the beggar Lazarus, at the door of the rich man, who lived out his misery in front of the presumptuousness of that lord (see *Lk* 16:20-21). There is always this combination of people in the Gospel.

In this case, the Lord teaches us how to pray, how to approach, how we must approach the Lord: with humility. There is a beautiful image in the liturgical hymn of the feast of Saint John the Baptist. It says that the people came to the Jordan to receive baptism, "naked in soul and foot": to pray with the naked soul, unembellished, without dressing up in one's own virtues. He, we read at the beginning of the Mass, forgives all sins but needs us to show Him our sins, with our nakedness. To pray in this way, exposed, with a naked soul, without covering up, without trusting even in what I have learned about the way to pray... To pray, you and I, face to face, with a naked soul. This is what the Lord teaches us. Instead, when we go to the Lord, a bit too sure of ourselves, we fall into the presumptuousness of this man [the Pharisee], or of the elder son, or of that rich man who lacked nothing. We will have the same sureness from the other side. "I will go to the Lord ... I want to go, to be educated ... and I will speak to Him face to face, practically...". This is not the way. The way is by lowering oneself. Lowering oneself. The way is reality. And the only man who, in this parable, had understood reality, was the tax collector : "You are God and I am a sinner". This is reality. But I say that I am a sinner not with the mouth: with the heart. To feel that one is a sinner.

Let us not forget this, which the Lord teaches us: justifying oneself is arrogance, it is pride, it is exalting oneself. It is dressing oneself up as something that one is not. And the miseries remain within. The Pharisee justified himself. [Instead he needed to] Confess directly his own sins, without justifying them, without saying: "But no, I did this but it was not my fault...". The naked soul. The naked soul.

May the Lord teach us to understand this, this attitude to begin to pray. When we begin prayer with our justifications, with our certainties, it will not be a prayer:

it will be speaking to the mirror. Instead, when we begin prayer with true reality – "I am a sinner" – it is a good step towards letting the Lord look upon us. May Jesus teach us this.

Sunday, March 22, 2020

Fourth Sunday of Lent (A)

Holy Mass[14]

Introduction

In these days, we hear the news of many deaths: men and women who die alone, without being able to say goodbye to their loved ones. Let us think of them and pray for them. But also for their families, who cannot accompany their loved ones in their passing. Our special prayer is for the deceased and their relatives.

Homily – What happens when Jesus passes

This passage from the Gospel of John (see 9:1-41) speaks for itself. It is a proclamation of Jesus Christ and also a catechesis. I would like only to highlight one thing. There is a phrase of Saint Augustine that has always struck me: "I fear Christ when He passes" (*Timeo Dominum Transeuntem*). "I am afraid that Jesus will pass". "But why are you afraid of the Lord? – "I am afraid of not being aware that it is Christ, and letting Him pass by". One thing is clear: In Jesus's presence, the heart's true sentiments flourish, true attitudes emerge. It is a grace and so Augustine was afraid he might let Him pass by without realizing He was passing.

---

[14] Liturgy of the Word: *1 Sam* 16:1, 6-7, 10-13; *Psalm* 22(23); *Eph* 5:8-14; *Jn* 9:1-41.

It is clear here: He heals a blind man and a scandal ensues. Then, the best and the worst of people comes out. The blind man, the wisdom of the blind man, the way he responds is surprising. He was used to moving with his hands, he could sense danger, he could sense dangerous things that might make him slip. And he moves like a blind man. He uses clear, precise argumentation, and then he even uses irony, he permits himself this luxury.

The doctors of the Law knew all the laws, all of them, all of them. But they were stuck there. They did not understand when God was passing by. They were rigid, attached to their habits. Jesus Himself says so, in the Gospel: attached to habits. And if in order to conserve these habits, they had to commit an injustice, it wasn't a problem, because the habits said that was not justice; and that rigidity led them to commit injustices. That narrow-mindedness came out in front of Christ.

Only this. I advise you all to take the Gospel today, chapter 9 of the Gospel of John, and to read it, at home, calmly. Once, twice, to understand well what happens when Jesus passes: that the sentiments come out. To understand well what Augustine tells us: I am afraid of the Lord when He passes, that I will not realize and I will not recognize Him. And I will not convert. Do not forget: read chapter 9 of *John* once, twice, three times, taking all the time you like.

Angelus

Dear Brothers and Sisters, good morning!

At the center of the liturgy of this fourth Sunday of Lent there is the theme of *light*. The Gospel (see *Jn* 9:1-41) recounts the episode of the man blind from birth, to whom Jesus gives sight. This miraculous sign confirms Jesus's affirmation that "I am the light of the world" (v. 5), the light that brightens our darkness. Jesus is thus. He operates illumination on two levels: a physical level and a spiritual level: the blind person first receives the *sight* of the eyes and then is led to *faith* in the "Son of Man" (v. 35), that is, in Jesus. It is all a journey. Today it would be good if you were all to take a copy of the Gospel according to John, chapter nine, and read this passage: it is so good and it will do us good to read it once or twice more. The wonders that Jesus performs are not spectacular gestures, but have the purpose of leading to faith through a journey of inner transformation.

The doctors of the law - who were there, in a group - persist in not admitting the miracle, and ask the healed man insidious questions. But he disconcerts them with the power of reality: "One thing I do know. I was blind and now I see" (v. 25). Amidst the distrust and hostility of those who surround him and interrogate him, incredulous, he takes a route that leads him to gradually discover the identity of the One who opened his eyes and to confess his faith in Him. At first he considers Him a prophet (see v. 17); then he recognizes Him as one Who comes from God (see v. 33); finally he welcomes Him as the Messiah and prostrates himself before Him (see vv. 36-38). He understood that by giving him sight Jesus displayed "the works of God" (see v. 3).

May we too have this experience! With the light of faith he who was blind discovers his new identity. He is now a "new creature", able to see his life and the world around him in a new light, because he has entered into communion with Christ, he has entered into another dimension. He is no longer a beggar marginalized by the community; he is no longer a slave to blindness and prejudice. His path of enlightenment is a metaphor for the path of liberation from sin to which we are called. Sin is like a dark veil that covers our face and prevents us from clearly seeing ourselves and the world; the Lord's forgiveness takes away this blanket of shadow and darkness and gives us new light. The Lenten period that we are living is an opportune and valuable time to approach the Lord, asking for His mercy, in the different forms that Mother Church proposes to us.

The healed blind man, who now sees both with the eyes of the body and with those of the soul, is the image of every baptized person, who immersed in Grace has been pulled out of the darkness and placed in the light of faith. But it is not enough to *receive* the light, one must *become light*. Each one of us is called to receive the divine light in order to manifest it with our whole life. The first Christians, the theologians of the first centuries, used to say that the community of Christians, that is the Church, is the "mystery of the moon", because it gave light but it was not its own light, it was the light it received from Christ. We too can be "mystery of the moon": giving light received from the sun, which is Christ, the Lord. Saint Paul reminds us of this today: "Live as children of light; for the fruit of the light consists in all goodness, righteousness and truth" (*Eph* 5:8-9). The seed of new life placed in us in Baptism is like the spark of a fire, which first of all purifies us, burning the evil in our hearts, and allows us to shine and illuminate. With the light of Jesus.

May Mary Most Holy help us to imitate the blind man of the Gospel, so that we can be flooded with the light of Christ and set out with Him on the way of salvation.

After the Angelus

Dear Brothers and Sisters,

In these trying days, while humanity trembles due to the threat of the pandemic, I would like to propose to all Christians that together we lift our voices towards Heaven. I invite all the Heads of the Churches and the leaders of every Christian community, together with all Christian of the various confessions, to invoke the Almighty, the omnipotent God, to recite at the same time the prayer that Jesus, our Lord, taught us. I, therefore, invite everyone to do this several times a day, but all together, to *recite the Our Father this coming Wednesday, March 25, at noon,* all together. On that day on which many Christians recall the annunciation to the Virgin Mary of the Incarnation of the Word, may the Lord listen to the united prayer of all of His disciples who are preparing themselves to celebrate the victory of the Risen Christ.

With this same intention, this coming Friday, March 27, at 6:00pm, I will preside over a moment of prayer on the *sagrata* of Saint Peter's Basilica, before the empty square. I invite everyone to participate spiritually through the means of communication. We will listen to the Word of God, we will lift up our supplication, we will adore the Blessed Sacrament, with which at the end, I will give the

Urbi et Orbi blessing, to which will be connected the possibility of receiving the plenary indulgence.

To the pandemic caused by the virus, we want to respond with the universality of prayer, of compassion, of tenderness. Let us remain united. Let us make our closeness felt toward those persons who are the most lonely and tried. Our closeness to the doctors, the healthcare workers, nurses, volunteers... Our closeness to the authorities who must impose stringent measures, but for our own good. Our closeness to the police, to the soldiers who try always to keep order on the streets, to ensure that the things the government asks to be done for the good of all are implemented. Closeness to all.

I express my closeness to the populations of Croatia, struck this morning by an earthquake. May the Lord give them the strength and solidarity to face this calamity.

And do not forget: today, take the Gospel and read calmly, slowly, the ninth chapter of John. I will do it too. It will do us all good.

And to all I wish a blessed Sunday. Do not forget to pray for me. Enjoy your meal and *arrivederci*.

Monday, March 23, 2020

Holy Mass[15]

Introduction

Let us pray today for the people who, due to the pandemic, are starting to have economic problems, as they cannot work and all this has an effect on the family. Let us pray for people who have this problem.

Homily – We must pray with faith, perseverance and courage

This father asks for health for his son (see *Jn* 4:43-54). The Lord rebukes everyone a little, but also him: "Unless you people see signs and wonders you will never believe" (see v. 48). The official, instead of remaining silent, goes forward and says to Him, "Sir, come down before my child dies" (v. 49). And Jesus answers, "Go, your son will live" (v. 50).

It takes three things to make a true prayer. The first is *faith*: "If you have no faith…" And very often, prayer is merely oral, made using the mouth, but it does not come from the faith of the heart; or it is a weak faith… Let us think of another father, that of the possessed son, when Jesus answers: "Everything is possible for one who has faith"; how the father says clearly: "I do believe, help my unbelief!" (see *Mk* 9:23-24). Faith in prayer. Praying with faith, both when we pray outside [in a place of worship],

[15] Liturgy of the Word: *Is* 65:17-21; *Psalm* 29(30); *Jn* 4:43-54.

and when we come here, and the Lord is there: do I have faith or is it a habit? Let us be attentive in prayer: let us not fall into the habit without the awareness that the Lord is there, that I am speaking with the Lord and that He is capable of solving the problem. The first condition for a true prayer is faith.

The second condition that Jesus teaches us is *perseverance*. Some ask, but grace does not come: they do not have this perseverance, because in the end they do not need it, or they do not have faith. And Jesus Himself teaches us the parable of that man who goes to his neighbor at midnight to ask for bread: the perseverance of knocking on the door (see *Lk* 11:5-8). Or the widow, with the dishonest judge: she insists and insists and insists: it is perseverance (see *Lk* 18:1-8). Faith and perseverance go together, because if you have faith, it is sure that the Lord will grant you what you ask. And if the Lord makes you wait, knock, knock, knock: in the end the Lord will give you the grace. But He (the Lord) does not do this to make Himself sought after, or because He says it's "better to wait", no. He does it for our own good, so that we take it seriously. Take prayer seriously, not like parrots: *blah blah blah* and nothing more. Jesus Himself rebukes us: "Do not babble like the pagans, who think that they will be heard because of their many words" (see *Mt* 6:7-8). No, it is perseverance, there. It is faith.

And the third thing that God wants in prayer is *courage*. Someone might think: it takes courage to pray and to stay before the Lord? It does. The courage to stay there asking and going ahead, rather, almost - almost, I don't want to say something heretical - but almost like threatening the Lord. The courage of Moses before God, when God wanted to destroy his people and put him at the head of another people. He says: "No. I will stay with the people" (see *Ex* 32:7-14). Courage, the courage of Abraham, when he negotiates Sodom's salvation: "And if there were thirty, and if there were twenty-five, and if there were twenty…": There was courage there (see *Gn* 18:22-33). This virtue of courage is so necessary. Not only for apostolic action but also for prayer.

Faith, perseverance and courage. In these days, in which it is necessary to pray, to pray more, let us think about whether we pray in this way: with faith that the Lord can intervene, with perseverance and courage. The Lord does not let us down, He does not disappoint. He makes us wait, He takes His time, but He does not disappoint. Faith, perseverance and courage.

Tuesday, March 24, 2020

Holy Mass[16]

Introduction

I have received the news in these days, several doctors and priests have died, I don't know if there were some nurses, who were infected, who caught this disease because they were serving the sick. Let us pray for them, for their families, and I thank God for the example of heroism who give themselves in caring for the sick.

Homily - The disease of sloth and the water that regenerates us

Today's liturgy makes us reflect on water, water as a symbol of salvation, because it is a means of salvation, but water is also a means of destruction: think of the flood… But in these readings, water is for salvation.

In the first Reading (see *Ez* 47:1-9, 12), that water that leads to life, that heals the waters of the sea, a new water that heals. And in the Gospel (see *Jn* 5:1-16), the pool, that pool where the sick went, full of water, to heal themselves, because it was said that every now and then the waters moved, as if it were a river, because an angel descended from heaven to move them, and the first who threw themselves into the waters were healed. And so many sick people lay there: "In these lay a large number of ill, blind,

---

[16] Liturgy of the Word: *Ez* 47:1-9, 12; *Psalm* 45(46); *Jn* 5:1-16.

lame and crippled" (v. 3), waiting to be healed, waiting for the water to move.

There was a man there who had been ill for thirty-eight years - thirty-eight years there, waiting to be healed. This makes us think, doesn't it? It's a bit too long… because someone who wants to be healed arranges to have someone who helps him, he moves, he is quick, smart… But this man, thirty-eight years there, to the point that one doesn't know if he is ill or dead… "When Jesus saw him lying there and knew that he had been ill for a long time, He said to him, 'Do you want to be well?'". And the answer is interesting: he does not say yes, he complains. Of the illness? No. The sick man answers: "Sir, I have no one to put me into the pool when the water is stirred up; while I am on my way, someone else gets down there before me" (v. 7). Jesus says to him: "Rise, take up your mat, and walk" (v. 8). "Immediately the man became well" (v. 9).

That man's attitude makes us think. Was he sick? Yes, perhaps he had some form of paralysis, but it seems he could walk a little. But his heart was sick, his soul was sick, he was sick with pessimism, he was sick with sadness, he was sick with apathy. This is the disease the man had: "Yes, I want to live, but…", he was there. And his answer is not, "Yes, I want to be healed!" No, it was to complain: "The others arrive first, always the others". His answer to Jesus's offer to heal him is a complaint about others. And in this way, he spent thirty-eight years complaining about others. And he did nothing to heal himself.

It was a sabbath: we have heard what the doctors of the Law did (vv. 10-13). But the key is the encounter with Jesus, afterwards: "Jesus found him in the temple area and said to him, 'Look, you are well; do not sin any more, so that nothing worse may happen to you'" (v. 14). That man was in sin, not because he had done something grave, no: the sin of surviving and complaining about the life of others; the sin of sadness which is the seed of the devil, of that incapacity to make a decision about one's own life, and instead to look at the life of others so as to complain. Not to criticize them: to complain. "They go first, I am the victim of this life": complaints, they breathe complaints, these people.

If we make a comparison with the man blind from birth, which we listened to last Sunday (see *Jn* 9): with what joy, how decisively did he welcome his healing, and also with how much determination did he go to speak with the doctors of the Law! This [paralytic] merely went and informed them: "Yes, it is he". Period (see v. 15). Without engaging with life... He makes me think of many of us, of the many Christians who live in this state of apathy, incapable of doing anything but complaining about everything. And apathy is a poison, it is a fog that surrounds the soul and does not allow one to live. And it is also a drug, because if you taste it often enough, you come to like it. And you become addicted to sadness, addicted to apathy. It is like the air you breathe. And this is a rather habitual sin among us: sadness, apathy; I would not say melancholy, but it is close.

It will do us good to reread this chapter 5 of John, to understand this disease, to which we can all fall prey. Water is to save us. "But I cannot save myself" – "Why?" – "Because it is the fault of others". And I stay there for thirty-eight years.... Jesus healed me: one does not see the reaction of the others who are healed, who take their mat and dance, sing, give thanks, tell all the world! No, he just goes on. The others say to him that it should not be done, and he says, "The one who healed me said yes", and goes on his way. And then, instead of going to Jesus, to thank Him and all, he informs: "It was He". A grey life, but grey from this evil spirit that is apathy, sadness, melancholy".

Let us think, of water, of that water that is the symbol of our strength, of our life, the water that Jesus used to regenerate us: Baptism. And let us think also of ourselves, if any of us are in danger of slipping into that apathy, into that "neutral" sin: the neutral sin is this, neither white nor black, one does not know what it is. And this is a sin the devil uses to annihilate our spiritual life and also our life as people. May the Lord help us understand how bad and how evil this sin is.

Wednesday, March 25, 2020

Solemnity of the Annunciation of the Lord

Holy Mass[17]

Introduction

Today, Feast of the Incarnation of the Lord, the Daughters of Charity of Saint Vincent de Paul, who direct, who have served in the Santa Marta Dispensary for 98 years, and are here at Mass, are renewing their vows together with their sisters in every part of the world. I would like to offer the Mass today for them, for their Congregation which always works with the sick, the poorest, as it has been here for 98 years, and for all the Sisters who are working at the moment taking care of the sick and also risking their lives and giving their lives.

Homily - Faced with mystery

The evangelist Luke (see 1:26-38) was able to know about this [event] only from the account given by Our Lady. Listening to Luke, we have heard Our Lady who tells about this mystery. We are faced with mystery. Perhaps the best thing we can do now is to reread this passage, thinking that it is Our Lady who recounts it.

[rereads the text of the Gospel]

In that time, the angel Gabriel was sent by God to a city in Galilee, called Nazareth, to a virgin, betrothed to a

---

[17] Liturgy of the Word: *Is* 7:10-14; 8:10; *Psalm* 39(40); *Heb* 10:4-10; *Lk* 1:26-38.

man of the house of David, named Joseph. The virgin was called Mary. He came to her and said: "Hail, favored one! The Lord is with you". But she was greatly troubled by these words and wondered what a greeting like this might mean. The angel said to her, "Do not be afraid, Mary, for you have found favor with God. Behold, you will conceive in your womb and bear a son, and you shall name Him Jesus. He will be great and will be called Son of the Most High, and the Lord God will give Him the throne of David His father, and He will rule over the house of Jacob forever, and of His kingdom there will be no end". And Mary said to the angel, "How can this be, since I have no relations with a man?" And the angel said to her, "The Holy Spirit will come upon you, and the power of the Most High will overshadow you. Therefore the child to be born will be called holy, the Son of God. And behold, Elizabeth, your relative, has also conceived a son in her old age, and this is the sixth month for her who was called barren; for nothing will be impossible for God." And Mary said, "Behold, I am the handmaid of the Lord. May it be done to me according to your word". And the angel departed from her.

This is the mystery. And now the sisters will renew their vows.

Thursday, March 26, 2020

Holy Mass[18]

Introduction

In these days of great suffering, there is great fear. The fear of the elderly who are alone in nursing homes, or hospitals, or in their own homes, and do not know what will happen. The fear of those who do not have regular jobs and are thinking about how to feed their children. They foresee they may go hungry. The fear of many civil servants. At this moment they are working to keep society functioning and they might get sick. There is also the fear, there are the fears, of each one of us. Each one knows what their own fears are. We pray to the Lord that He might help us to trust, and to tolerate and conquer these fears.

Homily - Knowing our idols

In the first Reading there is the scene of the mutiny of the people. Moses went to the Mount to receive the Law: God gave it to him, in stone, written by His own hand. But the people were bored and flocked around Aaron, and said, "But this Moses, it's been some time that we don't know where he is, where he has gone, and we are without a leader. Give us a god who helps us to go forward". And Aaron, who later will be a priest of God - but there he

[18] Liturgy of the Word: *Ex* 32:7-14; *Psalm* 105(106); *Jn* 5:31-47.

was a priest of stupid things, of idols – said, "But yes, give me all the gold and silver you have". And they gave him everything, and he made that golden calf (see *Ex* 32:1-7).

In the Psalm, we heard God's lament: "They fashioned a calf at Horeb and worshipped an image of metal, exchanging the God who was their glory for the image of a bull that eats grass" (*Ps* 106:19-20). And here, in this moment, at the beginning of the Reading: "The Lord spoke to Moses, 'Go down now, because your people, whom you brought out of Egypt have apostasized. They have been quick to leave the way I marked out for them; they have made themselves a calf of molten metal and have worshiped it and offered it sacrifice. 'Here is your God, Israel,' they have cried, 'who brought you up from the land of Egypt!'" (*Ex* 32:7-9). A true apostasy! From the Living God to idolatry. They did not have the patience to await Moses' return: they wanted novelty, they wanted something, a liturgical show, something…

I would like to point out a few things about this. First of all, this idolatrous nostalgia of the people; in this case, they thought of the idols of Egypt, but the nostalgia to return to the idols, to return to the worst, not to know how to wait for the Living God. This nostalgia is an illness, and it is also ours. One begins to walk enthusiastically toward freedom, but then the complaints begin: "But yes, this is a difficult moment, the desert, I am thirsty, I want water, I want meat… but in Egypt we ate onions, good things, and here there aren't any…". Idolatry is always selective: it makes one think of the good things it gives, but it does not let you see the bad things. In this case, they thought about how they were at the table, with these meals that were so good, that they liked so much, but they forgot that it was the table of slavery. Idolatry is selective.

Then, another thing: idolatry makes you lose everything. Aaron, to make the calf, asked them to give him their gold and silver; but it was the gold and the silver that the Lord had given them, when He said to them, "Ask the Egyptians to lend you gold", and then they went away with the gold. It is a gift from the Lord, and with the Lord's gift they make an idol (*Ex* 11:1-9). And this is very bad. But this mechanism also happens to us: when we do things that lead us to idolatry, we become attached to things that distance us from God. We make another god with the gifts that the Lord has given us - with our intelligence, with our will, with our love, with our heart . . . We use God's very gifts to make idols.

Yes, some of you might say to me, "But I don't have idols at home. I have the Crucifix, an image of Our Lady, which are not idols..." - No, no: in your heart. And the question that we must ask today is: what is the idol you have in your heart, in my heart? That hidden escape where I feel good, where I distance myself from the Living God. And we also have an attitude, with idolatry, that is very cunning: we know how to hide the idols, like Rachel did when she fled from her father and she hid them in the camel's saddle and among the clothes. We too have concealed many idols among the clothing of our heart.

The question I would like to ask today is: what is my idol? That idol of mine, of worldliness ... Idolatry also reaches piety because they wanted the golden calf not for a circus, no, for worship: "They bowed down before it" (see *Ps* 106:19 and *Ex* 32:8). Idolatry leads you to a mistaken religiosity, rather, very often worldliness, which is idolatry, makes you change the celebration of a Sacrament into a worldly party. For example, I don't know, I think, let's think, I don't know, let us imagine a wedding celebration. You don't know if it is a Sacrament in which the newlyweds truly give everything and love each other before God, and promise to be faithful before God and receive the grace of God, or if it is a fashion show, of how this, that and the other are dressed... worldliness. It is idolatry. This is an example. Because idolatry does not stop – it always increases.

The question I would like to ask us all today, all of us, is: what are my idols? Each one has his or her own. What are my idols? Where do I hide them? May the Lord not find us at the end of our lives, and say to us: "You apostasized. You deviated from the way that I marked out for you. You prostrated yourself before an idol".

Let us ask the Lord for the grace of recognizing our own idols. And if we cannot banish them, at least to keep them in the corner...

Friday, March 27, 2020

Holy Mass[19]

Introduction

News has arrived in these days of how many people are beginning to worry in a more general way for others; they are thinking of the families who don't have enough to get by, of the elderly people who are alone, of the sick in hospital. And they are praying so that some type of help might arrive. This is a good sign. Let us thank the Lord for inspiring these sentiments in the hearts of the faithful.

Homily – The courage to keep silent

The first Reading is almost like an anticipated news report about what happened to Jesus. It is a news report in advance. It is a prophecy. It seems to be an historical description of what happened later. What did the wicked say? «Let us lie in wait for the virtuous man, since he annoys us and opposes our way of life, reproaches us for our breaches of the law and accuses us of playing false to our upbringing. Before us he stands, a reproof to our way of thinking, the very sight of him weighs our spirits down; his way of life is not like other men's. If the virtuous man is God's son, God will take his part and rescue him from the clutches of his enemies" (*Wis* 2:12). What comes to our mind is what they said to Jesus on the Cross: "If you are

---

[19] Liturgy of the Word: *Wis* 2:1, 12-22; *Psalm* 33(34); *Jn* 7:1-2, 10, 25-30.

the Son of God, come down. Let Him come to save you" (see *Mt* 27:40). And then their plan of action: let us put Him to the test "with cruelty and torture, and thus explore this gentleness of his and put his endurance to the proof. Let us condemn him to a shameful death since He will be looked after - we have His word for it" (see *Wis* 2:19). It is truly a prophecy of what happened. And the Jews sought to kill Him, the Gospel says. They even go to arrest Him, the Gospel tells us, "but because His time had not yet come no one laid a hand on Him" (*Jn* 12:30).

This prophecy is too detailed. This plan of action of these wicked people is truly one detail after another. It does not spare anything. Let us put Him to the test with violence and torments, and try His spirit of gentleness... Let us sneak up on Him... Let us lay a trap for Him [to see] if He falls... This is not simple hatred. This is not a plan of action that is bad - certainly - of one party against another. This is something else. This is called hounding: when the demon, who is always behind every type of hounding, seeks to destroy and does not spare any means. The beginning of the Book of Job comes to mind, which is prophetic regarding this. God is satisfied with the way Job lives. The devil says, "Yes, because he has everything. He has no trials! Put him to the test!" (*Job* 1:1-12; 2:4-6). So, first the devil takes away his goods, and then he takes away his health, and Job never, never distanced himself from God. But the devil, this is what he does: hounding. Always. Behind every form of hounding, the devil is there to destroy God's work. Behind an argument or an enemy, the devil might be behind it from afar, with the normal temptations. But with this type of wanting to have it in for someone, there is no doubt. The devil is present there.

This hounding is quite subtle. Let us think how the devil not only hounded Jesus, but also the persecution of Christians, how he tries most sophisticated means to lead them to apostasy, to distance themselves from God. This is, as we say in everyday conversation, this is diabolic. Yes, diabolic intelligence.

Some Bishops from one of the countries that endured an atheistic dictatorship told me about this, and, even going into the finest detail. For instance, the Monday after Easter teachers had to ask the children: "What did you eat yesterday?" And some of the children would reply, Eggs". And those who said "eggs" were followed to see if they were Christians, because in those countries they would eat eggs on Easter Sunday. Even to this point, to see, to spy, to find out where there was a Christian, in order kill him or her. This is dogged persecution. And this is the devil.

And what should one do in the moment of being hounded? There are two things to be done: to dialogue with these people is not possible because they have their own ideas, fixed ideas, which the devil has sown in their hearts. We have heard what their plan of action is. What can one do? What Jesus did: remain silent. It is striking when we read in the Gospel that before all of these accusations, to all these things, Jesus was silent. In the face of the hounding spirit, only silence, never justification. Jesus spoke, He explained. When He understood that there were no words, silence. And in silence, Jesus lived His passion. It is the silence of the just one in the face of dogged fury. This is valid even for - we can say - the little, everyday types of hounding, when someone thinks someone might be talking behind his or her back, they say things and then nothing comes out in the open... stay silent. Silence. Endure and tolerate the hounding of gossip. Gossip is even a form of hounding, social hounding. It is a type of hounding that is not as strong as this, but it is hounding to destroy the other because the person is a disturbance, a nuisance.

Let us ask the Lord for the grace to fight against the evil spirit, to dialogue when we need to dialogue, but before the spirit of hounding, to have the courage to remain silent and allow the others to speak. The same goes when facing these small forms of daily hounding that is gossip: let them speak. In silence, before God.

Extraordinary moment of prayer before Saint Peter's Basilica[20]

Homily

"When evening had come" (*Mk* 4:35). The Gospel passage we have just heard begins like this. For weeks now it has been evening. Thick darkness has gathered over our squares, our streets and our cities; it has taken over our lives, filling everything with a deafening silence and a distressing void, that stops everything as it passes by; we feel it in the air, we notice in people's gestures, their glances give them away. We find ourselves afraid and lost. Like the disciples in the Gospel we were caught off guard by an unexpected, turbulent storm. We have realized that we are on the same boat, all of us fragile and disoriented, but at the same time important and needed, all of us called to row together, each of us in need of comforting the other. On this boat... are all of us. Just like those disciples, who

[20] Liturgy of the Word: *Mk* 4:35-41.

spoke anxiously with one voice, saying "We are perishing" (v. 38), so we too have realized that we cannot go on thinking of ourselves, but only together can we do this.

It is easy to recognize ourselves in this story. What is harder to understand is Jesus's attitude. While His disciples are quite naturally alarmed and desperate, He is in the stern, in the part of the boat that sinks first. And what does he do? In spite of the tempest, He sleeps on soundly, trusting in the Father; this is the only time in the Gospels we see Jesus sleeping. When He wakes up, after calming the wind and the waters, He turns to the disciples in a reproaching voice: "Why are you afraid? Have you no faith?" (v. 40).

Let us try to understand. In what does the lack of the disciples' faith consist, as contrasted with Jesus's trust? They had not stopped believing in Him; in fact, they called on Him. But we see how they call on him: "Teacher, do you not care if we perish?" (v. 38). *Do you not care*: they think that Jesus is not interested in them, does not care about them. One of the things that hurts us and our families most when we hear it said is: "Do you not care about me?" It is a phrase that wounds and unleashes storms in our hearts. It would have shaken Jesus too. Because He, more than anyone, cares about us. Indeed, once they have called on Him, He saves His disciples from their discouragement.

The storm exposes our vulnerability and uncovers those false and superfluous certainties around which we have constructed our daily schedules, our projects, our habits and priorities. It shows us how we have allowed to become dull and feeble the very things that nourish, sustain and strengthen our lives and our communities.

The tempest lays bare all our prepackaged ideas and forgetfulness of what nourishes our people's souls; all those attempts that anaesthetize us with ways of thinking and acting that supposedly "save" us, but instead prove incapable of putting us in touch with our roots and keeping alive the memory of those who have gone before us. We deprive ourselves of the antibodies we need to confront adversity.

In this storm, the façade of those stereotypes with which we camouflaged our egos, always worrying about our image, has fallen away, uncovering once more that (blessed) common belonging, of which we cannot be deprived: our belonging as brothers and sisters.

"Why are you afraid? Have you no faith?" Lord, your word this evening strikes us and regards us, all of us. In this world, that you love more than we do, we have gone ahead at breakneck speed, feeling powerful and able to do anything. Greedy for profit, we let ourselves get caught up in things, and lured away by haste. We did not stop at your reproach to us, we were not shaken awake by wars or injustice across the world, nor did we listen to the cry of the poor or of our ailing planet. We carried on regardless, thinking we would stay healthy in a world that was sick. Now that we are in a stormy sea, we implore you: "Wake up, Lord!".

"Why are you afraid? Have you no faith?" Lord, you are calling to us, calling us to faith. Which is not so much believing that you exist, but coming to you and trusting in you. This Lent your call reverberates urgently: "Be converted!", "Return to me with all your heart" (*Joel* 2:12). You are calling on us to seize this time of trial as a time of choosing. It is not the time of your judgement, but of

our judgement: a time to choose what matters and what passes away, a time to separate what is necessary from what is not. It is a time to get our lives back on track with regard to you, Lord, and to others. We can look to so many exemplary companions for the journey, who, even though fearful, have reacted by giving their lives. This is the force of the Spirit poured out and fashioned in courageous and generous self-denial. It is the life in the Spirit that can redeem, value and demonstrate how our lives are woven together and sustained by ordinary people - often forgotten people - who do not appear in newspaper and magazine headlines nor on the grand catwalks of the latest show, but who without any doubt are in these very days writing the decisive events of our time: doctors, nurses, supermarket employees, cleaners, caregivers, providers of transport, law and order forces, volunteers, priests, religious men and women and so very many others who have understood that no one reaches salvation by themselves. In the face of so much suffering, where the authentic development of our peoples is assessed, we experience the priestly prayer of Jesus: "That they may all be one" (*Jn* 17:21). How many people every day are exercizing patience and offering hope, taking care to sow not panic but a shared responsibility. How many fathers, mothers, grandparents and teachers are showing our children, in small everyday gestures, how to face up to and navigate a crisis by adjusting their routines, lifting their gaze and fostering prayer. How many are praying, offering and interceding for the good of all. Prayer and quiet service: these are our victorious weapons.

"Why are you afraid? Have you no faith?" Faith begins when we realize we are in need of salvation. We are

not self-sufficient; by ourselves we flounder: we need the Lord, like ancient navigators needed the stars. Let us invite Jesus into the boats of our lives. Let us hand over our fears to him so that he can conquer them. Like the disciples, we will experience that with Him on board there will be no shipwreck. Because this is God's strength: turning to the good everything that happens to us, even the bad things. He brings serenity into our storms, because with God life never dies.

The Lord asks us and, in the midst of our tempest, invites us to reawaken and put into practice that solidarity and hope capable of giving strength, support and meaning to these hours when everything seems to be floundering. The Lord awakens so as to reawaken and revive our Easter faith. We have an anchor: by His cross we have been saved. We have a rudder: by His cross we have been redeemed. We have a hope: by His cross we have been healed and embraced so that nothing and no one can separate us from his redeeming love. In the midst of isolation when we are suffering from a lack of tenderness and chances to meet up, and we experience the loss of so many things, let us once again listen to the proclamation that saves us: he is risen and is living by our side. The Lord asks us from his cross to rediscover the life that awaits us, to look towards those who look to us, to strengthen, recognize and foster the grace that lives within us. Let us not quench the wavering flame (see *Is* 42:3) that never falters, and let us allow hope to be rekindled.

Embracing His cross means finding the courage to embrace all the hardships of the present time, abandoning for a moment our eagerness for power and possessions in order to make room for the creativity that only the Spirit is capable of inspiring. It means finding the courage to create spaces where everyone can recognize that they are called, and to allow new forms of hospitality, fraternity and solidarity. By His cross we have been saved in order to embrace hope and let it strengthen and sustain all measures and all possible avenues for helping us protect ourselves and others. Embracing the Lord in order to embrace hope: that is the strength of faith, which frees us from fear and gives us hope.

"Why are you afraid? Have you no faith?" Dear brothers and sisters, from this place that tells of Peter's rock-solid faith, I would like this evening to entrust all of you to the Lord, through the intercession of Mary, Health of the People and Star of the stormy Sea. From this colonnade that embraces Rome and the whole world, may God's blessing come down upon you as a consoling embrace. Lord, may you bless the world, give health to our bodies and comfort our hearts. You ask us not to be afraid. Yet our faith is weak and we are fearful. But you, Lord, will not leave us at the mercy of the storm. Tell us again: "Do not be afraid" (*Mt* 28:5). And we, together with Peter, "cast all our anxieties onto you, for you care about us" (see *1 Pt* 5:7).

Saturday, March 28, 2020

Holy Mass[21]

Introduction

In these days, in some parts of the world, we are beginning to see consequences – some consequences – of the pandemic; one is hunger. We are beginning to see people who are hungry because they cannot work; because they did not have a regular job, or due to many other circumstances. We are beginning to see the "aftermath" that will come later, but it is beginning now. We pray for the families who are beginning to find themselves in need because of the pandemic.

Homily – The People of God follow Jesus and do not tire

"Then each went to his own house" (*Jn* 7:53). After debating everyone returned to their own convictions. There is a division within the people: the people who follow Jesus and who listen to Him – they are not aware of the time spent listening to Him, for the Word of Jesus enters the heart – and the group of the Doctors of the Law who reject Jesus *a priori* because, in their opinion, He was not observing the Law. The people were divided in two camps: The people who loved Jesus and followed Him, and the group of the intellectuals of the Law, the leaders of Israel, the leaders of the people. This is clear when the guards went

---

[21] Liturgy of the Word: *Jer* 11:18-20; *Psalm* 7; *Jn* 7:40-53.

to the chief priests who asked them: "Why haven't you brought him?" And the guards answered: "There has never been anybody who has spoken like him." But the Pharisees answered them: "So, you have been led astray as well? Have any of the authorities believed in him? Any of the Pharisees? This rabble knows nothing about the Law – they are damned (*Jn* 7:45-49). And this small group of the elite, the Doctors of the Law, despise Jesus. And they also despise the people, "that crowd" which is ignorant and does not know anything. The holy, faithful People of God believe in Jesus, they follow him. And this small group of the *elite*, the doctors of the law, they separate themselves from the people and do not welcome Jesus. But why? They were illustrious, intelligent, they had studied. But they had a great defect: they had forgotten their own belonging to the people.

The people of God follow Jesus… They cannot explain why, but they follow Him. He enters their hearts and they do not get tired. Let us think of the day of the multiplication of the loaves. They were with Jesus the entire day, to the point that the Apostles say to Jesus, 'Send them away so that they can go buy something to eat' (see *Mk* 6:36). Even the Apostles distanced themselves, they did not despise the People of God, but they did not take them into consideration either. "Send them to eat". Jesus's response: "You give them something to eat" (see *Mk* 6:37). He brings them back to the people.

This division between the *elite* of the religious leaders and the people is a problem that emerged a long time ago. Let us also think of the behavior of the sons of Eli in the temple, in the Old Testament: they used the people of God. And if any of them that was a bit atheistic comes to fulfil the Law, they said: "They are superstitious". Contempt for the people, Contempt for people "who are not as educated as we who have studied, who know..." Instead, the People of God have a huge grace: the sense of knowing where the Spirit was, even though they were sinners like us, that sense of knowing the path to salvation.

The problem of the *elite*, of the *elite* clerics like these, is that they had lost the memory of their own belonging to the People of God. They had become sophisticated. They had risen to another social class. They felt authoritative. This is clericalism that we see here. "But how come - I have heard in these days - these nuns and priests who are healthy, they go to the poor to give them something to eat and they can get the coronavirus? Why don't you say to the Mother Superior not to allow the sisters to leave the house, say to the bishop not to let the priests go out! They are for the Sacraments! It is the government who needs to provide food". This is what people are saying in these days: the same theme. "These are second class people. We are the upper class and should not get our hands dirty with the poor".

So many times I think: they are good people - priests, sisters - who do not have the courage to go and serve the poor. Something is missing. It is the same thing that the Doctors of the Law were lacking. They lost their memory, they lost what Jesus felt in His heart - that He was a part of His own people. They have lost the memory of what God said to David, "I took you from the flock". They forgot the memory of their own belonging to the flock.

And so each one goes back to their own home (see *Jn* 7:35). A division. Nicodemus, he saw something and it made him restless. Maybe he was not that courageous, too diplomatic; but he was restless. He went to Jesus, he was faithful to what he could be faithful to. He tried to mediate and quoted the Law, "But surely the Law does not allow us to pass judgement on a man without giving him a hearing and discovering what he is about?" (*Jn* 7:51) They responded, but not with anything from the Law: "Are you a Galilean too? Go into the matter, and see for yourself: prophets do not come out of Galilee" (*Jn* 7:52). And so the story ended this way.

We might think even today of so many qualified men and women in God's service who are good and who go to serve the people, of many priests who do not separate themselves from the people. The other day, I saw a photograph of a priest of a mountain area, of many villages, where it snows. He brought the ostensorium in the snow to the small villages in order to give benediction. It did not matter that it was snowing or that the cold metal of the ostensorium was burning his hands. The only thing that mattered was bringing Jesus to the people.

Let us think, each one of us, what side we are on, if we are in the middle, a little indecisive, if we have the same feelings as the People of God, of the faithful People of God who can never fail: it is this *infallibilitas in credendo*. Let us think of the *elite* that detaches itself from the people of God, of that clericalism. Perhaps the advice that Paul gave to his disciple, the bishop, the young bishop, Timothy would do all of us good: "Remember your mother and your grandmother" (see 2 *Tm* 1:5). If Paul advised this it was because he knew well the danger of where this sense of *elitism* leads.

Sunday, March 29, 2020

Fifth Sunday of Lent (A)

Holy Mass[22]

Introduction

I think of the many people who are weeping: isolated people, people in quarantine, elderly people on their own, people who are hospitalized and those in therapy, parents who see that, since they have no salary, they cannot afford to feed their children. Many people are weeping. Let us too accompany them from our hearts. And it would not do us any harm to weep a little, as our Lord wept for all His people.

Homily – The Sunday of weeping

Jesus had friends. He loved them all, but He had friends with whom He had a special relationship, as one does with friends, of greater love, of greater trust… Very, very often, He stayed at the house of these siblings: Lazarus, Martha, Mary… And Jesus felt pain for the sickness and death of His friend. He arrives at the tomb and is deeply moved. He asks, very troubled: "Where have you laid him?" (see *Jn* 11:34). And Jesus breaks out in tears. Jesus, God and man, weeps. There is another time in the Gospel that says that Jesus wept: when He wept over Jerusalem (see *Lk* 19:41-42). With what tenderness Jesus weeps! He

---

[22] Liturgy of the Word: *Ez* 37:12-14; *Psalm* 129(130); *Rom* 8:8-11; *Jn* 11:1-45.

weeps from the heart. He weeps with love. He weeps with His friends who weep. Jesus's tears. Perhaps He wept at other times in his life, we do not know; certainly on the Mount of Olives. But Jesus weeps out of love, always.

He is deeply moved and very troubled, and weeps. How many times we have heard this emotion of Jesus, with that repeated phrase: "His heart was moved with compassion" (see *Mt* 9:36; *Mt* 13:14). Jesus cannot look at the people and not feel compassion. His eyes are connected with His heart. Jesus sees with His eyes, but He sees with His heart and is capable of weeping.

Today, faced with a world that suffers greatly, many people who suffer the consequences of this pandemic, I wonder: Am I capable of weeping, as Jesus would certainly have done and does now? Is my heart like Jesus's? And if it is too hard, [even if] I can speak and do good in order to help, if my heart is not entering in and I am not capable of weeping, ask the Lord for this grace: Lord, that I might weep with You, weep with your people who are suffering right now. Many are weeping today. And we, from this altar, from this sacrifice of Jesus, of Jesus who was not ashamed of weeping, let us ask for the grace to weep. May today be for everyone like a Sunday of tears.

Angelus

Dear Brothers and Sisters, good morning!

The Gospel passage of this fifth Sunday of Lent is that of the resurrection of Lazarus (see *Jn* 11:1-45). Lazarus was the brother of Martha and Mary; they were good friends of Jesus. When He arrives in Bethany, Lazarus has already been dead for four days; Martha runs towards the Master and says to Him: "If you had been here, my brother would not have died!" (v. 21). Jesus replies to her: "Your brother will rise again" (v. 23) and adds: "I am the resurrection and the life. The one who believes in me will live, even though they die" (v. 25). Jesus makes Himself seen as the Lord of life, He Who is capable of giving life even to the dead. Then Mary and other people arrive, all in tears, and so Jesus - the Gospel says - "was deeply moved in spirit and troubled ... Jesus wept" (vv. 33, 35). With this turmoil in his heart, He has the tomb opened and cries aloud: "Lazarus, come out!" (v. 43). And Lazarus emerges with "his hands and feet wrapped with strips of linen, and a cloth around his face" (v. 44).

Here we are able to touch with our hand the fact that God is life and gives life, yet takes on the drama of death. Jesus could have avoided the death of His friend Lazarus, but He wanted to share in our pain for the death of people dear to us, and above all He wished to demonstrate God's dominion over death. In this Gospel passage we see that man's faith and the omnipotence of God, of God's love seek each other and finally meet. It is like a dual street: the faith of man and the omnipotence of God's love that seek each other and finally meet. We see this in the cry of Martha and Mary, and all of us with them: "If you had been here!". And God's answer is not a speech, no, God's answer to the problem of death is Jesus: "I am the resurrection and the life"... have faith. Amid grief, continue to have faith, even when it seems that death has won. Take away the stone from your heart! Let the Word of God restore life where there is death" .

Today, too, Jesus repeats to us: "Take away the stone". God did not create us for the tomb, He created us for life, beautiful, good, joyful. But "through the devil's envy death entered the world, and those who belong to his company experience it" (*Wis* 2:24) says the Book of Wisdom, and Jesus Christ came to free us from its bonds.

Therefore, we are called to take away the stones of all that smacks of death: for example, the hypocrisy with which faith is lived, is death; the destructive criticism of others, is death; offence, slander, is death; the marginalisation of the poor, is death. The Lord asks us to take away these stones from our hearts, and life will then flourish again around us. Christ lives, and he who welcomes Him and follows Him comes into contact with life. Without Christ, or outside of Christ, not only is life not present, but one falls back into death.

The resurrection of Lazarus is also a sign of the regeneration that takes place in the believer through Baptism, with full integration with the Paschal Mystery of Christ. Through the action and power of the Holy Spirit, the Christian is a person who journeys in life as a new creature: a creature for life and that goes towards life.

May the Virgin Mary help us to be compassionate like her Son Jesus, Who made our pain His own. May each of us be close to those who are in difficulty, becoming for them a reflection of God's love and tenderness, which liberates from death and makes life victorious.

After the Angelus

Dear Brothers and Sisters,

In these past days, the Secretary General of the United Nations launched an appeal for an "immediate global ceasefire in all corners of the world", invoking the current Covid-19 crisis, which does not recognize borders. An appeal for a total ceasefire.

I myself join those who have welcomed this appeal and I invite everyone to follow it up by ceasing any form of hostility, promoting the creation of humanitarian aid routes, openness to diplomacy, and attentiveness to those who find themselves in situations of grave vulnerability.

May our joint fight against the pandemic bring everyone to recognize the great need to reinforce brotherly and sisterly bonds as members of one human family. In particular, may it inspire a renewed commitment to overcome rivalries in the leaders of nations and those parties involved. Conflicts are not resolved through war! Antagonism and differences must be overcome through dialogue and a constructive search for peace.

In this moment my thoughts turn in a special way to all those people who suffer the vulnerability of being compelled to live in a group: rest homes, barracks... In particular I would like to mention those in prison. I read an official note of the Commission for Human Rights which talks about the problem of overcrowded prisons, which could become a tragedy. I ask the authorities to be sensitive to this serious problem and to take the necessary measures to avoid future tragedies.

I wish everyone a blessed Sunday. Please, do not forget to pray for me; I will do so for you. Enjoy your meal, and *arrivederci*.

Monday, March 30, 2020

Holy Mass[23]

Introduction

Let us pray today for the many people who are not succeeding in coping and remain in fear because of the pandemic. May the Lord help them to arise, to have the strength to cope for the good of society and the entire community.

Homily – Trust in God's mercy

In the Responsorial Psalm we recited the prayer: "The Lord is my shepherd; there is nothing I shall want; Fresh and green are the pastures where He gives me repose. Near restful waters He leads me, to revive my drooping spirit. He guides me along the right path; He is true to His name. If I should walk in the valley of darkness no evil would I fear. You are there with your crook and your staff; with these you give me comfort" (*Ps* 23:1-4).

This is the experience of the two women, whose story we read in the two Readings. An innocent woman, falsely accused, calumniated, and a sinful woman. Both of them condemned to death. The innocent and the sinful. The Fathers of the Church saw a figure of the Church in these women: holy but with sinful children. They would

---

[23] Liturgy of the Word: *Dn* 13:1-9, 15-17, 19-30, 33-62; *Psalm* 22(23); *Jn* 8:1-11.

use a beautiful Latin expression: the Church is the '*casta meretrix*' – the holy Church with her sinful children. Both women were desperate, humanly desperate. Susanna trusts in the Lord.

There are also two groups of people, of men; both groups had positions in the church: the judges and the Doctors of the Law. They were not ecclesiastics but they were at the service of the Church, in the tribunal and in the teaching of the Law. Different. Those who accused Susanna were corrupt: the corrupt judge, the emblematic figure in history. Also in the Gospel, Jesus takes up, in the parable of the persistent widow, the corrupt judge who did not believe in God and did not care about others. The corrupt. The Doctors of the Law were not corrupt, but hypocrites.

And these women, one fell into the hands of hypocrites, the other into the hands of the corrupt. There was no way out. "If I should walk in the valley of darkness no evil would I fear. You are there with your crook and your staff; with these you give me comfort" (*Ps* 23:4). Both women were in a valley of darkness, they were heading there: a valley of darkness, toward death. The first, explicitly entrusts herself to the Lord, and the Lord intervenes. The second, poor woman, knows she is guilty. She is ashamed in front of all the people – because there were people present in both situations. The Gospel does not say it, but surely she was praying inside, asking for some type of help.

What does the Lord do with these people? He saves the innocent woman, he does her justice. He forgives the sinful woman. He condemns the corrupt judges. He helps the hypocrites convert themselves and before other people Jesus says: "Really? Let him who is without sin among you be the first to throw a stone" (see *Jn* 8:7), and one by one they went away. The Apostle John says, with a touch of irony: "When they heard this, they went away one by one beginning with the eldest" (*Jn* 8:9). He allows a time in which they can repent. He does not forgive the corrupt ones, simply because the corrupt person is incapable of asking for forgiveness, he has gone beyond that point. He is tired… no, it is not that he is tired, but it is that he is not capable. Corruption has taken away from him that capacity that all of us have to be ashamed, to ask for forgiveness. No, those who are corrupt are sure of themselves, they go ahead and destroy and continue to exploit people such as this woman, everything, everything… they keep going. They put themselves in place of God.

The Lord responds to the women. He frees Susanna from the corrupt men, He makes her go forward. To the other: "Neither do I condemn you. Go, and sin no more" (*Jn* 8:11). He allows her to go. And [He does] this in front of the people. In the first case they praise God, in the second case the people learn. They learn about God's mercy.

Each one of us has our own story. Each one of us has our own sins. And if we do not remember, think about them: we will find them. Thank God if you find them, because if you do not find them, you are corrupt. Each one of us has his or her own sins. Let us look to the Lord, who does justice, but who is extremely merciful. Let us not be ashamed to be in the Church: let us be ashamed of being sinners. The Church is Mother to all. Let us thank God that we are not corrupt, that we are sinners. May each one of us, seeing how Jesus acted in these cases, entrust ourselves to God's mercy and pray, trusting in God's mercy, asking for forgiveness because God "guides me along the right path; He is true to His name. If I should walk in the valley of darkness no evil would I fear. You are there with your crook and your staff; with these you give me comfort." (*Ps* 23:3-4).

Tuesday, March 31, 2020

Holy Mass[24]

Introduction

We pray today for those who are homeless, at this moment in which everyone is supposed to be at home. May society, men and women, be aware of this situation and help them, and may the Church welcome them.

Homily – Look at the crucifix in the light of redemption

A serpent is certainly not a friendly animal: it is always associated with evil. Even in revelation, the serpent is specifically the animal that the devil uses in order to cause sin. In the Book of Revelation the devil is called the "ancient serpent", the one who from the beginning bites, poisons, destroys, kills. This is why it cannot succeed. If you want to succeed as one who proposes beautiful things, these are fantasies: we believe in them and so we sin. This is what happened to the people of Israel: they could no longer put up with the journey. They were tired. And the people spoke against God and Moses. It is always the same music. "Why have you brought us up out of Egypt to die in the desert? Here there is no bread and no water, and we loathe this worthless food, this manna." (see *Num* 21: 4-5). And their imagination - as we have read in the past days - always returned to Egypt: "We were doing well

---

[24] Liturgy of the Word: *Num* 21:4-9; *Psalm* 101(102); *Jn* 8:21-30.

there. We ate well". It also seems that the Lord could not bear His people at that moment. He got angry. The wrath of God is seen at times. And so, "the Lord sent among the people saraph serpents, which bit the people so that many Israelites died" (*Num* 21:5). At that time the serpent was always the image of evil. In seeing the serpents, the people saw their sin, what they had done wrong. They went to Moses and said: "We have sinned in complaining against the Lord and you. Pray the Lord to take the serpents from us" (*Num* 21:7). They repent. This is the story in the desert. Moses prayed for the people and the Lord said to Moses: "Build a serpent and set it on a pole. Every one who is bitten, when he sees it, shall live" (*Num* 21:8).

I wonder is this not idolatry? The serpent is there, an idol which gives me health... It cannot be understood. It cannot be understood logically, because it is a prophecy, it is a proclamation of what will happen. Because we have also heard a similar prophecy in the Gospel: "When you have lifted up the Son of a man, then you will know that I Am and that I do nothing on my own" (*Jn* 8:28) Jesus lifted up: on the cross. Moses made a serpent and set it on a pole. Jesus will be lifted up like the serpent to bring salvation. But the core of the prophecy is that Jesus made Himself into sin for us. He did not sin; He made Himself sin. As Saint Peter says in his letter, "He bore all of our sins in Himself" (see *1 Pt* 2:24) And so, when we gaze on the crucifix, we think about the Lord who suffers, and all of that is true. But let us pause a moment in order to arrive at the center of that truth: at this moment You seem to be the greatest sinner. You made Yourself sin. He took upon Himself all of our sins, He annihilated Himself. The cross, it is true, is a torture: there was a vendetta by the doctors of the law who did not want Him. All of that is true. But the truth that comes from God is that He came into the world to take our own sins upon Himself to the point of making Himself into sin. All sin. Our sins are there."

We need to make it a habit of looking at the crucifix in this light, which is the truest, it is the light of redemption. In Jesus made sin we see the utter defeat of Christ. He did not pretend to die, He did not pretend to suffer, alone, abandoned… "Father, why have you forsaken me?" (see *Mt* 27:46; *Mk* 15:34). A serpent: I am lifted up like a serpent, like that which is all sin.

It is not easy to understand this and if we think about it, we will never arrive at a conclusion. We can only contemplate, pray, and give thanks.

Wednesday, April 1, 2020

Holy Mass[25]

Introduction

Today I would like to pray for all those who work in the media, who are working to communicate, today, so that people are not isolated; for the education of children, to help us to bear this time of isolation.

Homily – Remain in the Lord

In these days, the Church has us listen to the eighth chapter of John. There is a heated discussion between Jesus and the doctors of the Law. Above all, He is trying to reveal His true identity: John tries to bring us close to this argument to clarify the identity both of Jesus and of the doctors. Jesus backs them into a corner, making them see their own contradictions. In the end they find no way out other than to insult. It is one of the saddest pages, it is a blasphemy. They insult Our Lady. But speaking of identity, Jesus speaks to the Jews who had believed in Him, advising them, "If you make my word your home you will indeed be my disciples" (*Jn* 8:31). He returns to that word very dear to the Lord, which He will repeat several times, and then at the Last Supper: abide with me. Stay with the Lord. Abide with the Lord. He does not say, "Study well, and learn all the arguments well": that is taken for grant-

---

[25] Liturgy of the Word: *Dn* 3:14-20, 46-50, 91-92, 95; *Dn* 3:52-56; *Jn* 8:31-42.

ed. He goes to the most important thing, that which is most dangerous in life if we don't do it: to remain. "Hold to my teaching", remain in my word (*Jn* 3:31). And those who hold to the word of Jesus have their own Christian identity. And what is it? "You are really my disciples" (*Jn* 8:31). The Christian identity is not an ID card that says, "I am a Christian": no. It is discipleship. If you abide in the Lord, in the Word of the Lord, in the life of the Lord, you will be a disciple. If you do not remain, you will be one who sympathizes with the doctrine, who follows Jesus as a man who did a lot of good, who is very good, who has the right values... but discipleship is the true identity of Christians.

And it will be discipleship that gives us freedom: the disciple is a free person because he or she remains in the Lord. And to abide in the Lord, to remain in the Lord, what does it mean? Letting oneself be guided by the Holy Spirit. A disciple is a person who allows him or herself to be guided by the Spirit, and is therefore a person who is rooted in the tradition but can embrace the new, a free person. Free. Never subject to ideology, to doctrine within the Christian life, doctrine that can be disputed. He or she remains in the Lord, and is inspired by the Spirit. When we sing to the Spirit, we say that He dwells in the soul (see *Inno Veni, Sanctae Spiritus*), that dwells in us. But this is true only if we remain in the Lord.

I ask the Lord the grace that He might allow us to know the wisdom to remain in Him and to know that familiarity with the Spirit: the Holy Spirit gives us freedom, and this is an anointing. To remain in the Lord is to be a disciple, and a disciple is anointed, one who is anointed by the Spirit, who has received the anointing of the Spirit and carries it forward. This is the way that Jesus makes us see, the path of freedom and also of life. And discipleship is the anointing received by those who remain in the Lord.

May the Lord make us understand this. It is not easy. Even the doctors did not understand it. It cannot be understood only with the head: it is understood with the mind and the heart, this wisdom of the anointing of the Holy Spirit which makes us disciples.

Thursday, April 2, 2020

Holy Mass[26]

Introduction

In these days of pain and sadness, many hidden problems are coming to the fore. In the newspaper today, there is a photo that touches the heart: many homeless people in a city, huddling in a parking lot, under observation... There are so many homeless people today. Let us ask Mother Teresa of Calcutta to awaken in us a sense of closeness to the many people, such as the homeless, who in society, in normal life, live hidden from view but whom we see in this way in this moment of crisis.

Homily – The three dimensions of Christian life: election, promise, covenant

"The Lord remembers His covenant forever". We repeated this in the Responsorial Psalm (see *Ps* 105:8). The Lord does not forget. He never forgets. Yes, there is only one case in which He forgets: when He forgives sins. After forgiving He loses His memory, He does not remember the sins. In other cases God does not forget. His fidelity is memory. His fidelity with His people. His fidelity with Abraham is a memory of the promise He had made. God chose Abraham to take a certain road. Abraham was chosen, he was chosen. God chose him. Then in that election

---

[26] Liturgy of the Word: *Gn* 17:3-9; *Psalm* 104(105); *Jn* 8:51-59.

He promised him an inheritance and today, in the passage of the book of Genesis, there is another step. "As for me, this is my covenant with you" (*Gn* 17:4). A covenant. A covenant that makes him see his fruitfulness in the future: "You shall become the father of a multitude of nations" (17:4). The election, the promise and the covenant are the three dimensions of the life of faith, the three dimensions of Christian life. Each one of us has been chosen. No-one chooses to be Christian among the possibilities that the religious "market" offers. He or she has been chosen. We are Christians because we have been chosen. In this election there is a promise, there is the promise of hope, and its sign is fruitfulness: Abraham will be the father of a multitude of nations... you will be fruitful in faith (see 17:5-6). Your faith will flourish in works, in good deeds, in works of fruitfulness too, a fruitful faith. But you must - the third step - observe the covenant with me (see 17:9). And the alliance is fidelity, being faithful. We have been chosen, the Lord has made a promise to us, and now He asks for a covenant. A covenant of fidelity. Jesus says that Abraham exalted with joy thinking, seeing his day, the day of great fruitfulness, that son of his - Jesus was a son of Abraham (see *Jn* 8:56) - who came to remake creation, which is more difficult than making it, the liturgy says . He came to redeem our sins, to free us. A Christian is a Christian not because he can show you his baptismal certificate: the baptismal certificate is just a piece of paper. You are Christian if you say yes to the Lord's choice of you, if you follow the promises the Lord has made, and you live the covenant with the Lord: this is Christian life. The sins on the way are always against these three dimensions: not accepting one's election, and so we follow many idols and many things that are not of God. Not accepting hope in the promise; which is looking far away to the promise, greeting the promises from afar, as the letter to the Hebrews says (see *Heb* 6:12; 8:6), and wanting the promises to be today with the little idols we make; and forgetting the covenant, living without the covenant, as if we were without the covenant. Fruitfulness and joy, that joy of Abraham who saw Jesus's day and was filled with joy (see *Jn* 8:56). This is the revelation that today the Word of God gives us regarding our Christian existence. May it be like that of our Father: aware of being chosen, joyful to go toward a promise, and faithful in fulfilling the covenant.

Friday, April 3, 2020

Holy Mass[27]

Introduction

There are people who are beginning now to think about the aftermath: the aftermath of the pandemic. Of all the problems that will arise: problems of poverty, work, hunger… Let us pray for all of the people who help today, but also think of tomorrow, to help us all.

Homily – Our Lady of Sorrows, mother and disciple

On this Passion Friday, the Church recalls the sorrows of Mary, Our Lady of Sorrows. This veneration of the people of God has existed for centuries. Hymns have been written in honor of Our Lady of Sorrows: she was at the foot of the cross and they contemplate her there, suffering. Christian piety has collected Our Lady's sorrows and speaks of the "seven sorrows". The first, just forty days after the birth of Jesus, is Simeon's prophecy that speaks of a sword that will pierce her heart (see *Lk* 2:35). The second sorrow is the flight to Egypt to save her Son's life (see *Mt* 2:13-23). The third sorrow, those three days of anguish when the boy remained in the temple (see *Lk* 2:41-50). The fourth sorrow, when Our Lady meets Jesus on the way to Calvary (see *Jn* 19:25). The fifth sorrow of Our Lady is the death of Jesus, seeing her son there, crucified, naked, dy-

[27] Liturgy of the Word: *Jer* 20:10-13; *Psalm* 17(18); *Jn* 10:31-42.

ing. The sixth sorrow, Jesus's descent from the cross, dead, when she takes Him in her arms as she held Him in her arms more than thirty years before in Bethlehem. The seventh sorrow is Jesus's burial. Thus, Christian piety follows this path of Our Lady who accompanies Jesus. It is good for me, late in the evening, when I pray the Angelus, to pray these seven sorrows as a remembrance of the Mother of the Church, how the Mother of the Church gave birth to us all with so much pain.

Our Lady never asked anything for herself, never. Yes, for others: let us think of Cana, when she goes to speak with Jesus. Never did she say: "I am the mother, look at me: I will be the queen mother". She never said it. She never asked anything important for herself within the apostolic college. She agrees simply to be a Mother. She accompanied Jesus like a disciple, because the Gospel shows that she followed Jesus: with her friends, pious women, she followed Jesus, she listened to Jesus. One time someone recognized her: "Ah, here is the mother". "Your mother is here" (see *Mk* 3:31) ... She followed Jesus. All the way to Calvary. And there, on her feet... surely, the people would have said: "But, poor woman, how she must be suffering", and the evil ones surely would have said: "But, she is guilty too, because if she had brought Him up well he would not have ended up this way". She was there, with the Son, with the Son's humiliation.

Honor Our Lady and say: "This is my Mother", because she is a Mother. And this is the title she received from Jesus, right there, at the moment of the Cross (see *Jn* 19:26-27). Your *children*, you are *Mother*. He did not make her prime minister or give her "functional" titles. Only "Mother". And then, the Acts of the Apostles show her in prayer with the apostles as Mother (see *Acts* 1:14). Our Lady did not want to take away any title from Jesus; she received the gift of being His Mother and the duty to accompany us as Mother, to be our Mother. She did not ask for herself to be a quasi-redeemer or a co-redeemer: no. There is only one Redeemer and this title cannot be duplicated. She is merely disciple and Mother. And thus, it is as Mother we need to think of her, seek her and pray to her. She is the Mother. In the Mother Church. In the maternity of Our Lady we see the maternity of the Church who welcomes everyone, the good and the evil ones: everyone.

Today it would be good to stop a moment and think about Our Lady's pain and sorrows. She is our Mother. And how she bore them, how she bore them well, with strength, with tears: they were not false tears, it was truly a heart destroyed with sorrow. It would be good to stop a moment and say to Our Lady: "Thank You for accepting to be Mother when the Angel said it to You, and thank You for accepting to be Mother when Jesus said it to You."

Video Message to Italian Families and to the world in this time of pandemic

Dear friends, good evening!

This evening I have the chance to enter your homes in a different way than usual. If you allow me, I would like to have a conversation with you for a few moments, in this time of difficulty and of suffering. I can imagine you in your families, living an unusual life to avoid contagion. I am thinking of the liveliness of children and young people, who cannot go out, attend school, live their lives. I have in my heart all the families, especially those who have a loved one who is sick or who have unfortunately experienced mourning due to the coronavirus or other causes. These days I often think about people who are alone, and for whom it is more difficult to face these moments. Above all I think of the elderly, who are very dear to me.

I cannot forget those who are sick with coronavirus, people who are in hospital. I am aware of the generosity of those who put themselves at risk for the treatment of this pandemic or to guarantee the essential services to society. So many heroes, every day, at every hour! I also remember how many are in financial straits and are worried about work and the future. A thought also goes out to prison inmates, whose pain is compounded by fear of the epidemic, for themselves and their loved ones; I think of the homeless, who do not have a home to protect them.

It is a difficult time for everyone. For many, very difficult. The Pope knows this and, with these words, he wants to tell everyone of his closeness and affection. Let us try, if we can, to make the best use of this time: let us be generous; let us help those in need in our neighborhood; let us look out for the loneliest people, perhaps by telephone or social networks; let us pray to the Lord for those who are in difficulty in Italy and in the world. Even if we are isolated, thought and spirit can go far with the creativity of love.

We will celebrate Holy Week in a truly unusual way, which manifests and sums up the message of the Gospel, that of God's boundless love. And in the silence of our cities, the Easter Gospel will resound. The Apostle Paul says: "And He died for all, that those who live should no longer live for themselves, but for Him Who died for them and was raised again" (2 *Cor* 5:15). In the risen Jesus, life conquered death. This Paschal faith nourishes our hope. I would like to share it with you this evening. It is the hope of a better time, in which we can be better, finally freed from evil and from this pandemic. It is a hope: hope does not disappoint; it is not an illusion, it is a hope.

Beside each other, in love and patience, we can prepare a better time in these days. Thank you for allowing me into your homes. Make a gesture of tenderness towards those who suffer, towards children, and towards the elderly. Tell them that the Pope is close and pray, that the Lord will soon deliver us all from evil. And you, pray for me. Have a good dinner. See you soon!

Saturday, April 4, 2020

Holy Mass[28]

Introduction

In these turbulent, difficult and painful times, people often have the possibility of doing one thing or another, many of them good. But there is also the possibility some might get the idea of doing something not so good, to take advantage of the situation, to profit personally from it. We pray today that the Lord might grant an upright and transparent conscience to everyone, that they might allow God to look on them without shame.

Homily – The process of temptation

The doctors of the law, even the high priests, had been restless for a while because strange things were happening in the Land. First there was this John, but in the end they left him alone because he was a prophet, he baptized there and the people went there, but there were no other consequences. Then came this Jesus, whom John had pointed out. He began to perform signs and miracles, but above all to speak to the people and they understood, and followed Him, but Jesus did not always observe the law and this is what made them very restless. "This is a revolutionary, a peaceful revolutionary… He attracts people to himself, the people follow him…" (see *Jn* 11:47-48). And these ideas made them talk to each other: "But look, I don't

[28] Liturgy of the Word: *Ez* 37:21-28; *Jer* 31:10-13; *Jn* 11:45-56.

like this... or that…", and this was the topic of their conversations and also of their concern. Then some of them went to Him in order to test Him, and the Lord always had a clear response which had not come to the minds of the doctors of the law. Let us think of that woman who had been married seven times, she had been widowed seven times: "But in heaven which of the seven of her husbands will be her husband?" (see *Lk* 20:33) He responded clearly and they went away a little embarrassed because of Jesus's wisdom, and other times they went away humiliated, as in the case of the woman caught in adultery who they wanted to stone and Jesus said in the end: "The one among you who has not sinned let him cast the first stone" (see *Jn* 8:7) and the Gospel says that they went away, beginning with the elders, humiliated in that moment. This prompted these conversations among them: "We have to do something, this is not right…". Then they sent soldiers to arrest Him and they returned saying: "We could not bring Him in because no one ever spoke like this man" … "You too have let yourselves be deceived" (see *Jn* 7:45-49): angry because not even the soldiers could arrest Him. And then, after the resurrection of Lazarus – the piece that we have heard today – many Jews went there to see the sisters and Lazarus, but some to see what had happened in order to report, and some of them went to the Pharisees and told them what Jesus had done (see *Jn* 11:45). Others believed in Him.

And those people who went there, the usual gossips, who spend their lives spreading gossip… they went to tell them. At this moment, this group that had formed among the doctors of the law had a formal meeting: "He is so dangerous, we have to make a decision. What should we do? This man performs many signs" – they recognize the miracles - "If we let Him continue, everyone will believe in Him. It is dangerous. They will follow Him and they will separate themselves from us" - the people were not attached to them - "The Romans will come and destroy our temple and our nation" (see *Jn* 11:48). There is some truth here, but not the whole truth. It was a justification. Because that they had found equilibrium with their occupiers, but they hated the Roman occupiers, but politically they had found an equilibrium. Thus they spoke among themselves. One of them, Caiaphas - the most radical - the high priest said: "You fail to see that it is better for one man to die for the people, than for the whole nation to be destroyed" (*Jn* 11:50). This was the high priest and he made the proposal: "Let us get rid of Him".

And John says: "He did not speak in his own person, it was as high priest that he made this prophecy that Jesus was to die for the nation... From that day they were determined to kill him." (see *Jn* 11:51-53) It was a process, a process that began with minor restlessness during John the Baptist's days and finished here with the doctors of the law and the high priests. A process that continually got stronger, a process in which the decisions that had to be made became increasingly sure, but no one said clearly: "This man needs to be gotten rid of." The way that the doctors of the law proceed is precisely a model of how temptation works in us, because it was truly the devil who was behind this, who wanted to destroy Jesus, and temptation in us truly works like this: it begins with something small, a desire, an idea, it grows, it infects others and in the end it justifies itself. These are the three steps of the temptation of the devil in us and the three steps of the temptation that the devil worked in the person of the doctor of the law. It began with something small, but it grew and grew until it began to infect others, it became real, and in the end it justified itself: "it is necessary that one die for the people" (see *Jn* 11:50), the total justification. And everyone went home calmly. They said: "This is the decision we had to make". And all of us, when we are conquered by temptation, we end up feeling calm, because we have found a justification for this sin, for this sinful attitude, for this life which is against God's law.

We should have the custom of identifying this process within us. That process that changes our hearts from good to bad, that leads us to a downward slope. A thing that grows, grows, grows slowly, then it infects others, in the end it justifies itself. It is rare that temptations come all at once, the devil is astute. And he knows how to take this path, the same one he took to arrive at Jesus's condemnation. When we recognize that we are in sin or that we have fallen, yes, we must go and ask the Lord for forgiveness, this is the first step that we must take. But then we must say: "How did I fall into this? How did this process begin in my soul? How did it grow? Whom have I infected? And in the end how did I justify myself in order to fall?" The life of Jesus is always an example for us. The things that happened to Jesus are things that also will happen to us: the temptations, the justifications, good people around us - and perhaps we do not listen to them - and bad people in the moment of temptation. We surround ourselves with them in order to allow the temptation to get stronger. But let us never forget: always, behind a sin, behind a fall, there is a temptation that began small, that grew, that infected us, and in the end we find a justification to fall. May the Holy Spirit enlighten us in this interior awareness.

Sunday, April 5, 2020

Palm Sunday (A)

Holy Mass[29]

Homily – Jesus, Servant and Saviour

Jesus "emptied himself, taking the form of a servant" (*Phil* 2:7). Let us allow these words of the Apostle Paul to lead us into these holy days, when the word of God, like a refrain, presents Jesus as *servant*: on Holy Thursday, He is portrayed as the servant who washes the feet of His disciples; on Good Friday, He is presented as the suffering and victorious servant (see *Is* 52:13); and tomorrow we will hear the prophecy of Isaiah about Him: "Behold my servant, whom I uphold" (*Is* 42:1). God saved us *by serving us*. We often think we are the ones who serve God. No, He is the one who freely chose to serve us, for He loved us first. It is difficult to love and not be loved in return. And it is even more difficult to serve if we do not let ourselves be served by God.

But - just one question - how did the Lord serve us? By giving His life for us. We are dear to Him; we cost Him dearly. Saint Angela of Foligno said she once heard Jesus say: "My love for you is no joke". His love for us led Him to sacrifice Himself and to take upon Himself our sins. This astonishes us: God saved us by taking upon Himself all the punishment of our sins. Without complaining, but

---

[29] Liturgy of the Word: *Mt* 21:1-11; *Is* 50:4-7; *Psalm* 21(22); *Phil* 2:6-11; *Mt* 26:14–27:66.

with the humility, patience and obedience of a servant, and purely out of love. And the Father *upheld* Jesus in His service. He did not take away the evil that crushed Him, but rather strengthened Him in his suffering so that our evil could be overcome by good, by a love that loves to the very end.

The Lord served us to the point of experiencing the most painful situations of those who love: *betrayal* and *abandonment*.

Betrayal. Jesus suffered betrayal by the disciple who sold Him and by the disciple who denied Him. He was betrayed by the people who sang hosanna to Him and then shouted: "Crucify Him!" (*Mt* 27:22). He was betrayed by the religious institution that unjustly condemned Him and by the political institution that washed its hands of Him. We can think of all the small or great betrayals that we have suffered in life. It is terrible to discover that a firmly placed trust has been betrayed. From deep within our heart a disappointment surges up that can even make life seem meaningless. This happens because we were born to be loved and to love, and the most painful thing is to be betrayed by someone who promised to be loyal and close to us. We cannot even imagine how painful it was for God who *is* love.

Let us look within. If we are honest with ourselves, we will see our infidelities. How many falsehoods, hypocrisies and duplicities! How many good intentions betrayed! How many broken promises! How many resolutions left unfulfilled! The Lord knows our hearts better than we do. He knows how weak and irresolute we are, how many times we fall, how hard it is for us to get up and how difficult it is to heal certain wounds. And what did

He do in order to come to our aid and serve us? He told us through the Prophet: "I will heal their faithlessness; I will love them deeply" (*Hos* 14:5). He healed us by taking upon himself our infidelity and by taking from us our betrayals. Instead of being discouraged by the fear of failing, we can now look upon the crucifix, feel His embrace, and say: "Behold, there is my infidelity, you took it, Jesus, upon yourself. You open your arms to me, you serve me with your love, you continue to support me… And so I will keep pressing on".

Abandonment. In today's Gospel, Jesus says one thing from the Cross, one thing alone: "My God, my God, why have you forsaken me?" (*Mt* 27:46). These are powerful words. Jesus had suffered the abandonment of His own, who had fled. But the Father remained for Him. Now, in the abyss of solitude, for the first time He calls Him by the generic name "God". And "in a loud voice" He asks the question "why?", the most excruciating "why?": "Why did you too abandon me?". These words are in fact those of a Psalm (see 22:2); they tell us that Jesus also brought the experience of extreme desolation to His prayer. But the fact remains that He Himself experienced that desolation: He experienced the utmost abandonment, which the Gospels testify to by quoting His very words.

Why did all this take place? Once again, it was done for our sake, to *serve* us. So that when we have our back to the wall, when we find ourselves at a dead end, with no light and no way of escape, when it seems that God Himself is not responding, we should remember that we are not alone. Jesus experienced total abandonment in a situation He had never before experienced in order to be one with us in everything. He did it for me, for you, for all of us; He did it to say to us: "Do not be afraid, you are not alone. I experienced all your desolation in order to be ever close to you". That is the extent to which Jesus served us: He descended into the abyss of our most bitter sufferings, culminating in betrayal and abandonment. Today, in the tragedy of a pandemic, in the face of the many false securities that have now crumbled, in the face of so many hopes betrayed, in the sense of abandonment that weighs upon our hearts, Jesus says to each one of us: "Courage, open your heart to my love. You will feel the consolation of God who sustains you".

Dear brothers and sisters, what can we do in comparison with God, who served us even to the point of being betrayed and abandoned? We can refuse to betray Him for whom we were created, and not abandon what really matters in our lives. We were put in this world to love Him and our neighbors. Everything else passes away, only this remains. The tragedy we are experiencing at this time summons us to take seriously the things that are serious, and not to be caught up in those that matter less; to rediscover that *life is of no use if not used to serve others*. For life is measured by love. So, in these holy days, in our homes, let us stand before the Crucified One - look upon the Crucified One! - the fullest measure of God's love for us, and before the God who serves us to the point of giving his life, and, - fixing our gaze on the Crucified One - let us ask for the grace to *live in order to serve*. May we reach out to those who are suffering and those most in need. May we not be concerned about what we lack, but what good we can do for others.

Behold my servant, whom I uphold. The Father, who sustained Jesus in His Passion also supports us in our efforts to serve. Loving, praying, forgiving, caring for others, in the family and in society: all this can certainly be difficult. It can feel like a *via crucis*. But the path of service is the victorious and life giving path by which we were saved. I would like to say this especially to young people, on this Day which has been dedicated to them for thirty-five years now. Dear friends, look at the *real heroes* who come to light in these days: they are not famous, rich and successful people; rather, they are those who are giving themselves in order to serve others. Feel called yourselves to put your lives on the line. Do not be afraid to devote your life to God and to others; it pays! For life is a gift we receive only when we give ourselves away, and our deepest joy comes from saying yes to love, without ifs and buts. To truly say yes to love, without ifs and buts. As Jesus did for us.

Angelus

Dear Brothers and Sisters,

Before concluding this liturgy, I would like to greet all those taking part via the means of social communication. In particular, my thoughts turn to young people all over the world, who are living today's World Youth Day, celebrated at the diocesan level, in an unprecedented way. The handing over of the Cross from the youth of Panama to those of Lisbon was to have taken place today. This very significant gesture has been postponed to Christ the King Sunday, this coming November 22. While waiting for that moment, I urge you young people to nurture and witness the hope, generosity and solidarity that we all need at this difficult time.

Tomorrow, [Monday] April 6, is the United Nations International Day of Sport for Development and Peace. Many sporting events have been suspended during this period. However, the best fruits of sports are emerging: resistance, team spirit, fraternity, giving the best of oneself.... So, let's launch sports for peace and development once again.

Dear friends, let us journey in faith toward Holy Week when Jesus suffers, dies and rises. The people and families who are unable to participate in the liturgical celebrations are invited to gather together in prayer at home, also aided by the means of technology. Let us spiritually gather around the sick and their families, and all those who care for them with self-denial. Let us pray for the deceased in the light of paschal faith. Everyone is present in our hearts, in our thoughts, in our prayers.

May we learn from Mary, that inner silence, that gaze of the heart, that loving faith, so as to follow Jesus on the way of the cross that leads to the glory of the Resurrection. She walks with us and sustains our hope.

Monday, April 6, 2020

Holy Mass[30]

Introduction

I am thinking of a serious problem that exists in many parts of the world. I would like us to pray for the problem of overcrowded prisons. Where there is overcrowding - there are many people there - there is the danger, in this pandemic, that it ends up as a grave tragedy. Let us pray for those responsible, for those who need to make decisions in this regard, so that they might find a just and creative way to solve the problem.

Homily – Seeking Jesus in the poor

This passage ends with an observation: "The chief priests decided to kill Lazarus as well, since it was on his account that many of the Jews were leaving them and believing in Jesus" (*Jn* 12:10-11). The other day we saw the process of temptation: the initial seduction, the illusion, then it grows - second step - and the third, it grows, it spreads and one justifies oneself. But there is another step. It goes on and it never stops. Therefore it was not enough to put Jesus to death; now Lazarus too, as he was a living witness.

But today I would like to pause on one of Jesus's words. Six days before the Passover - we are right at the doorway of the Passion - Mary performs this contempla-

[30] Liturgy of the Word: *Is* 42:1-7; *Psalm* 26(27); *Jn* 12:1-11.

tive gesture. Martha was serving, as in the other pssage, and Mary opens the door to contemplation. And Judas thinks about money, and thinks about the poor, but "not because he cared about the poor, but because he was a thief; he was in charge of the common fund and used to help himself to the contributions" (v. 6). This story of the unfaithful administrator is always current: they are always around, even at a high level. Think about some charitable or humanitarian organisations that have many, many employees, with a structure full of people, and only forty per cent of donations arrive at the poor because sixty per cent goes to pay the salaries of many people. This is a way of taking money from the poor. But Jesus is the answer. And this is where I want to stop. "You have the poor with you always" (*Jn* 12:8). This is a truth. "You have the poor with you always". There are poor people. There are many of them: there are the poor people we see, but they are just a small part; the majority of poor people are those we do not see: the hidden poor.

And we do not see them because we enter into this culture of indifference which denies their existence: "No, no, there aren't many of them, we don't see them; yes, maybe that case"..., minimizing the reality of the poor. But there are so very many.

Or even, if we enter into that culture of indifference, there is a habit of seeing the poor as ornaments in a city, like statues; yes, they are there, we see them; yes, that old woman who begs, that other one... But as if it were something normal. The poor are part of the decoration of the city. But the great majority are the poor victims of economic policies, of financial policies. Some recent statistics summarize it thus: there is a lot of money in the hands of the few, and great poverty suffered by many. And this is the poverty of many people, the victims of the structural injustice of the world economy. Many poor people are ashamed; many of them are from the middle class and go to *Caritas* secretly, and are ashamed to ask for help. The poor are far more numerous than the rich; far more. And what Jesus said is true: "You have the poor with you always". But do I see them? Am I aware of the situation? In particular, the hidden reality, those who are ashamed to say that they can't make it to the end of the month.

I remember that in Buenos Aires they told me that the building of an abandoned factory, empty for years, was inhabited by around fifteen families, who had arrived in the preceding months. I went there. They were families with children and each had claimed a part of the abandoned factory to live in. Looking closer, I saw that each family had good furniture, indicative of the middle class, with a television set. But they ended up there because they couldn't pay their rent. The new poor, who are forced to leave their homes because they can't afford the rent, go there. This is the injustice of the economic or financial system that led them to this. And there are very many of them, to the point that we will meet them at the judgement. The first question Jesus will ask is: "How did you get on with the poor? Did you give them something to eat? When they were in prison, did you visit them? In hospital, did you see them? Have you helped the widow, the orphan? Because that is where I was". And on this we will be judged. We will not be judged for the luxury in which we live, or the journeys we make, or the social importance we have. We will be judged by our relationship with the poor. But if today I ignore the poor, if I cast them aside, if I think they do not exist, the Lord will ignore me on the day of judgement. When Jesus says: “The poor will always be with you”, He means: “I will always be with you in the poor. I will be present there”. And this is not being a communist, this is the center of the Gospel. We will be judged on this.

TUESDAY, APRIL 7, 2020

Holy Mass[31]

Introduction

In these days of Lent we have seen the persecution that Jesus suffered, and how the doctors of the Law had it in for Him; He was judged with this dogged fury, even though He was innocent. I would like to pray today for all those people who suffer an unjust sentence as a result of persecution.

Homily – Persevering in service

The prophecy of Isaiah which we have heard is a prophecy of the Messiah, of the Redeemer, but also a prophecy of the people of Israel, of the people of God: we can say that it may be a prophecy of each one of us. Substantially the prophecy underlines that the Lord chose His servant from His mother's womb. Twice it says this (*Is* 49:1). From the beginning His servant was chosen, from birth or from before birth. The people of God was chosen before birth, each one of us. too. None of us fell to earth by chance. Each one has a destiny, a free destiny, the destiny of being chosen by God. I am born with the destiny of being a child of God, of being a servant of God, with the task of serving, constructing, building. Right from my mother's womb.

---

[31] Liturgy of the Word: *Is* 49:1-6; *Psalm* 70(71); *Jn* 13:21-33, 36-38.

The servant of Yahweh, Jesus, served unto death; it seemed to be a defeat, but it was a way of serving. And this underlines the way of serving that we must also take up in our own lives. To serve is to give of oneself, to give oneself to others. To serve is not about demanding some benefit for ourselves, other than serving. Serving is glory, and the glory of Christ is to serve up to the point of annihilating oneself, until death, death on the Cross (see *Phil* 2:8). Jesus is the servant of Israel. The people of God are servants, and when the people of God distance themselves from this attitude of service they become an apostate people. They distance themselves from the vocation that God gave them. And when we distance ourselves from this vocation of service, we distance ourselves from God's love. And we build our lives on the basis of other loves, very often idolatrous.

The Lord chose us from our mother's womb. There are falls in life: each one of us is a sinner and can fall, and has fallen. Only Our Lady and Jesus [are without sin]: all the others have fallen, we are sinners. But what is important is my attitude before God, who chose me, who anointed me as a servant. It is the attitude of a sinner who is capable of asking for forgiveness, like Peter, who swore, "I'll never deny You! Never, never, never", and then when the cock crows, weeps and repents (see *Mt* 26:75). This is the path of the servant: when he slips, when he falls, he asks for forgiveness.

Instead, when the servant is not capable of understanding that he has fallen, when passion takes hold of him in such a way that it leads him to idolatry, his heart is open to Satan who enters at night: this is what happened to Judas (see *Mt* 27:3-10).

But let us think today of Jesus the servant, faithful in service. His vocation is to serve, until death on the Cross (see *Phil* 2:5-11). Let us think about each one of us, part of the people of God: we are servants, our vocation is to serve, not to take advantage of our place in the Church. To serve. Always in service.

Let us ask for the grace to persevere in service. At times we slip and fall, but when this happens, let us ask for the grace to weep like Peter.

WEDNESDAY, APRIL 8, 2020

Holy Mass[32]

Introduction

Let us pray together today for people who during this time of the pandemic trade at the expense of the needy; who profit from the needs of others and sell them: the mafia, usurers and others. May the Lord touch their hearts and convert them.

Homily – Judas, where are you?

Holy Wednesday is also called "Spy Wednesday", the day in which the Church underlines Judas's betrayal. Judas sells the Master.

When we think of the fact of selling people what comes to mind is the slave trade from Africa to America – something from the past – then the business, for example, of the Yazidi girls sold to the Daesh: but this is something far away, this is something.... Even today people are sold. Everyday. There are Judases who sell their brothers and sisters, exploiting them for work, without a just pay, without recognizing their duties. Many times they even sell their dearest things. I think that in order to have a greater convenience a person is able to take his parents away and not see them anymore; to take them far away to safe old-age homes and not visit them anymore... He is selling

[32] Liturgy of the Word: *Is* 50:4-9; *Psalm* 68(69); *Mt* 26:14-25.

them. There is a very common saying that such a person is "capable of selling his or her own mother": and they sell her. Now they feel at peace, they are kept away: "You take care of them…".

Trafficking in human persons today is as it was in earlier times: it is done. And why is that? Jesus said why. He gave money the status of master. Jesus said: "You cannot serve God and money" (see *Lk* 16:13) – two masters. It is the only thing that Jesus compares, and each one of us needs to choose: either serve God and you will be free in adoration and service; or serve money and you will be a slave to money. This is the option; and many people want to serve both God and money. And this cannot be done. In the end they pretend to serve God in order to serve money. They are hidden exploiters, socially flawless, but under the table they even traffic in human beings: it does not matter to them. Human exploitation is selling one's neighbor.

Judas went away, but he left some disciples, who are not his disciples but the devil's. What Judas's life was like we do not know. He must have been a normal boy, perhaps, also with anxieties, because the Lord called him to be a disciple. He never never succeeded in being one. he did not have the mouth of a disciple and the heart of a disciple, as we heard in the first Reading. He was weak in his discipleship, but Jesus loved him… Then the Gospel makes us understand that he liked money. At Lazarus's house, when Mary anoints Jesus's feet with that expensive perfume, he makes the reflection and John emphasizes: "But he did not say this because he loved the poor: he was a thief" (see *Jn* 12:6) His love for money had led him beyond the rules: to stealing, and from stealing to betraying there is only one step, a very small one. Those who love money too much betray in order to have even more, always: this is a rule, it is a matter of fact. Judas, perhaps a good boy, with good intentions, ends up as a traitor to the point of going to the market to sell: "He went to the chief priests and said 'What are you prepared to give me if I hand him over to you?'" (see *Mt* 26:14). In my opinion, this man was out of his mind.

One thing that draws my attention is that Jesus never called him a "traitor"; He says that He will be betrayed, but He never called him a "traitor". He never said: "Go away, traitor!" Never! Rather, He calls him "friend", and kisses him. The mystery of Judas: what is the mystery of Judas? I do not know... Fr. Primo Mazzolari explained it better than me... Yes, I take comfort in contemplating that capital at Vezelay: how did Judas end up? I am not sure. Jesus makes a strong threat, here; he makes a strong threat: "Woe to that man by whom the Son of Man is betrayed. It would be better for that man if he had never been born" (see *Mt* 26:24). But does this mean that Judas is in Hell? I do not know. I look at the chapiter.[33] And I hear Jesus's word: "friend".

But it makes us think of another thing, that is more real, more current: the devil entered Judas, it was the devil who lead him to that point. And how did the story end? The devil is a poor paymaster: he is not a reliable paymaster. He promises everything, shows you everything and in the end leaves you alone in despair to hang yourself.

---

[33] Pope Francis is referring to the scene on the top of a column in the Basilica of St Mary Magdalene in Vèzelay in Burgundy.

Judas's restless heart is tormented by concupiscence and tormented by the love of Jesus – a love that failed to become love – tormented by this fog, he goes back to the priests and asks for forgiveness, asks for salvation. "What is that to us? It is your responsibility…" (see *Mt* 27:4): the devil speaks like this and leaves us in despair.

Let us think of the many institutionalized Judases in this world who exploit people. And think also of the small Judas that each one of us has within at the hour of choice: between loyalty or interest. Each one of us has the ability to betray, to sell, to choose for one's own interest. Each one of us has the opportunity to let ourselves be attracted by love of money or goods or future well-being. "Judas, where are you?" But I will ask each one of us: "You, Judas, the little Judas within me: where are you?"

Thursday, April 9, 2020

Mass of the Lord's Supper[34]

Homily – Eucharist, service, anointing

This is what we experience in today's celebration: the Lord who wants to remain with us in the *Eucharist*. And we become the Lord's tabernacles, carrying the Lord with us; to the point that He himself tells us: if we do not eat His body and drink His blood, we will not enter the kingdom of heaven. This is a mystery, bread and wine, the Lord with us, within us, inside us.

Service. This gesture is the condition to enter the kingdom of heaven. Yes, to serve... everyone. But the Lord, in the words He exchanged with Peter (see *Jn* 13:6-9), makes him realize that to enter the kingdom of heaven we must let the Lord serve us, that the servant of God be our servant. And this is hard to understand. If I do not let the Lord be my servant, do not let the Lord wash me, help me grow, forgive me, then I will not enter the kingdom of heaven.

And the *priesthood* too. Today I would like to be close to priests, to all priests, from the most recently ordained right up to the Pope. We are all priests. The bishops too, all of us... we are *anointed*, anointed by the Lord; anointed to confect the Eucharist, anointed to serve.

---

[34] Liturgy of the Word: *Ex* 12:1-8, 11-14; *Psalm* 115(116); *1 Cor* 11:23-26, *Jn* 13:1-15.

There is no Chrism Mass today – I hope we can have it before Pentecost, otherwise it will have to be postponed to next year – but I cannot let tonight's Mass pass by without remembering priests. Priests who offer their lives for the Lord, priests who are servants. In these days many of them have died, more than sixty here in Italy, while tending to the sick in hospital, together with doctors and nurses... They are "saints next door", priests who have given their lives in serving.

I think too of those who are far away. Today I received a letter from a priest, a chaplain in a prison far away, who told me how he was spending this Holy Week with the prisoners. A Franciscan priest. Priests who travel far to bring the Gospel and who die far away. A bishop told me once that the first thing he did on arriving in these mission posts was to go to the cemetery, to the graves of priests who gave their lives there, young priests who died from local diseases because they were not prepared, they didn't have the antibodies; and no one knew their names: anonymous priests. Then there are the parish priests in the countryside, pastors of four, five, seven little villages in the mountains, who go from one to the other, who know the people. One of them once told me that he knew the name of every person in his villages. I asked him, "Really?" And he told me "I even know the dogs' names!". They know everyone. Priestly closeness. Good, good priests.

Today I carry you in my heart and I carry you to the altar. Also priests who are slandered. This happens often today; they cannot walk about freely because people say bad things about them, referring to the scandal from discovering priests who have done bad things. Some of them have told me that they cannot go out wearing clerics because people insult them. Yet they carry on. Priests who are sinners, together with bishops and the Pope who is also a sinner, must not forget to ask forgiveness and learn how to forgive because they know that they need to ask forgiveness and to forgive. We are all sinners. Priests who suffer from crises, who do not know what to do, who live in darkness...

Today you are all with me, brother priests, at the altar, you who are consecrated. I say to you just one thing: do not be stubborn like Peter. Let your feet be washed. The Lord is your servant, He is close to you, and He gives you strength to wash the feet of others.

In this way, conscious of the need to be washed clean, you will be great dispensers of forgiveness. Forgive! Have a big heart that is generous in forgiving. This is the measure by which we will be judged. As you have forgiven, so you will be forgiven, in the same measure. Do not be afraid to forgive. Sometimes we have doubts; look to Christ. There, there is forgiveness for all. Be courageous, also in taking risks, in forgiving, in order to bring consolation. And if you cannot give sacramental pardon at this moment, then at least give the consolation of a brother to those you accompany, leaving the door open for people to return.

I thank God for the grace of the priesthood, we all give thanks. I thank God for you, priests. Jesus loves you! He asks only that you let him wash your feet.

Saturday, April 11, 2020

Easter Vigil in the Holy Night[35]

Homily – Let mercy be enkindled in the darkness of our hearts

"After the Sabbath" (*Mt* 28:1), the women went to the tomb. This is how the Gospel of this holy Vigil began: with the Sabbath. It is the day of the Easter Triduum that we tend to neglect as we eagerly await the passage from Friday's cross to Easter Sunday's Alleluia. This year however, we are experiencing, more than ever, the great silence of Holy Saturday. We can imagine ourselves in the position of the women on that day. They, like us, had before their eyes the drama of suffering, of an unexpected tragedy that happened all too suddenly. They had seen death and it weighed on their hearts. Pain was mixed with fear: would they suffer the same fate as the Master? Then too there was fear about the future and all that would need to be rebuilt. A painful memory, a hope cut short. For them, as for us, it was the darkest hour.

Yet in this situation the women did not allow themselves to be paralyzed. They did not give in to the gloom of sorrow and regret, they did not morosely close in on themselves, or flee from reality. They were doing something simple yet extraordinary: preparing at home the spices to anoint the body of Jesus. They did not stop

---

[35] Liturgy of the Word: *Gn* 1:1, 26-31; *Psalm* 103(104); *Ex* 14:15–15:1; *Ex* 15:1-6; *Is* 55:1-11; *Is* 12:2-6; *Psalm* 117(118); *Rom* 6:3-11; *Mt* 28:1-10.

loving; in the darkness of their hearts, they lit a flame of mercy. Our Lady spent that Saturday, the day that would be dedicated to her, in prayer and hope. She responded to sorrow with trust in the Lord. Unbeknownst to these women, they were making preparations, in the darkness of that Sabbath, for "the dawn of the first day of the week", the day that would change history. Jesus, like a seed buried in the ground, was about to make new life blossom in the world; and these women, by prayer and love, were helping to make that hope flower. How many people, in these sad days, have done and are still doing what those women did, sowing seeds of hope! With small gestures of care, affection and prayer.

At dawn the women went to the tomb. There the angel says to them: "Do not be afraid. He is not here; for He has risen" (vv. 5-6). They hear the words of life even as they stand before a tomb... And then they meet Jesus, the giver of all hope, who confirms the message and says: "Do not be afraid" (v. 10). *Do not be afraid, do not yield to fear*: This is the *message of hope*. It is addressed to us, today. These are the words that God repeats to us this very night.

Tonight we acquire a fundamental right that can never be taken away from us: *the right to hope*. It is a new and living hope that comes from God. It is not mere optimism; it is not a pat on the back or an empty word of encouragement, uttered with an empty smile. No! It is a gift from heaven, which we could not have earned on our own. Over these weeks, we have kept repeating, "All will be well", clinging to the beauty of our humanity and allowing words of encouragement to rise up from our hearts. But as the days go by and fears grow, even the boldest hope can dissipate. Jesus's hope is different. He plants in our hearts the conviction that God is able to make everything work unto good, because even from the grave he brings life.

The grave is the place where no one who enters ever leaves. But Jesus emerged for us; He rose for us, to bring life where there was death, to begin a new story in the very place where a stone had been placed. He, who rolled away the stone that sealed the entrance of the tomb, can also remove the stones in our hearts. So, let us not give in to resignation; let us not place a stone before hope. We can and must hope, because God is faithful. He did not abandon us; He visited us and entered into our situations of pain, anguish and death. His light dispelled the darkness of the tomb: today he wants that light to penetrate even to the darkest corners of our lives. Dear sister, dear brother, even if in your heart you have buried hope, do not give up: God is greater. Darkness and death do not have the last word. Be strong, for with God nothing is lost!

Courage. This is a word often spoken by Jesus in the Gospels. Only once do others say it, to encourage a person in need: "Courage; rise, [Jesus] is calling you!" (*Mk* 10:49). It is He, the Risen One, who raises us up from our neediness. If, on your journey, you feel weak and frail, or fall, do not be afraid, God holds out a helping hand and says to you: "Courage!". You might say, as did Don Abbondio (in Manzoni's novel), "Courage is not something you can give yourself" (*I Promessi Sposi,* XXV). True, you cannot give it to yourself, but you can receive it as a gift. All you have to do is open your heart in prayer and roll away, however slightly, that stone placed at the entrance to your heart so that Jesus's light can enter. You only need to ask him: "Jesus, come to me amid my fears and tell me too: Courage!" With you, Lord, we will be tested but not shaken. And, whatever sadness may dwell in us, we will be strengthened in hope, since with you the cross leads to the resurrection, because you are with us in the darkness of our nights; you are certainty amid our uncertainties, the word that speaks in our silence, and nothing can ever rob us of the love you have for us.

This is the Easter message, a message of hope. It contains a second part, the sending forth. "Go and tell my brethren to go to Galilee" (*Mt* 28:10), Jesus says. "He is going before you to Galilee" (v. 7), the angel says. The Lord goes before us; He goes before us always. It is encouraging to know that He walks ahead of us in life and in death; He goes before us to Galilee, that is, to the place which for Him and His disciples evoked the idea of daily life, family and work. Jesus wants us to bring hope there, to our everyday life. For the disciples, Galilee was also the place of remembrance, for it was the place where they were first called. Returning to Galilee means remembering that we have been loved and called by God. Each one of us has their own Galilee. We need to resume the journey, reminding ourselves that we are born and reborn thanks to an invitation given gratuitously to us out of love, there in our respective Galilees. This is always the point from which we can set out anew, especially in times of crisis and trial, remembering our Galilee.

But there is more. Galilee was the farthest region from where they were: from Jerusalem. And not only geographically. Galilee was also the farthest place from the sacredness of the Holy City. It was an area where people of different religions lived: it was the "Galilee of the Gentiles" (*Mt* 4:15). Jesus sends them there and asks them to start again from there. What does this tell us? That the message of hope should not be confined to our sacred places, but should be brought to everyone. For everyone is in need of reassurance, and if we, who have touched "the Word of life" (*1 Jn* 1:1) do not give it, who will? How beautiful it is to be Christians who offer consolation, who bear the burdens of others and who offer encouragement: messengers of life in a time of death! In every Galilee, in every area of the human family to which we all belong and which is part of us - for we are all brothers and sisters - may we bring the song of life! Let us silence the cries of death, no more wars! May we stop the production and trade of weapons, since we need bread, not guns. Let the abortion and killing of innocent lives end. May the hearts of those who have enough be open to filling the empty hands of those who do not have the bare necessities.

Those women, in the end, "took hold" of Jesus's feet (*Mt* 28:9); feet that had travelled so far to meet us, to the point of entering and emerging from the tomb. The women embraced the feet that had trampled death and opened the way of hope. Today, as pilgrims in search of hope, we cling to you, Risen Jesus. We turn our backs on death and open our hearts to you, for you are Life itself.

SUNDAY, APRIL 12, 2020

EASTER SUNDAY

Urbi et Orbi Message

Dear Brothers and Sisters, Happy Easter!

Today the Church's proclamation echoes throughout the world: "Jesus Christ is risen!" – "He is truly risen!".

Like a new flame this Good News springs up in the night: the night of a world already faced with epochal challenges and now oppressed by a pandemic severely testing our whole human family. In this night, the Church's voice rings out: "Christ, my hope, has arisen!" (Easter Sequence).

This is a different "contagion", a message transmitted from heart to heart – for every human heart awaits this Good News. It is the contagion of hope: "Christ, my hope, is risen!". This is no magic formula that makes problems vanish. No, the resurrection of Christ is not that. Instead, it is the victory of love over the root of evil, a victory that does not "by-pass" suffering and death, but passes through them, opening a path in the abyss, transforming evil into good: this is the unique hallmark of the power of God.

The Risen Lord is also the Crucified One, not someone else. In His glorious body He bears indelible wounds: wounds that have become windows of hope. Let us turn our gaze to Him that He may heal the wounds of an afflicted humanity.

Today my thoughts turn in the first place to the many who have been directly affected by the coronavirus: the sick, those who have died and family members who mourn the loss of their loved ones, to whom, in some cases, they were unable even to bid a final farewell. May the Lord of life welcome the departed into His kingdom and grant comfort and hope to those still suffering, especially the elderly and those who are alone. May He never withdraw His consolation and help from those who are especially vulnerable, such as persons who work in nursing homes, or live in barracks and prisons. For many, this is an Easter of solitude lived amid the sorrow and hardship that the pandemic is causing, from physical suffering to economic difficulties.

This disease has not only deprived us of human closeness, but also of the possibility of receiving in person the consolation that flows from the sacraments, particularly the Eucharist and Reconciliation. In many countries, it has not been possible to approach them, but the Lord has not left us alone! United in our prayer, we are convinced that He has laid His hand upon us (see *Ps* 138:5), firmly reassuring us: Do not be afraid, "I have risen and I am with you still!" (see *Roman Missal,* Entrance Antiphon, Mass of Easter Sunday).

May Jesus, our Passover, grant strength and hope to doctors and nurses, who everywhere offer a witness of care and love for our neighbors, to the point of exhaustion and not infrequently at the expense of their own health. Our gratitude and affection go to them, to all who work diligently to guarantee the essential services necessary for civil society, and to the law enforcement and military personnel who in many countries have helped ease people's difficulties and sufferings.

In these weeks, the lives of millions of people have suddenly changed. For many, remaining at home has been an opportunity to reflect, to withdraw from the frenetic pace of life, stay with loved ones and enjoy their company. For many, though, this is also a time of worry about an uncertain future, about jobs that are at risk and about other consequences of the current crisis. I encourage political leaders to work actively for the common good, to provide the means and resources needed to enable everyone to lead a dignified life and, when circumstances allow, to assist them in resuming their normal daily activities.

This is not a time for indifference, because the whole world is suffering and needs to be united in facing the pandemic. May the risen Jesus grant hope to all the poor, to those living on the peripheries, to refugees and the homeless. May these, the most vulnerable of our brothers and sisters living in the cities and peripheries of every part of the world, not be abandoned. Let us ensure that they do not lack basic necessities (all the more difficult to find now that many businesses are closed) such as medicine and especially the possibility of adequate health care. In light of the present circumstances, may international sanctions be relaxed, since these make it difficult for countries on which they have been imposed to provide adequate support to their citizens, and may all nations be put in a position to meet the greatest needs of the moment through the reduction, if not the forgiveness, of the debt burdening the balance sheets of the poorest nations.

This is not a time for self-centeredness, because the challenge we are facing is shared by all, without distinguishing between persons. Among the many areas of the world affected by the coronavirus, I think in a special way of Europe. After the Second World War, this continent was able to rise again, thanks to a concrete spirit of solidarity that enabled it to overcome the rivalries of the past. It is more urgent than ever, especially in the present circumstances, that these rivalries do not regain force, but that all recognize themselves as part of a single family and support one another. The European Union is presently facing an epochal challenge, on which will depend not only its future but that of the whole world. Let us not lose the opportunity to give further proof of solidarity, also by turning to innovative solutions. The only alternative is the selfishness of particular interests and the temptation of a return to the past, at the risk of severely damaging the peaceful coexistence and development of future generations.

This is not a time for division. May Christ our peace enlighten all who have responsibility in conflicts, that they may have the courage to support the appeal for an immediate global ceasefire in all corners of the world. This is not a time for continuing to manufacture and deal in arms, spending vast amounts of money that ought to be used to care for others and save lives. Rather, may this be a time for finally ending the long war that has caused such great bloodshed in beloved Syria, the conflict in Yemen and the hostilities in Iraq and in Lebanon. May this be the time when Israelis and Palestinians resume dialogue in order to find a stable and lasting solution that will allow both to live in peace. May the sufferings of the people who live in the eastern regions of Ukraine come to an end. May the terrorist attacks carried out against so many innocent people in different African countries come to an end.

This is not a time for forgetfulness. The crisis we are facing should not make us forget the many other crises that bring suffering to so many people. May the Lord of life be close to all those in Asia and Africa who are experiencing grave humanitarian crises, as in the Province of Cabo Delgado in the north of Mozambique. May He warm the hearts of the many refugees displaced because of wars, drought and famine. May He grant protection to migrants and refugees, many of them children, who are living in unbearable conditions, especially in Libya and on the border between Greece and Turkey. And I do not want to forget the island of Lesbos. In Venezuela, may He enable concrete and immediate solutions to be reached that can permit international assistance to a population suffering from the grave political, socio-economic and health situation.

Dear Brothers and Sisters,

Indifference, self-centeredness, division and forgetfulness are not words we want to hear at this time. We want to ban these words for ever! They seem to prevail when fear and death overwhelm us, that is, when we do not let the Lord Jesus triumph in our hearts and lives. May Christ, who has already defeated death and opened for us the way to eternal salvation, dispel the darkness of our suffering humanity and lead us into the light of his glorious day, a day that knows no end.

With these thoughts, I would like to wish all of you a happy Easter.

Monday, April 13, 2020

Easter Monday of the Angel

Holy Mass[36]

Introduction

Today, let us pray for government leaders, scientists and politicians who are beginning to research a way out of the pandemic, though its "aftermath" has already begun: may they find the right way, always for the good of their people.

Homily – Choose to proclaim so as not to fall into our sepulchres

Today's Gospel presents us with an option, an everyday option, a human option but one that has applied since that day: the choice between the joy and hope of the resurrection of Jesus, and nostalgia for the tomb.

The women go forward in bringing the proclamation (see *Mt* 28:8): God always begins with women, always. They open up the way. They do not doubt: they know; they had seen Him, they had touched Him. They had also seen the empty tomb. It is true that the disciples could not believe it and said: "But these women are probably a little too imaginative"... I don't know, they had their doubts. But the women were sure and in the end they continued on this path until today: Jesus is risen, He is alive among us! (see *Mt* 28:9-10) And then there is the other choice:

---

[36] Liturgy of the Word: *Acts* 2:14, 22-33; *Psalm* 15(16); *Mt* 28:8-15.

it is better not to live, with the empty tomb. This empty tomb will bring us many problems. And the decision to hide the fact. As always: when we do not serve God, the Lord, we serve the other god, money. Let us remember what Jesus said: there are two masters, the Lord God and the lord of money. One cannot serve both of them. And to get away from this fact, this reality, the priests and the doctors of the Law chose the other road, the one offered by the lord of money and they paid: they paid for silence (see *Mt* 28:12-13). The silence of the witnesses. One of the guards confessed as soon as Jesus died: "Truly this man was the Son of God!" (*Mk* 15:39). These poor men do not understand, they are afraid because their life is at stake... and they went to the priests, to the doctors of the Law. And they paid: they paid for their silence, and this, dear brothers and sisters, this is not a bribe: this is corruption, pure corruption. If you do not confess Jesus Christ the Lord, think about why: where the seal on your sepulcher is, where corruption is. Many people do not confess Jesus because they do not know Him, because we have not announced Him consistently, and this is our fault. But when before the evidence one takes this road, it is the road of the devil, it is the road of corruption. You're paid and you keep quiet.

Even today, in front of the coming - which we hope will come soon - the coming end of this pandemic, there is the same option: we will either make a stake on life, in favor of the resurrection of our people, or we will make a stake on the god of money, turning back to the tomb of hunger, slavery, war, the making of weapons, of children without an education... the tomb is there. May the Lord, both in our personal life and in our social life, always help us to choose proclamation: the proclamation that is a horizon, that is open, always; may He lead us to choose the good of the people. And never to fall into the tomb of the god money.

Regina Coeli

Today, Easter Monday of the Angel, the joyous proclamation of Christ's Resurrection resounds. The Gospel passage (see *Mt* 28:8-15) narrates that the frightened women, quickly left Jesus's tomb which they had found empty. But Jesus himself appears to them on the way, saying: "Do not be afraid; go and tell my brethren to go to Galilee, and there they will see me" (v. 10). With these words, the Risen One entrusts the women with a missionary mandate for the Apostles. Indeed, they offered an admirable example of faithfulness, of dedication, and of love for Christ throughout the time of His public life, as well as during His passion. Now they are rewarded by Him with this gesture of attention and predilection. The women always at the beginning: Mary at the beginning, women at the beginning.

First, the women, then the disciples, and Peter in particular, bear witness to the reality of the resurrection. Jesus had foretold to them a number of times that, after His passion and cross, He would rise again. But the disciples had not understood because they were not yet ready. Their faith needed a leap in quality that could only be inspired by the Holy Spirit, the gift of the Risen One.

At the beginning of the Book of the Acts of the Apostles, we hear Peter declare with frankness, courage and candour: "This Jesus God raised up, and of that we all are witnesses" (*Acts* 2:32). As if to say: "I put myself on the line for Him. I give my life for Him": And later, he would give his life for Him. From that moment on, the proclamation that Christ is risen has spread everywhere and has reached the four corners of the earth, becoming the message of hope for everyone. Jesus's Resurrection tells us that death does not have the last word, but rather life does. In raising his Only-begotten Son, God the Father has fully manifested His love and His mercy for humanity of all time.

If Christ has risen, it is possible to look with hope at every event of our existence, even the most difficult ones, those charged with anguish and uncertainty. This is the Easter message that we are called to proclaim with words, and above all through the witness of life. May this news resound in our homes and in our hearts: "Christ, my hope, has arisen!" (Easter Sequence). May this certainty strengthen the faith of every baptized person and above all, encourage those who are facing greater suffering and difficulty.

May Mary, the silent witness of the death and resurrection of her son, Jesus, help us to believe strongly in this mystery of salvation. When it is welcomed with faith, it can change our lives. This is the Easter wish that I renew to each of you. I entrust it to her, our Mother, whom we now invoke with the prayer, the Regina Caeli.

After the Regina Coeli

Dear Brothers and Sisters,

We have heard that women proclaimed Jesus's Resurrection to the disciples. Today I would like to call to mind the efforts that so many women are making in order to take care of others, even during this health crisis: women doctors, nurses, agents of law enforcement and prisons, employees in stores providing basic necessities..., and many mothers and sisters and grandmothers who are confined to their homes with their entire family, with children, the elderly, and the disabled. At times, they are at risk of enduring violence due to a living situation in which they bear a burden that is too heavy. Let us pray for them, so that the Lord may grant them strength, and our communities may support them together with their families. May the Lord give us the courage of women, to always go forward.

This Easter week I would like to remember with closeness and affection all the countries that are being seriously affected by the coronavirus, some of them with large numbers of people infected and deceased, in particular Italy, the United States of America, Spain, France … the list is long. I pray for them. And do not forget that the Pope prays for you and is close to you.

I renew my heartfelt Easter greetings to everyone. Let us remain united in prayer and in the commitment to help each other as brothers and sisters.

Enjoy your lunch. *Arrivederci!*

Tuesday, April 14, 2020

Holy Mass[37]

Introduction

We pray that the Lord might give us the grace of unity among us. In these difficult times, may He allow us to discover the communion that binds us and the unity which is always greater than any division.

Homily – The grace of fidelity

Peter's preaching on the day of Pentecost cuts to the heart of people: "He whom you crucified is risen" (see *Acts* 2:36). "When they heard this they were cut to the heart and said to Peter and the rest of the apostles, 'Brothers, what shall we do?'" (*Acts* 2:37). And Peter is clear: "Repent. Repent. Change your life. You who received God's promise and you who distanced yourselves from God's Law, because of many of your own things, your idols and many things … convert yourselves. Return to faithfulness" (see *Acts* 2:38). Converting oneself means returning to faithfulness. Faithfulness, that human attitude that is not very common in people's lives, in our own lives. There are always illusions that attract our attention, and often we follow after these illusions. Faithfulness: in good times and in bad. There is a passage in the Second Book of Chronicles that is very striking to me. It is from the twelfth Chapter, at

[37] Liturgy of the Word: *Acts* 2:36-41; *Psalm* 32(33); *Jn* 20:11-18.

the beginning. "When the kingdom was consolidated – it reads – King Rehoboam felt secure and abandoned the law of the Lord, and so did all Israel with him" (see *2 Chr* 12: 1). This is what the Bible says. It is a historical event, but it is a universal event. Many times, when we feel secure, we begin to make plans and we slowly drift away from the Lord. We do not remain faithful. My security is no longer that which the Lord gives me. It is an idol. This is what happened to Rehoboam and the people of Israel. He felt secure – a consolidated kingdom – and abandoned the law and began to worship idols. Sure, we might say: "Father, I don't kneel before idols". No, perhaps you do not kneel, but it is true that you seek them and often adore idols in your heart. Self-assuredness opens the door to idols.

But is feeling secure a bad thing? No, it is a grace: being secure, but being secure in the knowledge that the Lord is with me. But when there is security and I am at the center, I drift away from the Lord, like King Rehoboam, and I become unfaithful. It is very difficult to preserve faithfulness. The whole history of Israel, and the whole history of the Church, is full of infidelity. Full of it. It is full of egotistical behaviour and self-assuredness that lead the people of God to abandon the Lord, to lose that faithfulness, the grace of faithfulness. Even among us, between people, faithfulness is certainly not a cheap virtue. One is not faithful to another, to another… "Repent, return to faithfulness to God" (see *Acts* 2:38).

And in the Gospel, the icon of fidelity: that faithful woman who had not forgotten all that the Lord had done for her. She was there, faithful before the impossible – a tragedy. Hers is a faithfulness that led her to think she could carry away His body (see *Jn* 20:15) A weak but faithful woman. The icon of fidelity of Mary of Magdalene, apostle of the apostles.

Today let us ask the Lord for the grace of faithfulness: to thank Him when He gives us security, but never to think that these are "my" securities and always to look beyond our securities; the grace to be faithful even before the tomb and the collapse of so many illusions.

A faithfulness that remains always, but that is not easy to maintain. May He, the Lord, preserve it.

Wednesday, April 15, 2020

Holy Mass[38]

Introduction

Let us pray today for the elderly, especially those who are isolated or in nursing homes. They are afraid, afraid of dying alone. They are experiencing this pandemic. They see this pandemic as aggressive to them. They are our roots, our story, our history. They have given us the faith, our traditions, our sense of homeland. Let us pray for them, that the Lord might be close to them in this moment.

Homily – Faithfulness is our response to God's fidelity

Yesterday we reflected on Mary Magdalene as the icon of fidelity: fidelity to God. But how is this fidelity to God? To what God? Precisely to God who is faithful.

Our fidelity is nothing more than a response to God's fidelity. God who is faithful to His word, who is faithful to His promise, who walks with His people carrying out the promise close to His people. Faithful to the promise: God, who continually reveals Himself as a Savior of His people because He is faithful to His promise. God, who is capable of re-doing things, of re-creating, as He did with this man crippled from birth whose feet He recreated, He healed him (see *Acts* 3:6-8), the God who heals, the God who al-

[38] Liturgy of the Word: *Acts* 3:1-10; *Psalm* 104(105); *Lk* 24:13-35.

ways brings consolation to His people. The God who recreates. A new recreation: this is His faithfulness to us. A recreation that is more wonderful than creation.

A God who goes forward and does not tire of working – we say "working", *"ad instar laborantis"* (see Saint Ignatius of Loyola, *Spiritual Exercises*, 236), as the theologians say – to lead His people forward, He is not afraid of getting "tired", let us put it that way… like that Shepherd who, when he goes back home realizes that a sheep is missing and he leaves, he returns back to seek the sheep that got lost there (see *Mt* 18:12-14). A shepherd who does the extraordinary, but out of love, out of fidelity… And our God is a God who does the extraordinary but not for pay: gratuitously. It is the fidelity of gratuitousness, of abundance. It is the fidelity of that father who is capable of going up onto the terrace many times to see if his son is returning, and who never grows tired of going up there: he waits to throw a party (see *Lk* 15:21-24). God's faithfulness is a feast, it is joy, it is such a joy that it makes us behave like this crippled man: he entered the temple walking, jumping, praising God (see *Acts* 3:8-9). God's faithfulness is a feast, a free feast. A feast for all of us.

God's fidelity is a patient fidelity: he is patient with His people, He listens to them, He guides them, He explains slowly to them and He warms their hearts, as He did with these two disciples who were going far away from Jerusalem: He warms their heart so that they might return home (see *Lk* 24:32-33). God's faithfulness is what we do not know: what happened in that dialogue, but it is the generous God who sought after Peter who had denied him. We only know that the Lord rose and appeared to Simon: we do not know what happened in that dialogue (see *Lk* 24:34). But we do know that it was God's faithfulness that sought Peter out. God's fidelity always precedes us, and our faithfulness is always a response to that faithfulness that precedes us. It is God who always precedes us. It is like the flower of the almond tree, in spring: it flowers first.

To be faithful is to praise this fidelity, to be faithful to this fidelity. It is a response to this fidelity.

Thursday, April 16, 2020

Holy Mass[39]

Introduction

In these days I have been reproached because I have forgotten to thank a group of people who are also working. I thanked doctors, nurses, volunteers… "But you have forgotten pharmacists": they too have been working hard to help the sick get better. Let us pray for them as well.

Homily – To be filled with joy

In these days, in Jerusalem, people had many feelings: fear, amazement, doubt. "In those days, while the healed cripple clung to Peter and John, all the people were astonished…" (*Acts* 3:11): there was not a tranquil environment because things were happening that were not understood. And the Lord went to His disciples. Even they knew that He had already risen, even Peter knew it because he had spoken with Him that morning. These two who returned from Emmaus knew it, but when the Lord appeared they were afraid. "They were startled and frightened, thinking they saw a ghost" (*Lk* 24:37); they had the same experience on the lake, when Jesus came walking on the water. But at that time Peter, had been courageous and placed his bet on the Lord, saying: "But if it is you, bid me to walk on the water" (see *Mk* 14:28). But this day Peter was quiet; he had spoken

---

[39] Liturgy of the Word: *Acts* 3:11-26; *Psalm* 8; *Lk* 24:35-48.

with the Lord, that morning, and nobody knows what they had said to each other in that dialogue and so he remained silent. But they were so filled with fear, upset, they thought they were seeing a ghost. And He said: "Why are you so agitated, and why are these doubts rising in your hearts? Look at my hands, my feet..." He lets them see His wounds (see *Lk* 24:38-39). That treasure that Jesus took with Him to Heaven to show to the Father and intercede for us. "Touch me and see for yourselves; a ghost has no flesh and bones." And then there is a phrase that gives me a lot of consolation and for this reason, this passage of the Gospel is one of my favorites: "But they didn't believe for joy..." (see *Lk* 24:41) again, and were full of astonishment, the joy prevented them from believing. Their joy was so great that "No, this cannot be true. This joy is not real, it is too much joy". And this keeps them from believing. Joy. They were both filled with joy and paralysed by joy. And joy is one of the desires that Paul has for his community in Rome: "May the God of hope fill you with all joy" (see *Rom* 15:13), he says. To fill with joy, to be filled with joy. It is the experience of the greatest consolation, when the Lord makes us understand that this is something different from being happy, positive or radiant... No, it is something different. To be joyful...but filled with joy, an overflowing joy that really gets us. And this is why Paul wishes the Romans that "the God of hope might fill you with joy". And that word, that expression, to fill with joy is repeated many, many times. For example, what happened in the jail, when Paul saves the life of the jailer who was about to commit suicide after the doors had been opened by the earthquake, and then he proclaims the Gospel to him, he baptizes him, and the jailer, the Bible says, was "filled with joy" for having believed (see *Acts* 16: 29-34).

The same happened with the minister of economy of Candace, when Philip baptized him; he disappeared, he went on his way "filled with joy" (see *Acts* 8:39). The same happened on the day of the Ascension: the disciples returned to Jerusalem, says the Bible, "filled with joy" (see *Lk* 24:52). It is the fullness of consolation, the fullness of Lord's presence. Because, as Paul says to the Galatians, "joy is the fruit of the Holy Spirit" (see *Gal* 5:22). It is not the consequence of emotions that emerge because of something marvellous... No, it is something more. This joy that fills us is the fruit of the Holy Spirit. Without the Spirit, we cannot have joy. To receive the joy of the Spirit is a grace. I am reminded of the last numbers, the last paragraphs of Paul VI's Exhortation *Evangelii nuntiandi* (see nos. 79-80), when he speaks of joyful Christians, of joyful evangelizers, and not of those who are always down. Today is a good day to read it. Filled with joy. This is what the Bible says to us: "But they didn't believe for joy...". Their joy was so great that they did not believe. There is a passage in the book of Nehemiah that will help us today in this reflection on joy. The people, after returning to Jerusalem, rediscovered the book of the law; they discovered it again - because they knew the law by heart, they could not find the book of the law - they had a great feast and all the people gathered together to listen to the priest Ezra reading the book of the law. The people were moved and wept, they wept with joy because they had found the very book of the law and they wept, it was joyful, the weeping... In the end when the priest Ezra finished, Nehemiah said to the people: "Be calm, do not weep anymore, preserve this joy because the joy in the Lord is your strength" (see *Neh* 8:1-12). This word from the book of Nehemiah will help us today. The great strength that we have to transform, to preach the Gospel, to go forward as witnesses of life is the joy of the Lord which is a fruit of the Holy Spirit. Today, let us ask Him to grant us this fruit.

Friday, April 17, 2020

Holy Mass[40]

Introduction

Today I would like us to pray for expectant mothers, pregnant women who will become mothers and are restless and concerned. A question: "What kind of world will my child be born into?" Let us pray for them, that the Lord may give them courage to raise these children trusting that it will certainly be a different world, but it will always be a world that the Lord will love greatly.

Homily – Familiarity with the Lord

The disciples were fishermen: indeed, Jesus had called them when they were at work. Andrew and Peter were working with the nets. They left their nets and they followed Jesus (see *Mt* 4:18-20). John and James, the same: they left the father and the youths who worked with them and followed Jesus (see *Mt* 4:21-22). They received their call precisely as they worked as fishermen. And today's passage from the Gospel, this miracle, the miraculous catch, makes us think of another miraculous catch, the one Luke tells us about (see *Lk* 5:1-11): the same thing happened there too. They caught something when they didn't think they were going to be able to catch anything. After Jesus had preached He told them to go out to sea. "But we

---

[40] Liturgy of the Word: *Acts* 4:1-12; *Psalm* 117(118); *Jn* 21:1-14.

have been working all night and we haven't caught anything!" And Jesus said, "Go". And Peter said, "On your word we will cast out the nets". The quantity was so great, says the Gospel, that "astonishment ... seized him and all those with him" (*Lk* 5:9), upon seeing that miracle. Today, in that other catch of fish one does not speak about astonishment. We can see a certain naturalness, we can see that there has been some progress, a journey of knowing the Lord, of intimacy with the Lord. I would say the right word would be that they have grown in *familiarity* with the Lord. When John sees this, he says to Peter: "But it is the Lord!", and Peter tucks in his garment and jumps into the sea in order to go to the Lord (*Jn* 21:7). The first time he kneeled before Him and said: "Depart from me, Lord, for I am a sinful man" (see *Lk* 5:8). This time he says nothing, it is more natural. No one asked, "Who are you?". They knew that He was the Lord: it was natural, the encounter with the Lord. The apostles' familiarity with the Lord had grown.

We Christians too, in our journey of life, are in this state of walking, of progressing in familiarity with the Lord. The Lord, I could say, is a bit "down to earth", but He is down to earth because He walks with us, we recognize that it is Him. No one asks Him, here, "Who are you?": they knew that He was the Lord. It is an everyday familiarity with the Lord, that of the Christian. And certainly, they ate breakfast together, with fish and bread, certainly they spoke about many things naturally. This familiarity with the Lord, of Christians, is always in community. Yes, it is intimate, it is personal, but within the community. A familiarity without community, a familiarity without bread, a familiarity without the Church, without the people, without the sacraments, is dangerous. It can become, let's say, a gnostic familiarity, a familiarity for me by myself, detached from the people of God. The apostles' familiarity with the Lord is always a community familiarity. It always takes place at the table, a sign of the community. It was always with the Sacrament, always with the Bread.

I say this because someone made me reflect on the danger that we are living in this moment, this pandemic that has made us all communicate, even religiously, through the means of communication. Even this Mass, we are all communicants, but not together, we are spiritually together. The people gathered are few. There is a large number of people: we are together, but not together. The Sacrament too: today you receive the Eucharist, but the people linked up with us, only spiritual communion. And this is not the Church: this is the Church in a difficult situation, which the Lord permits, but the ideal of the Church is always with the people and with the Sacraments. Always.

Before Easter, when the news emerged that I would celebrate Easter in an empty Saint Peter's Basilica, a bishop wrote to me, a good bishop, good; and he rebuked me. "But how come, Saint Peter's is so big, why not put at least thirty people in there, so that you can see there are people? There won't be any danger". I thought: "But, what does he have in mind, to tell me this?" I didn't understand, at the time. But since he is a good bishop, very close to the people, he wanted to say something to me. When I find him, I will ask him. Then I understood. He was saying to me, "Be careful not to make the Church virtual, viral; not to make the sacraments virtual, not to make the people of God virtual. The Church, the sacraments, the people of

God are concrete. It is true that in this moment we must provide this familiarity with God in this way, but so as to come out of the tunnel, not to stay inside it. And this is the familiarity of the apostles: not gnostic, not virtual, not selfish, for each one of us, but a concrete familiarity, in the people. Familiarity with the Lord in everyday life, familiarity with the Lord in the sacraments, in the midst of the people of God. They went on a journey of maturation in their familiarity with the Lord. Let us learn how to do this as well. From the very first moment, they understood that familiarity was different to what they had imagined, and they arrived at this. They knew that there was the Lord, and they shared everything: the community, sacraments, the Lord, peace, feasting.

May the Lord teach us this intimacy with Him, this familiarity with Him but in the Church, with the sacraments, with the faithful holy people of God.

Saturday, April 18, 2020

Holy Mass[41]

Introduction

Yesterday I received a letter from a sister who works as a sign language translator for the deaf and mute, and she told me about the very difficult work that healthcare workers, nurses, and doctors have to do with disabled people affected by COVID-19. Let us pray for those who are always at the service of those who have different abilities, but who do not have the abilities that we have.

Homily – The gift of the Holy Spirit: frankness, courage, parrhesia

The chief priests, the elders, the scribes were astonished seeing these men and the boldness with which they spoke, and knowing they were uneducated people, perhaps they didn't even know how to write. They did not understand: "But it is something we cannot understand, how these people are so courageous, they have this boldness" (*Acts* 4:13). This word is very important, and becomes the style typical of Christian preachers, especially in the Acts of the Apostles: frankness, boldness, courage. It means all of this. It says so clearly. It comes from the Greek root that means all of this, and we, too, use this word very frequently, the Greek word itself, *parrhesia,* to indicate frankness and courage. And they saw this frankness, this courage,

[41] Liturgy of the Word: *Acts* 4:13-21; *Psalm* 117(118); *Mk* 16:9-15.

this *parrhesia* in them, and they did not understand. Boldness. The courage and the frankness with which the first apostles preached... For example, the Book of the Acts of the Apostles is full of this: it says that Paul and Barnabas sought to explain the mystery of Jesus to the Hebrews with frankness, and that they preached the Gospel with frankness (see *Acts* 13:46).

But there is a verse in the Letter to the Hebrews that I like a lot, when the author of the Letter to the Hebrews realizes that there is something in the community that is waning, that something is being lost, that these early Christians are becoming lukewarm. And he says this – I don't remember the citation well... he says "Remember the days past when ... you endured a great contest of suffering. ... Do not throw away your confidence" (see *Heb* 10:32-35). "Start again", recover the frankness, the Christian courage to go ahead. One cannot be Christian without this boldness: if it does not come, you are not a good Christian. If you do not have courage, if to explain your position you slip and slide on ideological positions or casuistical explanations, then you lack that boldness, you lack that Christian style, the freedom to speak, to say everything. Courage. And we see that the chief priests and the scribes are victims of this boldness, because it backs them into a corner – they do not know what to do. Realizing that "they were unschooled, ordinary men, they were astonished and they took note that these men had been with Jesus. But since they could see the man who had been healed standing there with them, there was nothing they could say" (*Acts* 4:13-15). Instead of accepting the truth as it could be seen, their hearts were so closed that they sought the way of diplomacy, the way of compromise: "Let's frighten them a little, tell them that they will be punished, and we'll see if that way they are silent" (see *Acts* 4:16-17). They were truly backed into a corner by this boldness; they did not know how to get out of it. But it did not come to mind to them to say, "Could this be true?", because their hearts were already closed, they were hard: their hearts were corrupt. This is one of the tragedies: the strength of the Holy Spirit, that manifests itself in this boldness of preaching, in this folly of preaching, cannot enter into corrupt hearts. Therefore, let us be careful: sinners yes, corrupt never. And never arrive at this corruption, which manifests itself in many forms. .. But, they were backed into a corner and did not know what to say. And in the end, they found a compromise: "Let's threaten them a bit, frighten them a little", and they invited them, they called them back and ordered them, they invited them not to say at any moment, nor to teach, the name of Jesus. "Let us make peace: go in peace but do not speak in the name of Jesus, do not teach" (see *Acts* 4:18). Peter knew them: he was not born courageous. He was a coward, he denied Jesus. But what happened, now? They answer: "Which is right in God's eyes: to listen to you, or to Him? You be the judges! As for us, we cannot help speaking about what we have seen and heard" (*Acts* 4:19-20). But where does this courage come from, to this coward who denied the Lord? What happened in the heart of this man? The gift of the Holy Spirit: frankness, courage, *parrhesia*, is a gift, a grace that the Holy Spirit gives on the day of Pentecost. Right after receiving the Holy Spirit they went out to preach: somewhat courageously, as it was something new to them. This is consistency, the mark of the Christian, the true Christian: he or she is courageous and tells all the truth, because he or she is consistent.

And this consistency is what the Lord appeals to when He sends them out. After Mark's summary in the Gospel: " When he had risen, early on the first day of the week..." (16: 9) - a summary of the resurrection - He "rebuked them for their unbelief and hardness of heart because they had not believed those who saw Him after He had been raised" (v. 14). But with the strength of the Holy Spirit - it is Jesus's greeting, "Receive the Holy Spirit" (*Jn* 20:22) - He said to them, "Go into the whole world and proclaim the Gospel to every creature" (*Mk* 16:15). Go with courage, go with boldness, do not be afraid. Do not - I return to the verse in the Letter to the Hebrews - "Do not throw away your confidence", do not throw away this gift of the Holy Spirit (see *Heb* 10:35). The mission is born right there. It is that gift that makes us courageous, bold in the proclamation of the Word.

May the Lord help us always to be like that, courageous. This does not mean imprudent: no, no. Courageous. Christian courage is always prudent, but it is courage.

Sunday, April 19, 2020

Second Sunday of Easter (Feast of the Divine Mercy) (A)

Holy Mass[42]

Homily – God's mercy always lifts us up

Last Sunday we celebrated the Lord's resurrection; today we witness the resurrection of His disciple. It has already been a week, a week since the disciples had seen the Risen Lord, but in spite of this, they remained fearful, cringing behind "closed doors" (*Jn* 20:26), unable even to convince Thomas, the only one absent, of the resurrection. What does Jesus do in the face of this timorous lack of belief? He returns and, standing in the same place, "in the midst" of the disciples, He repeats His greeting: "Peace be with you!" (*Jn* 20:19, 26). He starts all over. The resurrection of His disciple begins here, from this *faithful and patient mercy*, from the discovery that God never tires of reaching out to lift us up when we fall. He wants us to see Him, not as a taskmaster with whom we have to settle accounts, but as our Father who always raises us up. In life we go forward tentatively, uncertainly, like a toddler who takes a few steps and falls; a few steps more and falls again, yet each time his father puts him back on his feet. The hand that always puts us back on our feet is mercy: God knows

---

[42] Liturgy of the Word: *Acts* 2:42-47; *Psalm* 117(118); *1 Pt* 1:3-9; *Jn* 20:19-31.

that without mercy we will remain on the ground, that in order to keep walking, we need to be put back on our feet.

You may object: "But I keep falling!". The Lord knows this and He is always ready to raise you up. He does not want us to keep thinking about our failings; rather, He wants us to look to Him. For when we fall, He sees children needing to be put back on their feet; in our failings He sees children in need of His merciful love. Today, in this church that has become a shrine of mercy in Rome, and on this Sunday that Saint John Paul II dedicated to Divine Mercy twenty years ago, we confidently welcome this message. Jesus said to Saint Faustina: "I am love and mercy itself; there is no human misery that could measure up to my mercy" (*Diary*, September 14, 1937). At one time, the Saint, with satisfaction, told Jesus that she had offered him all of her life and all that she had. But Jesus's answer stunned her: "You have not offered me the thing that is truly yours". What had that holy nun kept for herself? Jesus said to her with kindness: "My daughter, give me your failings" (October 10, 1937). We too can ask ourselves: "Have I given my failings to the Lord? Have I let Him see me fall so that He can raise me up?" Or is there something I still keep inside me? A sin, a regret from the past, a wound that I have inside, a grudge against someone, an idea about a particular person… The Lord waits for us to offer Him our failings so that He can help us experience His mercy.

Let us go back to the disciples. They had abandoned the Lord at His Passion and felt guilty. But meeting them, Jesus did not give a long sermon. To them, who were wounded within, He shows His own wounds. Thomas can now touch them and know of Jesus's love and how much

Jesus had suffered for him, even though he had abandoned him. In those wounds, he touches with his hands God's tender closeness. Thomas arrived late, but once he received mercy, he overtook the other disciples: he believed not only in the resurrection, but in the boundless love of God. And he makes the most simple and beautiful profession of faith: "My Lord and my God!" (v. 28). Here is the resurrection of the disciple: it is accomplished when his frail and wounded humanity enters into that of Jesus. There, every doubt is resolved; there, God becomes *my God;* there, we begin to accept ourselves and to love life as it is.

Dear brothers and sisters, in the time of trial that we are presently undergoing, we too, like Thomas, with our fears and our doubts, have experienced our frailty. We need the Lord, who sees beyond that frailty an irrepressible beauty. With him we rediscover how precious we are even in our vulnerability. We discover that we are like beautiful crystals, fragile and at the same time precious. And if, like crystal, we are transparent before Him, His light – the light of mercy – will shine in us and through us in the world. As the Letter of Peter said, this is a reason for being "filled with joy, though now for a little while you may have to suffer various trials" (*1 Pt* 1:6).

On this feast of Divine Mercy, the most beautiful message comes from Thomas, the disciple who arrived late; he was the only one missing. But the Lord waited for Thomas. Mercy does not abandon those who stay behind. Now, while we are looking forward to a slow and arduous recovery from the pandemic, there is a danger that we will forget those who are left behind. The risk is that we may then be struck by an even worse virus, that of *selfish indifference*. A virus spread by the thought that life is better if it is better for me, and that everything will be fine if it is fine for me. It begins there and ends up selecting one person over another, discarding the poor, and sacrificing those left behind on the altar of progress. The present pandemic, however, reminds us that there are no differences or borders between those who suffer. We are all frail, all equal, all precious. May we be profoundly shaken by what is happening all around us: the time has come to eliminate inequalities, to heal the injustice that is undermining the health of the entire human family! Let us learn from the early Christian community described in the Acts of the Apostles. It received mercy and lived with mercy: "All who believed were together and had all things in common; and they sold their possessions and goods and distributed them to all, as any had need" (*Acts* 2:44-45). This is not some ideology: it is Christianity.

In that community, after the resurrection of Jesus, only one was left behind and the others waited for him. Today the opposite seems to be the case: a small part of the human family has moved ahead, while the majority has remained behind. Each of us could say: "These are complex problems, it is not my job to take care of the needy, others have to be concerned with it!". Saint Faustina, after meeting Jesus, wrote: "In a soul that is suffering we should see Jesus on the cross, not a parasite and a burden... [Lord] you give us the chance to practice deeds of mercy, and we practice making judgements" (*Diary*, September 6, 1937). Yet she herself complained one day to Jesus that, in being merciful, one is thought to be naive. She said, "Lord, they often abuse my goodness". And Jesus replied: "Never mind, don't let it bother you, just be merciful to everyone always" (December 24, 1937). To everyone: let us not think only of our interests, our vested interests. Let us welcome this time of trial as an opportunity to prepare for our collective future, a future for all without discarding anyone. Because without an all-embracing vision, there will be no future for anyone.

Today the simple and disarming love of Jesus revives the heart of His disciple. Like the apostle Thomas, let us accept mercy, the salvation of the world. And let us show mercy to those who are most vulnerable; for only in this way will we build a new world.

Regina Coeli

Dear Brothers and Sisters,

On this Second Sunday of Easter, it was meaningful to celebrate the Eucharist here, in the Church of the Holy Spirit in Saxony, which St John Paul II wanted to be the Shrine of Divine Mercy. The Christian response to the storms of life and history cannot but be mercy: compassionate love among us and toward everyone, especially toward those who suffer, who have more difficulties, and are more abandoned... Not devotionalism, or mere assistance, but compassion, that comes from the heart. Divine Mercy comes from the Heart of Christ, of the Risen Christ. It flows from the wound in His side that is always open, open for us, who are always in need of pardon and comfort. May Christian mercy also inspire a just sharing among the nations and their institutions, to conform the current crisis in the spirit of solidarity.

I extend greetings to our brothers and sisters who belong to the Oriental Churches, who today celebrate the Feast of Easter. Together, let us proclaim: "The Lord is truly risen!" (*Lk* 24:34). Above all, at this moment of trial, let us feel what a great gift and hope it is that comes from being risen with Christ! In particular, I rejoice with the Eastern Catholic communities who, for ecumenical reasons, celebrate Easter together with the Orthodox. May this fraternity be of comfort in those places where Christians are a small minority.

With Paschal joy, let us turn now to the Virgin Mary, Mother of Mercy.

Monday, April 20, 2020

Holy Mass[43]

Introduction

Let us pray today for the men and women who have a vocation to political life. Politics is a very high form of charity. For the political parties in the various countries, so that in this moment of pandemic they may seek together the good of the country and not the good of their own party.

Homily –To be born from the Spirit

This man Nicodemus is one of the leaders of the Jews, an authoritative man. He felt the need to go to Jesus and he went by night. He went by night because he had to be careful, as those who went to talk with Jesus were not looked upon well (see *Jn* 3:2). He was a Pharisee, a just man. Not all of the Pharisees were bad, no, there were also good Pharisees. He was a just Pharisee. He felt restless. He was a man who had read the prophets and knew that what Jesus was doing had been announced by the prophets. He felt that restlessness, and so he went to speak with Jesus.

"Rabbi, we know that you are a teacher who comes from God" (v. 2). This is a confession up to a certain point. "For no one could perform the signs that you do unless God were with him" (v. 2).

---

[43] Liturgy of the Word: *Acts* 4:23-31; *Psalm* 2; *Jn* 3:1-8.

And then he stops. He stops before the "therefore", and Jesus responds mysteriously, in a way that Nicodemus does not expect. He responds with the symbol of being born: "Unless a man is born from above, he cannot see the kingdom of God" (v. 3).

And he, Nicodemus, feels confused, he does not understand and takes Jesus's answer literally: "But how can someone who is already an adult be born again?" (see v. 4). To be born from on high, from the spirit. It is the leap forward that Nicodemus needs to make but he does not know how to make it. Because the spirit is unpredictable. The definition of the spirit that Jesus gives here is interesting: "The wind blows where it pleases you hear it sound but you cannot tell where it comes from or where it is going. That is how it is with all who are born of the Spirit" (v. 8), that is, free. A person who allows himself to be carried from one place to another by the Holy Spirit: this is the freedom of the Spirit. And one who does this is a docile person, and here we speak about docility to the Spirit.

Being a Christian is not only obeying the Commandments: we need to do that, this is true; but if you stop there, you are not a good Christian. Being a good Christian means letting the Spirit enter within you and lead you, lead you where He wants. In our Christian life very often we stop, like Nicodemus, before that "therefore". We do not know what step to take, we do not know how to do it, and we do not have the trust in God to make this step and let the Spirit enter. Being born again means letting the Spirit enter into us, so that I am led by the Spirit, not by myself, free, with this freedom of the Spirit, and you never know where it will end.

The Apostles, who were in the Cenacle when the Spirit came, went out to preach with that courage, that boldness (see *Acts* 2:1-13) … they did not know that this would have happened; and they did it, because the Spirit guided them. The Christian must never stop at the fulfilment of the Commandments; one must do this, but go beyond, towards that new birth that is birth in the Spirit, which gives you the freedom of the Spirit.

That is what happened to this Christian community in the first Reading. After John and Peter returned from the interrogation with the high priests, they went to their brothers and sisters, to their community, and told them everything the high priests and elders had said to them. And the community, when it heard this, was rather afraid (see *Acts* 4:23). And what did they do? They prayed. They did not stop at precautionary measures: "No, now we will do this, we'll be a bit calmer" – no. They prayed. So that the Spirit would tell them what they should do. They raised their voice to God, saying: "Lord!" (v. 24), and they prayed. This beautiful prayer in a dark moment, a moment in which they have to make decisions and do not know what to do. They want to be born from the Spirit, they open their heart to the Spirit, that He might tell them what to do.

And they say: "Herod, Pontius Pilate with the Pagan nations against Jesus" (v. 27). They tell the story and they say, "Lord, do something!" "Lord, take note of their threats" – those of the group of priests – "and tell your servants to proclaim your word with all boldness" (v. 29). They ask for the boldness, the courage, not to be afraid. "Stretch out your hand to heal and to work miracles and marvels through the name of Jesus" (v. 30). And when they finished their prayer "the house where they were assembled rocked, they were all filled with the Holy Spirit and began to proclaim the word of God boldly" (v. 31). A second Pentecost took place here.

Faced with difficulties, faced with a closed door, when they did not know how to go forward, they went to the Lord, they open their heart and the Spirit comes and gives them what they need, and they go out to preach, with courage. This is what it means to be born of the Spirit. This means not stopping at the "therefore", at the things we have always done, at the "therefore" after the Commandments, at the "therefore" after religious habits: no! This means being reborn. And how does one prepare to be reborn? With prayer. Prayer is what opens the door to the Spirit and gives us this freedom, this boldness, this courage of the Holy Spirit. You will never know where it will take you. But it is the Spirit.

May the Lord help us always to be open to the Spirit, as it will be He who leads us forward in our life of service to the Lord.

Tuesday, April 21, 2020

Holy Mass[44]

Introduction

There is a lot of silence at the moment. The silence can even be heard. May this silence, which is somewhat new to what we are accustomed, teach us how to listen, so that we might grow in our ability to listen. Let us pray for this.

Homily – The Holy Spirit: master of harmony

"To be born from above" (*Jn* 3:7) is to be born with the strength of the Holy Spirit. We cannot keep the Holy Spirit for ourselves; we can only allow Him to transform us. And our docility opens the door to the Holy Spirit; it is He who changes us, who works this transformation in us, this rebirth from on high. This is the promise that Jesus makes: to send the Holy Spirit (see *Acts* 1:8). The Holy Spirit is capable of wondrous things that we cannot even imagine.

An example is this first Christian community, which is not a fantasy, this is what they say here: it is a model, at which we can arrive when there is docility and one allows the Holy Spirit to enter and to transform. An ideal community, let's say. It is true that immediately after this, problems begin, but the Lord makes us see up to what

---

[44] Liturgy of the Word: *Acts* 4:32-37; *Psalm* 92(93); *Jn* 3:7-15.

point we can arrive if we are open to the Holy Spirit, if we are docile.

There is harmony in this community (see *Acts* 4:32-37). The Holy Spirit is the master of harmony; He is capable of making it, and He has made it happen here. It is what needs to happen in our hearts, many things in us must change to create harmony, because He Himself is harmony. Also the harmony between the Father and the Son: it is He, the love of harmony. And He, with harmony, creates these things such as this community, which was so harmonious. But then, history tells us – the same Book of the *Acts of the Apostles* – of many problems in the community. This is a model: the Lord has permitted this model of an almost "heavenly" community, to make us see where we should arrive.

But then the divisions began to appear in the community. The Apostle James, in the second chapter of his Letter, says: ""May your faith be immune from personal favoritism" (see *Jas* 2:1) because it was there. "Do not discriminate": the Apostles had to come out and admonish. And Paul, in the first Letter to the Corinthians, in Chapter 11, laments: "I have heard that there are divisions among you" (see *1 Cor* 11:18). Internal divisions begin in the community. We need to arrive at this ideal, but it is not easy. There are many things that divide a community, be it a Christian community, a parish community, a diocesan community, a community of priests or men and women religious… many things come to divide a community.

Looking at the things that divided the first Christian community, I find three. First, money. When the Apostle James says that personal favoritism is to be avoided, he gives an example. Because "if in your Church, in your assembly, someone comes in with a golden ring, they immediately bring him to the front of the community, and the poor person is left on the side" (see *Jas* 2:2-4). Money. Paul says the same thing: "The rich bring things to eat and they eat, and the poor are left standing" (*1 Cor* 11:20-22). We leave them there as if to say to them, "Take care of yourselves". Money divides, the love of money divides the community, it divides the Church.

How many times, in the history of the Church, where there have been doctrinal deviations - not always, but many times - has money been behind it! The money of power, whether it be political power or cash, always money. Money divides the community. This is why poverty is the mother of the community, poverty is the wall that guards the community. Money and personal interests divide. Even in the family: how many families have ended up divided over an inheritance? How many families? And they do not even speak to each other any more. So many families... over an inheritance. Money divides.

Another thing that divides a community is vanity, that desire to feel better than others. "I thank you Lord, because I am not like the others" (see *Lk* 18:11): the prayer of the Pharisee. Vanity, feeling that... and also the vanity of making myself seen, vanity in habits, in how we dress. How many times, not always, but how many times is the celebration of a Sacrament an example of vanity: who has the best clothes, who can throw the biggest party... Even there, vanity enters. And vanity divides. Because vanity leads you to behave like a peacock and where one is like a peacock, there is division, always.

A third thing that divides a community is gossip: it is not the first time I have said this, but it is true. It is reality. It is something the devil puts in us, almost a need to speak badly of others. "He's a good person...". "Yes, sure, but...", and then right away, that "but", that is like a rock, to discredit the other. And then straight away I say something I have heard, and in that way I put the other person down.

But the Spirit always comes with His strength to save us from this worldliness of money, vanity and gossip, because the Spirit is not of the world: He is against the world. He is capable of working these miracles, these great things.

Let us ask the Lord for this docility to the Spirit so that He might transform us, and transform our parish, diocesan and religious communities: that He might transform them in order always to go forward in harmony, the harmony that Jesus wants for the Christian community.

Wednesday, April 22, 2020

Holy Mass[45]

Introduction

At this moment, in which unity between ourselves and nations is very necessary, let us pray today for Europe, so that Europe might succeed in creating this fraternal unity the founding fathers dreamt of.

Homily – Let the light of God enter in us so we do not become like bats in the darkness

This passage from the Gospel of John, chapter 3 (see *Jn* 3:16-21), the dialogue between Jesus and Nicodemus, is a true theological treatise. Everything is here: *kerygma,* catechesis, theological reflection, *parenesis*… everything is here. Every time we read it we find more wealth, more explanations, more things that help us understand God's revelation. It would be good to read it many times in order to draw near to the mystery of the Redemption.

Today I will take just two points from all of this, two points that are in today's passage.

The first is the revelation of God's love. God loves us, and He loves us *madly,* as one of the saints used to say. God's love appears to be madness. He loves us: "God loved the world so much that He gave us His only son" (*Jn* 3:16). And He sent Him to die on the cross. And every time that we look at the cross, we find this love. The cruci-

---

[45] Liturgy of the Word: *Acts* 5:17-26; *Psalm* 33(34); *Jn* 3:16-21.

fix is truly the great book of God's love. It is not an object to put here or to place there, beautiful, not so beautiful, an antique, or modern, no. It is truly an expression of God's love. God loved us so much that He sent His Son, who annihilated Himself to the point of death on the cross, out of love. "God so loved the world that He gave His only Son" (see v. 16).

How many people, how many Christians spend time gazing at the crucifix? There they find everything, because they have understood, the Holy Spirit makes them understand that all knowledge, all God's love, all Christian wisdom is there. Paul speaks about this, explaining that all his human reasoning served him up to a certain point, but the true reasoning, the most beautiful way of thinking, but also that which explains everything, is Christ's cross: it is a scandal (see *1 Cor* 1:23), it is folly, but it is the way. And this is God's love. "God loved the world so much that He gave His only Son" (*Jn* 3:16). And why? "So that everyone who believes in Him may not be lost but may have eternal life". The love of God, who wants His children to be with Him.

To look at the Cross in silence, to look at the wounds, to look at the heart of Jesus, to look at it all: Christ crucified, the Son of God, annihilated, humiliated... out of love. This is the first point that were are shown today by this treatise of theology, which is Jesus's dialogue with Nicodemus.

The second point that will help us, too: "The light has come into the world, but men have shown they prefer darkness to the light because their deeds were evil" (*Jn* 3:19). Jesus also picks up this theme of light. There are people - we too, very often - who cannot live in the light because they are accustomed to the dark. The light blinds them, they are unable to see. *They are humans who are like bats*, which only know how to move about at night. And we too, when we are in sin, are in this state: we cannot tolerate the light. It is more convenient for us to live in darkness. The light hits us in the face, it makes us see what we do not want to see. What's worse is that the eyes of the soul, the more they live in darkness, the more they grow accustomed to it, and become ignorant of what light is. One loses a sense of light through growing more accustomed to the darkness. And many human scandals, so much corruption, prove this. Those who are corrupt do not know what the light is, they do not know. We too, when we are in a state of sin, distance ourselves from the Lord and become blind. We feel better when we are in the darkness and we move about in this way, without seeing, like the blind, as best we can.

Let us allow the love of God, who sent Jesus to save us, enter into us, and may the light that Jesus brings (see v. 19), the light of the Spirit, enter into us and help us to see things with God's light, with the true light and not the shadows that the lord of darkness gives us.

Two things, today: the love of God in Christ, in the crucifix, in daily life. And the question we can ask ourselves every day: "Do I walk in the light or do I walk in the darkness? Am I a child of God or have I ended up like a *poor bat*?"

Thursday, April 23, 2020

Holy Mass[46]

Introduction

In many places, one of the effects of this pandemic is being felt: many families are in need, they are hungry, and unfortunately usurers are profiting from them. This is another pandemic, another virus. A social pandemic: families who have a precarious job, who work day to day, or do not have a regular job, and do not have food to put on the table, and have children to feed. And then usurers come along and take what little they have. Let us pray. Let us pray for these families, for those many children of these families, for the dignity of these families, and let us pray also for the usurers, that the Lord might touch their hearts and convert them.

Homily – Jesus prays for us before the Father, showing His wounds

The first Reading continues the story that began with the healing of the crippled man at the Beautiful Gate of the Temple. The Apostles were taken before the Sanhedrin, and then they were sent to jail, then an angel freed them. And this morning, that same morning, they were supposed to be brought out of jail in order to be judged, but the angel freed them, and they went into the Temple and began to preach (see *Acts* 5:17-25). And that day the

---

[46] Liturgy of the Word: *Acts* 5:27-33; *Psalm* 33(34); *Jn* 3:31-36.

commander and the soldiers took the Apostles and presented them before the Sanhedrin (see v. 27); they had gone to take them from the Temple and took them before the Sanhedrin. And there, the high priest rebukes them. "We gave you a formal warning not to preach in this name (v. 28), that is, in Jesus's name, and what have you done? You have filled Jerusalem with your teaching, and seem determined to fix the guilt of this man's death on us" (v. 28). The Apostles, Peter above all, reproved the leaders for having killed Jesus. And Peter and the Apostles replied with the same story. "Obedience to God comes before obedience to men … and you are guilty" (see *Acts* 5:29-31). His accusation is so courageous and bold that one might ask: Is this the same Peter who denied Jesus? That Peter who was so fearful, that Peter who was even a coward? How in the world did he arrive at this point? And they even finish saying, "We are witnesses to all this, we and the Holy Spirit whom God has given to those who obey Him" (see v. 32). What was the journey this Peter took to arrive at this point, at this courage, at this boldness, to expose himself in this way? Because he could have arrived at a compromise with the priests, saying, "Calm down, we will take on a softer tone, we won't accuse you in public, we will leave you in peace", so as to arrive at a compromise.

The Church, throughout her history, has often had to do this in order to save the people of God. And at times, the Church has done this to save herself - not the Holy Church, but the Church's leaders. Compromises can be good and they can be bad. But the Apostles could have gotten out of this through a compromise. No! Peter said,

"No compromise, you are guilty" (see v. 30), and he said it courageously.

How did Peter reach this point? Because he was an enthusiastic man, a man who loved passionately, but he was also fearful. He was a man who was open to God to the point that God reveals to him that Jesus is Christ, the Son of God, but shortly afterwards - straight away - he gives in to the temptation of denying Jesus, he reaches the point of saying to Jesus, "No, Lord, that is not the way: let us take another": redemption without the Cross. And Jesus says to him, "Satan" (see *Mk* 8:31-33). A Peter who passed from temptation to grace, a Peter who is capable of kneeling before Jesus and saying, "Leave me for I am a sinful man" (see *Lk* 5:8), and then we see a Peter who tries to get by without being seen, and denies Jesus so as not to end up in jail (see *Lk* 22:54-62). Peter who is unstable, as he is very generous and also very weak. What is the secret, what is the strength that Peter received in order to get here? There is a verse that will help us understand this. Before the Passion, Jesus said to the Apostles, "Satan has desired to sift you like wheat" (*Lk* 22:31). This is the moment of temptation. You are going to be sifted like wheat. And to Peter He says, "but I have prayed for you so that your faith may not fail" (v. 32). This is Peter's secret: Jesus's prayer. Jesus prays for Peter, so that his faith will not fail him and that he may - Jesus says - confirm his brothers in faith. Jesus prays for Peter.

And what Jesus did for Peter, He does for all of us. Jesus prays for us all. He prays before the Father. We are used to praying to Jesus so that He might give us one grace or another, that He might help us, but we are not accustomed to contemplating Jesus who shows the Father His wounds, Jesus the intercessor, the mediator, Jesus who prays for us. And Peter was able to progress on this path from a coward to a courageous person with the gift of the Holy Spirit, thanks to Jesus's prayer.

Let us think about this a little, and let us turn to Jesus, grateful that He prays for us. Jesus prays for every one of us. Jesus is the intercessor. Jesus wanted to take His wounds with Him to show His Father the price of our salvation. We need to have more confidence; more than in our own prayers, in Jesus's prayer. "Lord, pray for me" – "But I am God, I can give you…" "Yes, but pray for me, because You are the intercessor". This is Peter's secret. "Peter, I have prayed for you that your faith will not fail" (*Lk* 22:32). May the Lord teach us how to ask Him for the grace to pray for each one of us.

Friday, April 24, 2020

Holy Mass[47]

Introduction

Let us pray today for teachers. They need to work hard to provide lessons via internet and in other ways. And let us also pray for students who need to take their exams in a way that they are not accustomed to. Let us accompany them with our prayer.

Homily – Christ forms the pastor's heart in closeness to the people of God

This sentence in this passage from the Gospel makes us think: "He said this to put him to the test, He Himself knew exactly what He was going to do" (see *Jn* 6: 6). And that is what Jesus had in mind when He asked Philip, "Where can we buy some bread for these people to eat?" (v. 5). He said it to put him to the test. He knew. Here we observe Jesus's behavior with the disciples. He continually put them to the test in order to teach them. And when they deviated from the function they were to perform, He would stop them and teach them.

The Gospel is filled with these actions of Jesus, intended to make His disciples grow and become pastors of the people of God, in this case bishops: pastors of the people of God. And one of the things Jesus loved the most was to be with the crowd, because this too is a symbol

---

[47] Liturgy of the Word: *Acts* 5:34-42; *Psalm* 26(27); *Jn* 6:1-15.

of the universality of redemption. And one of the things the Apostles did not like was the crowd. They liked being near the Lord, listening to the Lord, hearing everything that the Lord said. That day they went there to rest. That is what the other Gospels say. Because all four Gospels talk about this ... perhaps there were two multiplications of the loaves. They were coming back from a mission, and the Lord said, "Let's go and rest awhile" (see *Mk* 6:31). And so they went there. And the people noticed where they were going by the sea, and they ran ahead along the shore and waited for them there. And the disciples were not happy, because the crowd had ruined their break; they couldn't have this feast with the Lord. In spite of this, Jesus began to teach, they started to speak among themselves, and the hours went by. Jesus spoke and the people were happy. And [the disciples] said, "Our feast has been ruined, our rest has been ruined".

But the Lord sought closeness to the people, and tried to form the hearts of the pastors to be near the people of God in order to serve them. And they understood that they had been chosen, and they felt that they were in a privileged circle, a type of aristocracy, we might say, near to the Lord. And many times the Lord made gestures to correct them. For example, let us think of the children. The disciples protected the Lord, saying to them, "Oh no, don't go near Him, don't disturb Him... No, children belong with their parents". And Jesus? "Let the children come to me" (see *Mk* 10:13-16). And they did not understand. Then they understood. Or we can think of the road to Jericho, that other one who called "Jesus, Son of David, have mercy on me" (*Lk* 18:38), and a person said, "Keep quiet. Keep quiet. Let the Lord pass by! Do not disturb Him!" And

Jesus says, "But who is that? Bring him here" (see *Lk* 18:35-43). Once again the Lord [corrects them]. And in this way He teaches them about being near to the people of God.

It is true that the people of God tire the pastor, they are tiring: when there is a good pastor, things multiply, because the people always go to a good pastor for one reason or another. Once, a great pastor in a simple, humble quarter in my diocese, had the rectory like a normal house, like any other, and people would come and knock on the door or on the window at all times ... and once he said to me, "I would like to wall up the door and the window so they would let me get some rest". But he knew he was a pastor and that he needed to be with the people! And Jesus forms and teaches the disciples. He teaches the apostles this pastoral behavior, which is being near to the people of God. And the people of God are tiring, because they always ask us for concrete things; they always ask you for something real. Maybe they are mistaken in what they ask, but they are always concrete things. And so the pastor always needs to take care of these things.

The versions of the other evangelists of this episode show that the hours had passed and it was starting to get dark, but they say, "send the crowd away so that they can go to the surrounding villages and countryside and find food" (see *Lk* 9:12-13). Right at the moment that it began to get dark. But what were they thinking of? That their own party could begin, that selfishness that is not bad, it is understandable, they wanted to stay with their shepherd, with Jesus who is the great shepherd. And Jesus answers, to put them to the test, "You give them something to eat" (see v. 13). And this is what Jesus says today to all pastors: "You give them something to eat". "Are they anguished? Give them consolation. Are they lost? Give them a way out. Have they made mistakes? Help them to solve the problems. You give them, you give them...". And the poor apostle feels that he has to give, give, give... But from whom does he receive? Jesus teaches us: from the same One from whom Jesus receives. After this event, He bids farewell to the apostles and goes to pray: from the Father, from prayer. This dual closeness of the pastor is what Jesus tries to make the apostles understand so that they may become great pastors.

But very often the crowd errs, and here it has made a mistake, hasn't it? "The people, seeing this sign that He had given, said, 'This really is the prophet who is to come into the world.' Jesus, who could see they were about to come and take Him by force and make Him king, escaped back to the hills by Himself" (*Jn* 6:15-15). Maybe, maybe - but the Gospel does not say it - one of the apostles might have said to him, "Lord, let's take advantage of this and take power". Another temptation. And Jesus makes them see that this is not the way. The power of the pastor is service, he has no other power; and when he makes the mistake of taking another power, he ruins the vocation and becomes, I don't know, a manager of "pastoral enterprises", but not a pastor. *Structure* does not make pastoral ministry: it is the *heart of the pastor* that makes pastoral ministry. And the pastor's heart is what Jesus is teaching is now.

Let us ask the Lord today, for the pastors of the Church, that the Lord always speak to them, since He loves them so much; that He might speak to us always, that He might tell us how things are, that He explain to us and above all teach us not to be afraid of the people of God, not to be afraid to be near them.

Saturday, April 25, 2020

Holy Mass[48]

Introduction

Let us pray together today for those who provide mortuary services. What they do is very painful and very sad, and they feel the pain caused by this pandemic. Let us pray for them.

Homily – Faith must be transmitted, it must be offered, above all by witness

Today the Church celebrates Saint Mark, one of the four evangelists, very close to the Apostle Peter. The Gospel of Mark was the first to be written. It is simple, a simple style, very close. If you have a bit of time today, pick it up and read it. It is not long, and the simplicity with which Mark recounts the life of the Lord is pleasing.

In the Gospel we have just read - which is at the end of the Gospel of Mark - there is the sending forth by the Lord. The Lord reveals Himself as Savior, as the only Son of God; He revealed Himself to all Israel, all the people, especially and with more details to the apostles, to the disciples. This is the Lord's farewell, the Lord is going away:

---

[48] Liturgy of the Word: *1 Pt* 5:5-14; *Psalm* 88(89); *Mk* 16:15-20.

He left and "He was taken up into heaven: there at the right hand of God He took His place (*Mk* 16:19). But before leaving, when He appeared to the eleven, He said to them: "Go into the whole world; proclaim the Good News to every creature" (*Mk* 16:15). This is the missionary dimension of faith. Either faith has a missionary dimension, or it is not faith. Faith is not something only for myself, so that I may grow with faith: this is a gnostic heresy. Faith always leads you to come out of yourself, to go out. The transmission of faith; faith must be transmitted, it must be offered, above all by witness: "Go, so that the people see how you live" (see v. 15).

Someone once said to me, a European priest, from a European city: "There is a lot of unbelief, a lot of gnosticism in our city. Because the Christians do not have faith. If they had it they would certainly give it to the people". They lack this missionary dimension, because conviction is lacking at its root: "Yes, I am Christian, I am Catholic", as if it were a social habit. On your identity card, your name is this and that, and "I am Christian". It is a piece of information on an identity card. This is not faith! This is a cultural thing. Faith necessarily takes you out, it leads you to give it, because essentially faith must be transmitted. It is not something quiet. "Oh, so you mean, Father, that we all need to be missionaries and go to far-off countries?" No, this is a part of the missionary dimension. This means that if you have faith you must by necessity come out of yourself, and show your faith in society. Faith is social, it is for everyone. "Go into the whole world; proclaim the Good News to every creature" (*Mk* 16:15). This does not mean becoming someone who proselytizes, as if you were recruiting people to a football team or to a non-profit organization. It means that you show the revelation, so that the Holy Spirit might work in people through witness: as a witness, with service. Service is a way of life. If I say that I am a Christian, but I live like a pagan, that doesn't work, that doesn't convince anyone. If I say that I am a Christian, and I live like a Christian, this attracts. It is witness.

Once, in Poland, a university student asked me: "At university I have many atheist companions. What should I say to them to convince them?" "Nothing. The last thing you need to do is say something. Start to live, and they, seeing your witness, will ask you, 'Why do you live this way?'". Faith must be transmitted: not by convincing but by offering a treasure. "It is there, do you see it?"

And this is also the humility Saint Peter spoke about in the First Reading: "Wrap yourselves in humility to be servants of each other, because God refuses the proud and will always favor the humble" (*1 Pt* 5:5). How many times in the history of the Church have movements and aggregations been born, of men and women who wanted to convince others, to convert them... True proselytes. And how did they end? In corruption.

This passage of the Gospel is so tender! But where is the certainty? How can we be sure that by going out of ourselves we will be fruitful in the transmission of the faith? "Proclaim the Good News to every creature" (*Mk* 16:15) and you will work wonders (see vv. 17-18). And the Lord will be with us until the end of the world. In the transmission of ideologies there are teachers but when I act out of faith, the Lord accompanies me. I am never alone in the transmission of faith. It is the Lord with me who transmits faith. He promised: "I will be with you all days even till the end of the world" (see *Mt* 28:20).

Let us pray to the Lord that He help us to live our faith in this way: a faith with open doors, a transparent faith, not proselytism, but which shows itself: "I am this way". And with this healthy curiosity, may He help others to receive this message that will save them.

Sunday, April 26, 2020

Third Sunday of Easter (A)

Holy Mass[49]

Introduction

Let us pray today, in this Mass, for all the people who suffer from sadness, because they are alone or because they do not know what the future holds for them, or because they cannot support their family because they have no money, because they have no job. Many people suffer from sadness. Let us pray for them today.

Homily – Jesus is our pilgrim companion

Very often we have heard that Christianity is not merely a doctrine, nor a way of behaving, nor a culture. Yes, it is all this, but it is first and foremost an encounter. A person is Christian because he or she has encountered Jesus Christ, has let him or herself be encountered by Him.

This passage of the Gospel of Luke tells us about an encounter, so as to enable us to know better how the Lord acts and how we act. We are born with a seed of restlessness. God wants it thus: the restlessness of finding fullness, restlessness of finding God, very often always without knowing that we have this restlessness. Our hearts are restless, our hearts are thirsty: thirsty for the encounter

---

[49] Liturgy of the Word: *Acts* 2:14, 22-33; *Psalm* 15(16); *1 Pt* 1:17-21; *Lk* 24:13-35.

with God. Our hearts seek Him, many times on the wrong paths: it gets lost, then it returns, it seeks Him... On the other hand, God thirsts for the encounter to the point that He sent Jesus to meet us, to come towards this restlessness.

How does Jesus act? In this passage of the Gospel (see *Lk* 24:13-35), we see clearly that He respects our situation, He does not go ahead. Only at times, with the headstrong – think of Paul, when he is thrown down from the horse. But usually He goes slowly, respecting our pace. He is the Lord of patience. How much patience the Lord has with us, with each one of us!

The Lord walks next to us, as we have seen here with these two disciples. He listens to our restlessness, He knows it, and at a certain point He says something to us. The Lord likes to hear how we speak, to understand us well and to give the right answer to that disquiet. The Lord does not speed up His pace, He always keeps in step with us, very often slow, but His patience is thus.

There is an ancient rule of pilgrims, which says that the true pilgrim should go at the pace of the slowest person. And Jesus is capable of this, He does it, He does not speed up, He waits for us to take the first step. And when it is the right moment, He asks the question. In this case it is clear: "What are you discussing?" (see v. 17). He makes Himself appear ignorant to make us speak to Him. He likes it when we speak to Him. He likes to hear this, He likes us to speak to Him in this way, to listen to Him and to answer, He makes us talk. As if He were ignorant, but with great respect. And then He answers, He explains, up to the necessary point. Here He says to us: "Was it not necessary that the Messiah should suffer these things and enter into His glory?" Then "beginning with Moses and all the prophets, He interpreted to them what referred to Him in all the scriptures" (v. 26). He explains, He clarifies. I confess that I am curious to know how Jesus explained, to do the same. It was a beautiful catechesis.

And then the same Jesus who has accompanied us, who has drawn close to us, pretends to go on further, to see the extent of our restlessness. "Stay with us, for it is nearly evening and the day is almost over" (v. 29). And in this way we meet. But the encounter is not just a time to break bread here, but the entire journey. We meet Jesus in the darkness of our doubts, even in the ugly doubt of our sins, He is there to help us, in our anxieties... He is always with us.

The Lord accompanies us because He wants to meet us. That is why we say that the core of Christianity is an encounter: it is the encounter with Jesus. "Why are you a Christian? Why are you a Christian?" And a lot of people are unable to say. Some, by tradition. Others cannot say it, because they met Jesus, but they didn't realize it was an encounter with Jesus. Jesus is always looking for us. Always. And we have our restlessness. In the moment in which our restlessness meets Jesus, that is where the life of grace begins, life in its fullness, the life of the Christian journey.

May the Lord give us all this grace to meet Jesus every day; to know, to be aware that it is really He who is walking with us in all our moments. He is our pilgrim companion.

Regina Coeli

Dear Brothers and Sisters, good morning!

Today's Gospel, which takes place on the day of the Passover, describes the episode of the two disciples of Emmaus (*Lk* 24:13-35). It is a story that begins and ends on the move. There is in fact, the outbound journey of the disciples who, saddened by the epilogue of Jesus's story, leave Jerusalem and return home to Emmaus, walking some 11 kilometers. It is a journey that takes place during the day, much of it downhill. And there is the return journey: another 11 kilometers, but at nightfall, partly an uphill journey after the fatigue of the outward journey and the entire day. Two trips: one easy in daytime, and the other tiring at night. Yet the first takes place in sadness, the second in joy. In the first one, there is the Lord walking beside them, but they do not recognize Him; in the second one they do not see Him anymore, but they feel Him near them. In the first they are discouraged and hopeless; in the second they run to bring the good news of the encounter with the Risen Jesus to the others.

The two different paths of those first disciples tell us, Jesus's disciples today, that in life we have two opposite directions before us: there is the path of those who, like those two on the outbound journey, allow themselves to be paralyzed by life's disappointments and proceed sadly; and there is the path of those who do not put themselves and their problems first, but rather Jesus who visits us, and the brothers who await His visit, that is, our brothers and sisters who are waiting for us to take care of them. Here is the turning point: to stop orbiting around one's self; the disappointments of the past, the unrealized ideals, the many bad things that have happened in our life. Very often we tend to keep going around and around.... To leave that behind and to go forward looking at the greatest and truest reality of life: Jesus lives, Jesus loves me. This is the greatest reality. And I can do something for others. It is a beautiful reality: positive, bright, beautiful! This is the turning point: to go from thoughts about I to the reality of my God; going – with another play on words – from "if" [se in Italian] to "yes" [sì in Italian]. From "if" to "yes". What does this mean? "If he had freed us, if God had listened to me, if life had gone as I wanted, if I had this and that…", in a tone of complaint. This "if" is not helpful, it is not fruitful. It helps neither us nor others. Here are our "ifs", similar to those of the two disciples, whom however, move to a yes: "Yes, the Lord is alive, He walks with us. Yes, we continue our journey to announce it now, not tomorrow". "Yes, I can do this for the people so that they may be happier, so that people may better themselves, to help many people. Yes, yes I can". From "if" to "yes", from complaints to joy and peace, because when we complain, we are not joyful; we are in the grey, greyness, that grey air of sadness. And this does not help nor does it allow us to grow well. From "if" to "yes"; from complaints to the joy of service.

How did this change of pace, from "I" to "God", from "if" to "yes", occur within the disciples? By meeting Jesus: the two disciples of Emmaus first open their hearts to Him, then they listen to Him explain the Scriptures and then they invite Him home. These are three steps that we too can take in our homes: first, opening our hearts to Jesus, entrusting Him with the burdens, the hardships, the disappointments of life, entrusting the "ifs" to Him, and then, the second step, listening to Jesus, taking the Gospel in hand, reading this passage in chapter 24 of Luke's Gospel on this very day; third, praying to Jesus, in the same words as those disciples: "Lord, 'stay with us' (v. 29). Lord, stay with me. Lord, stay with all of us, because we need you to find the way. And without you, there is night".

Dear Brothers and Sisters, we are always journeying in life. And we become what we go towards. Let us choose the way of God, not of self; the way of "yes", not the way of "if". We will discover that there are no unexpected events, no uphill path, no night that cannot be faced with Jesus. May Our Lady, Mother of the journey, who by receiving the Word made her entire life a "yes" to God, show us the way.

After the Regina Coeli

Dear Brothers and Sisters,

Yesterday was United Nations World Malaria Day. While we are combatting the coronavirus pandemic, we must also continue our efforts to prevent and cure malaria, which threatens billions of people in many countries. I am close to all the sick, to those who care for them, and to those who work to ensure that every person has access to good basic healthcare.

I also address a greeting to all those in Poland who are participating today in the "National Scripture Reading Day". I have told you many times, and I would like to say once again, how important it is to get into the habit of reading the Gospel, for a few minutes, every day. Let us carry it in our pockets, in our bags. May it always be close to us, even physically, so that we read it a little every day.

In a few days' time, the month of May will begin, which is dedicated especially to the Virgin Mary. In a short Letter published yesterday, I invited all the faithful to pray the Holy Rosary this month, either with your families or on your own, and to recite one of the two prayers that I have made available to everyone. Our Mother will help us face this time of difficulty we are experiencing with greater faith and hope.

I wish you all a happy month of May, and a happy Sunday. Please do not forget to pray for me. Enjoy your lunch. *Arrivederci.*

Monday, April 27, 2020

Holy Mass[50]

Introduction

Let us pray today for artists, who have this very great capacity for creativity, and through beauty show to us the path to follow. May the Lord give all of us the grace of creativity in this moment.

Homily – Always return to the first encounter

The people who had heard Jesus during the whole day, and who then had the grace of the multiplication of the loaves and had seen the power of Jesus, wanted to make Him king. First they went to Jesus to listen to His word, and also to ask for the healing of the sick. They stayed to listen to Jesus the entire day without getting bored, without tiring: they were there, happy. When they then saw that Jesus gave them something to eat, something that they did not expect, they thought: "Well, He would be a good governor for us, and He will certainly be able to free us from the power of the Romans and bring the country forward". And they were keen to make Him king. Their intention had changed, because they saw and they thought, "Well … because a person who performs this miracle, who gives His people food to eat, could be a

---

[50] Liturgy of the Word: *Acts* 6:8-15; *Psalm* 118(119); *Jn* 6:22-29.

good governor" (see *Jn* 6:1-15). But they had forgotten at that moment the enthusiasm that Jesus's word had provoked in their hearts.

Jesus had distanced Himself and went to pray (see v. 15). Those people stayed there and the day after they looked for Jesus, "because He must be here", they said, because they had seen that He had not gotten into the boat with the others. And there was a boat there, it remained there (see *Jn* 6:22-24). But they did not know that Jesus had joined the others by walking on water (see vv. 16-21). And so they decided to go to the other side of the lake of Tiberias to look for Jesus and, when they saw Him, the first word they said to Him was: "Rabbi, when did you get here?" (v. 25). It is as if they were saying, "We don't understand, this is something very strange".

And Jesus makes them return to their first sentiment, what they were feeling before the multiplication of the loaves when they were listening to the word of God: "Amen, amen, I say to you, you are looking for me not because you saw signs, but because you ate the loaves and were filled" (v. 26). Jesus reveals their intention and says, "But you have changed your attitude". And instead of justifying themselves – "No, Lord, no" – they were humble. Jesus continues, "Do not work for bread that cannot last, but work for food that endures to eternal life, the kind of food the Son of Man is offering you, for on Him the Father, God Himself, has set His seal" (v. 6:27). And being good, they asked Him, "What must we do if we are to do the works that God wants?" (v. 28). And Jesus says, "Believe in the Son of God" (see v. 29). This is an example of how Jesus corrects the attitude of the people, of the crowd, because as they were journeying they gradually strayed from that first moment, from the first spiritual consolation, and took a path that was not the right one, a path more worldly than evangelical.

This makes us understand how many times we ourselves have started out on the path of following Jesus, with the values of the Gospel, and then halfway down the road we get another idea, we see some sign or other, and we stray and conform to something more temporal, more material, more worldly let's say, and we lose the memory of that first enthusiasm we had when we heard Jesus speak. The Lord always makes us return to that first encounter, the first moment when He looked at us, He spoke to us and He inspired in us the desire to follow Him.

This is a grace to ask of the Lord, because in life we will always have this temptation to stray because we see something else: "But that will go really well, but that's a good idea", and we distance ourselves. The grace to return to the first call, the first moment: to not forget, to not forget my history, when Jesus looked at me with love and said to me, "This is your path"; when Jesus, through many people, made me understand what the path of the Gospel is, and not other paths that are more worldly, with other values. To return to the first encounter.

Among the things that Jesus says on the morning of the Resurrection, it has always struck me that He says, "Do not be afraid. Go and tell my brothers to go to Galilee; there they will see me" (see *Mt* 28:10). Galilee was the place of the first meeting with Jesus. They met Him there. Each one of us has our own Galilee within us, that specific moment in which Jesus drew near to us and said to us, "Follow me". In life, what happens to those people happens to us: they say to Him right away, "But what should we do?", and then we distance ourselves and we seek other values, other hermeneutics, other things, and we lose the freshness of the first call. The author of the Letter to the Hebrews refers to this: "Remember the days past" (see *Heb* 10:32). Memory, the memory of the first encounter, the memory of "my Galilee", when the Lord looked at me with love and said, "Follow me".

Tuesday, April 28, 2020

Holy Mass[51]

Introduction

At this time, when indications have been given to start coming out of quarantine, we pray that the Lord will grant to His people, to all of us, the grace of prudence and obedience to these indications, so that the pandemic will not return.

Homily – The small everyday lynching of gossip

In the first Reading of these days we have heard about the martyrdom of Stephen: it is simple, how it happened. The doctors of the law did not tolerate the clarity of [his] doctrine, and as soon as it was proclaimed, they went out to ask people who declared they had heard it said that Stephen blasphemed against God, against the Law (see *Acts* 6:11-14). And after this, they pounced on him and stoned him: just like that, simply (see *Acts* 7:57-58). It is a structure of action, and is not the first: they did the same with Jesus too (see *Mt* 26:60-62). The people, who were there, tried to convince Him that he was a blasphemer, and cried out, "Crucify Him" (*Mk* 15:13). Acting like beasts. It is acting like beasts, to begin with false witness in order to arrive at "justice". In the Bible there are things of this nature: they did the same to Susanna (see *Dn* 13:1-64), they did the same to Naboth (see *I Kgs* 21:1-16), then

[51] Liturgy of the World: *Acts* 7:51–8:1; *Psalm* 30(31); *Jn* 6:30-35.

Aman tried to do the same thing with the people of God (see *Est* 3:1-14). Fake news, calumny that agitates people who then ask for justice. It is a lynching, a real lynching.

And so, they take him to the judge, so that the judge can give legal form to this: but he has already been judged. The judge would have to be very, very courageous to go against such a "popular" judgement, already made on purpose, prepared. It is the case of Pilate: Pilate saw clearly that Jesus was innocent, but he saw the people, and he washed his hands of Him (see *Mt* 27:24-26). It is a way of applying the law.

We see this today, too: even today it happens, in some countries, when they want to perform a *coup d'état* or get rid of a politician so that they do not go to elections, they do this: fake news, calumny, then they take it to a judge, one of those who like to practice the law with this "situationalist" positivism which is in vogue, and then it leads to a condemnation. It is a social lynching. And this is what was done to Stephen, this is how justice was done with Stephen: they bring to justice a person already judged by the people, who have been deceived.

This happens today, to the martyrs of today: judges do not have the possibility of bringing justice to those who have already been judged. Let us think of Asia Bibi, for example, whom we have seen: ten years in jail because she had been judged on the basis of calumny and a people who clamor for death. Faced with this avalanche of fake news that form opinion, very often nothing can be done, nothing can be done.

In relation to this I think a lot about the Shoah. The Shoah is a case in point. An opinion was created against a people, and then it became normal to say, "Yes, yes, they must be killed, they must be put to death". A way of proceeding in order to do away with people who are bothersome, who are disturbing to others.

We all know that this is not good, but what we do not know is that there are small everyday lynchings that seek to condemn people, to create a bad reputation among the people, to discard and condemn. The small daily lynchings of gossip, which creates an opinion. Very often we hear someone speak badly of someone else, and another says, "No, this person is a good person!" – "No, no, heard that...", and with that "I heard that...", an opinion is created that can finish a person. The truth is something else: the truth is testimony of what is true, of the things a person believes; the truth is clear, it is transparent. The truth does not tolerate pressure. Look at Stephen, martyr: the first martyr after Jesus. The first martyr. Think of the apostles: they all bore witness. And think of many martyrs, even the one we celebrate today, Saint Peter Chanel: it was gossip that created the opinion that he was against the king. Notoriety was created, and he was put to death. And think of us, of our tongue: very often we, with our comments, initiate a lynching of this type. And in our Christian institutions, we have seen many everyday lynchings born out of gossip.

May the Lord help us be just in our judgements, not to begin or follow this type of mass condemnation that gossip causes.

Wednesday, April 29, 2020

Holy Mass[52]

Introduction

Today is the feast day of Saint Catherine of Siena, Doctor of the Church, Patroness of Europe. Let us pray for Europe, for the unity of Europe, for the unity of the European Union: so that all together we might go forward as brothers and sisters.

Homily – The tangibility and simplicity of the small

In the First Letter of Saint John the Apostle there are many contrasts: between light and dark, lies and truth, sin and innocence (see *1 Jn* 1:5-7). But the Apostle always calls to concreteness, to truth, and he says that we cannot be in union with God while living in the darkness because He is light. It is either one thing or the other: a grey area is even worse, because the grey area makes you think you are walking in the light, because you are not in the dark, and this soothes you. The grey area is treacherous. Either one thing or another.

The Apostle continues: "If we say we have no sin in us; we are deceiving ourselves and refusing to admit the truth" (*1 Jn* 1:8). Because we have all sinned. We are all sinners. And here is something that might deceive us: saying that we are all sinners, as in the same way we say "Hello",

[52] Liturgy of the Word: *1 Jn* 1:5—2:2; *Psalm* 102(103); *Mt* 11:25-30.

or "Good morning", something habitual, even something social, so that we do not have a true awareness of sin. No: I am a sinner because of this, this and this. Concreteness: the concreteness of truth. The truth is always tangible; lies are ethereal, they are like the air, you cannot take hold of them. The truth is concrete. And you cannot go to confess your sins in an abstract way: "Yes, I… yes, once I lost my patience, another time…", in an abstract way. "I am a sinner". Concreteness: "I have done this. I thought that. I said this". Concreteness is what makes me feel I am a sinner in a specific and serious way, instead of keeping it up in the air.

Jesus says in the Gospel, "I bless you Father, Lord of heaven and of earth, for hiding these things from the learned and the clever and revealing them to mere children" (*Mt* 11:25). The concreteness of the little ones. It is good to listen to children when they come to confess: they do not say strange things, "up in the air"; they say concrete things, at times even too specific, as they have that simplicity that God gives to the little ones. I always remember a child who once came to tell me that he was sad because he had argued with his aunt. But then he continued. And I said, "But what did you do?" – "I was at home, I wanted to go out and play football" – he was a child – but the aunt (the mother wasn't there), said, "No, you can't go out, you must do your homework first". One word followed another, and eventually he told his aunt to go to hell. He was a child with a good geographical knowledge – he even told me the name of that place where he had sent his aunt! Children are like this: simple, concrete.

We too need to be simple, concrete. Concreteness leads you to humility, because humility is concrete. "We are all sinners" is something abstract. No: "I am a sinner because of this, this, and this". And this leads me to the shame of looking at Jesus and saying, "Forgive me". The true attitude of the sinner. "If we say we have no sin in us; we are deceiving ourselves and refusing to admit the truth" (*1 Jn* 1:8). This vague abstract attitude is a way of saying we are not sinners. "Yeah, I lost my patience one time", but everything is "up in the air". I am not aware of the reality of my sins. "But you know, we all do these things. I am sorry, I am sorry". No. "It pains me, I won't do it again, I don't want to do it again, I don't want to think it again". It is important that within us we name our sins. Concreteness. Because if we keep them up in the air, we end up in the dark. Let us become like the little ones, who say what they feel, what they think: they still have not learned the art of saying things that are "gift-wrapped" a bit, so that they are understood without saying. This is the art of adults, which very often is not good for us.

Yesterday I received a letter from a boy from Caravaggio, called Andrea. And he told me about himself. Letters from young people and children are beautiful, because they are concrete. And he told me that he had watched the Mass on the television and he had to "rebuke" me for something: I invite people to give a sign of peace and he said I can't say that, because in this time of the pandemic we can't touch each other. He does not see that you [here in the church] bow your heads without touching each other. But he has the freedom to say things as they are.

And we too, with the Lord, should have the freedom to say things as they are: "Lord, I am in sin, help me". Like Peter after the first miraculous catch: "Leave me, Lord, for I am a sinful man" (*Lk* 5:8). To have this wisdom of the concrete. Because the devil wants us to live in a tepid way, in the grey area, neither good nor bad, neither white nor black, but grey, a life that is not pleasing to the Lord. The Lord does not like those who are tepid, mediocre. Concreteness. So as not to be liars. "If we acknowledge our sins, then God who is faithful and just will forgive our sins" (*1 Jn* 1:9). He will forgive us when we are concrete. The spiritual life is so simple, so simple; but we make it complicated with these shades of grey, and in the end we never get there.

Let us ask the Lord for the grace of simplicity. May He give us this grace that He gives to the simple, to children, who say what they feel. They do not hide what they feel. Even if it is wrong, they say it. And with Him too, saying things: transparency. And not living a life that is neither one thing nor the other. The grace of the freedom to say these things; and also the grace of knowing well who we are before God.

Thursday, April 30, 2020

Holy Mass[53]

Introduction

Let us pray today for the deceased, those who have died in this pandemic; and in particular for, let us say, the anonymous deceased: we have seen the photographs of mass graves, many of them…

Homily – Without witness and prayer, apostolic preaching is not possible

"No one can come to me unless he is drawn by the Father" (*Jn* 6:44). Jesus recalls that even the prophets had prophesied that "they will all be taught by God" (v. 45). And God who draws us to the knowledge of the Son. Without this, no one can know Jesus. Yes, one can study, also study the Bible, even know how He was born, what He did, all this, yes. But to know Him from within, to know the mystery of Christ, is only for those who are drawn to this by the Father.

This is what happened to this minister of the economy of Ethiopia. We can see that he is a pious man, and that he had taken the time, amid his many business affairs, to go and worship God. He is a believer. And he was returning to his homeland, reading the prophet Isaiah (see *Acts* 8:27-28). The Lord takes Philip and sends him to that place, and He says, "Go up and meet the chariot" (v. 29).

---

[53] Liturgy of the Word: *Acts* 8:26-40; *Psalm* 65(66); *Jn* 6:44-51.

And he hears the minister reading Isaiah. He approaches him and asks, "Do you understand?" "How can I unless I have someone to guide me?" (v. 31). And so then he asks, "Who is saying this, a prophet?", and invites him to get into the carriage. During the journey – we don't know how long, I think at least a couple of hours – Philip explains, he explains Jesus (see v. 26-35).

That restlessness the man felt when reading the prophet Isaiah was indeed the Father, drawing him towards Jesus (see *Jn* 6:44). He had prepared him, He had brought him from Ethiopia to Jerusalem to worship God and then, with this reading, He had prepared his heart to reveal Jesus. As soon as he sees the water he asks, "Can I be baptized?" (see v. 36). And he believed.

And this – that no one can know Jesus without the Father having drawn him or her (see v. 44) – this is valid for our apostolate, for our apostolic mission as Christians. I also think of the missions. "What do you go to do in the missions?" "I go to convert people". "But stop, you will never convert anyone! It will be the Father who attracts those hearts to acknowledge Jesus". Going to the missions is to go and bear witness to one's own faith. Without witness, you will do nothing. To go to the missions, and there are some really good missionaries, is not merely about building big structures and things, and stopping there. No, the structures must be testimonies. You can make a hospital structure, an educational structure of great perfection, of great development, but if it is without Christian witness, your work will not be a work of witness, a work of the true proclamation of Jesus: it will be a charitable institution, very good, very good! – but nothing more.

If I want to go to the missions, if I want to carry out the apostolate, I must go with the disposition that the Father draws people to Jesus, and must bear witness to this. Jesus Himself says it to Peter, when he professes that He is the Messiah: "Blessed are you Simon, because it was the Father who revealed this to you" (see *Mt* 16:17). It is the Father who draws us to Him through our own witness. "I will do a lot of works here, there and everywhere, this and that", but without witness they are good things, but they are not the proclamation of the Gospel, there are not places that might give people knowledge of Jesus (see *Jn* 6:44). Work and witness.

"But what can I do so that the Father will make it His business to attract people?" It is prayer. This is prayer for the missions: to pray that the Father will draw people towards Jesus. *Witness and prayer*, they go together. Without witness and prayer one cannot carry out apostolic preaching, one cannot proclaim. You will give a good moral sermon, but the Father will not have the possibility of drawing people to Jesus. And this is the center: this is the center of our apostolate, that the Father may attract the people to Jesus (see *Jn* 6:44). Our witness opens the doors of the people and our prayer opens the heart of the Father, so that it may attract people. Witness and prayer. And this is not only for the missions, it is also for our work as Christians. Do I truly bear witness to Christian life, with my style of life? Do I pray for the Father to draw people to Jesus?

This is the great rule for our apostolate, everywhere, and in a special way for the missions. To go to the missions is not to carry out proselytism. Once a woman - a good person, you could see she had good will - came up to me with two young people, a boy and a girl, and she said to me: "This boy, Father, was a protestant and I converted him; I convinced him. And this girl was...", I don't know, animist, I don't know what she said, "and I converted her". And the woman was good, good. But she was mistaken. I lost my patience a little and I said to her, "Listen, you haven't converted anyone; it was God who touched the heart of the people. And do not forget: witness, yes; proselytism, no".

Let us ask the Lord for the grace to live our work with witness and prayer, so that He, the Father, may draw people to Jesus.

Friday, May 1, 2020

Holy Mass[54]

Introduction

Today is the feast of Saint Joseph the Worker, and it is also Workers' Day. Let us pray for all workers. For all of them. May no one be without employment, and may all be fairly paid, that they might earn both the dignity of their work and the beauty of rest.

Homily – Work is the vocation of man

"God created" (*Gn* 1:27). A Creator. He created the world, He created man, and He gave man and woman a mission to manage: to work with and bring forward creation. And the Bible uses the word "work" to express this activity of God: He "completed the work He had been doing. He rested on the seventh day … after all His work of creating" (*Gn* 2:2). To the point that work is none other than the continuation of God's work: human work is man's vocation received from God at the end of the creation of the universe.

Work makes the human person similar to God, because with work man is a creator, capable of creating, of creating many things; also of creating a family to raise. The human person is a creator, and creates through work.

---

[54] Liturgy of the Word: *Gn* 1:26—2:3; *Psalm* 89(90); *Mt* 13:54-58.

This is his vocation, and it says in the Bible that "God saw all He had made, and indeed it was very good" (*Gn* 1:31). That is, work had goodness within itself and creates the harmony of things - beauty, goodness - and involves man in everything: in his thought, his actions, everything. Man is involved in work. It is man's first vocation: to work. And this gives dignity to man. The dignity that makes him resemble God. The dignity of work.

Once, a man went to Caritas, a man who had no employment and went to ask for help for his family. An employee of *Caritas*, who gave him something to eat, said to him, "At least you can take some food home". "But this is not enough for me", was the answer. "I want to earn the food I take home". He was lacking the dignity, that dignity of "making" the bread himself, through work, and taking it home. The dignity of work, which is trampled on, unfortunately.

Throughout history we have read about the brutality inflicted on slaves: they were brought from Africa to America - I think of that history that touches my own land - and we say, "What barbarism!" But there are many slaves today too, many men and women who are not free to work; they are forced to work in order to survive, nothing more. They are slaves: it is forced labor. It is forced labor, unjust, ill-paid, and which leads men and women to live with their dignity trampled underfoot. There are many, many throughout the world. Many. In the newspapers a few months ago we read, in a country in Asia, of how a man had beaten to death an employee who earned less than half a dollar a day, because he had done something badly. Today's slavery is our "indignity", because it takes away the dignity of men, of women, all of us. "No, I work, I have my dignity". Yes, but your brothers and sisters do not. "Yes, Father, it is true, but this, since it is very far away from me, I struggle to understand it. But they are among us; yes, here among us. Think of the day workers, who are made to work for minimum pay, and not for eight, but for twelve or fourteen hours a day: this happens today, here. Throughout the world, and also here. I think of the domestic worker who does not receive a fair wage, who has no social security assistance, insurance, no pension provision: this does not only happen in Asia. It happens here.

Every injustice inflicted on a person who works tramples on human dignity; and also the dignity of the one who does this injustice. It lowers the level and we end up with that tension that exists between a dictator and a slave. Instead, the vocation that God gives us is so good: to create, to re-create, to work. But this can be done when the conditions are right and the dignity of the person is respected.

Today let us join with many men and women, believers and non-believers, who commemorate Workers' Day, the day of work, for those who fight for justice in the world of work, for those - the good employers - who manage their businesses fairly, even if they themselves lose as a result. Two months ago I spoke on the telephone to a businessman, here in Italy, who asked me to pray for him because he did not want to lay off any of his workers, and said, "Because to lay off one of them is like firing myself". This conscience of so many employers who are good, who take care of their employees as if they were their own children. Let us pray for them too. And let us ask Saint Joseph, with this beautiful image [a statue standing near the altar] with the tools of his trade in his hand, that he might help us fight for the dignity of work, so that there may be work for everyone and that the work may be dignified. Not slave labor. May this be our prayer today.

Saturday, May 2, 2020

Holy Mass[55]

Introduction

Let us pray today for the government leaders who have the responsibility of taking care of their peoples in this moment of crisis. For heads of state, government presidents, legislators, mayors, regional presidents... so that the Lord may help them and give them strength, because their work is not easy. And that when there are differences among them, they may understand that in moments of crisis they must be very united for the good of the people, because unity is superior to conflict.

Today, Saturday May 2, we are joined in prayer by 300 prayer groups which are called "*madrugadores*" in Spanish, that is, "early birds". They are people who rise early in the morning in order to pray. They are joining us now, at this moment.

Homily – Learning to live in moments of crisis

The first Reading begins: "The Churches throughout Judea, Galilee and Samaria were now left in peace, building themselves up, living in the fear of the Lord, and filled with the consolation of the Holy Spirit, and growing in number" (*Acts* 9:31). A time of peace. And the Church grew. And Church was calm and serene, it had the com-

---

[55] Liturgy of the Word: *Acts* 9:31-42; *Psalm* 115(116); *Jn* 6:60-69.

fort of the Holy Spirit, the consolation. They were beautiful times... This was followed by the healing of Aeneas, and then Peter raises Tabitha, also known as Dorcas, from the dead. Things that are done in peacetime.

But there were times that were not peaceful, in the early Church: times of persecutions, difficult times, times that put believers in crisis. Times of crisis. One such moment of crisis is recounted today in the Gospel of John (see 6:60-69). This passage from the Gospel is the end of a series that begins with the multiplication of the loaves, when they wanted to make Jesus king. Jesus goes to pray, and the next day they can't find Him; they go to look for Him and Jesus reproaches those who seek Him because they are looking for something to eat instead of the bread of eternal life. And this whole story finishes here. They say to Him, "Give us this bread", and Jesus explains that the bread He will give is His very own body and blood.

"At that time, some of them said, 'This is a hard teaching. Who can accept it?'" (v. 60). Jesus had said that those who had not eaten His body and His blood would not have eternal life. Jesus also said, "Whoever eats my flesh and drinks my blood has eternal life, and I will raise them up at the last day" (see v. 54). These are the things Jesus said. "This is a hard teaching" (v. 60), the disciples think. "It is too hard. Something isn't right. This man has gone beyond the limits". And this is the moment of crisis. There were moments of peace and moments of crisis. Jesus knew that the disciples were murmuring among themselves. There is a distinction here between disciples and apostles. There were the 72 or more disciples, whereas the apostles were the Twelve. Jesus "had known from the beginning which of them did not believe and who would betray Him" (v. 64). And in the face of this crisis, He reminds them: "This is why I told you that no one can come to me unless the Father has enabled them" (v. 65). He speaks again of being drawn by the Father, that the Father attracts people to Jesus. And this is how the crisis is resolved.

And after this, "many of His disciples left Him and stopped going with Him" (v. 66). They distance themselves from Him. "This man is a bit dangerous, a bit... with these doctrines... Yes, He is a good man, He preaches and heals, but when He starts doing strange things... Please, let's go" (see v. 66). And the disciples of Emmaus did the same thing, on the morning of the Resurrection: "But yes, it's strange: the women say that the tomb... but this doesn't look good, let's go away before the soldiers come and crucify us" (see *Lk* 24:22-24). The soldiers who were guarding the tomb did the same: they had seen the truth, but then they preferred to sell their secret: "Let's be sure, let's not get involved in these stories, they are dangerous" (see *Mt* 28:11-15).

A moment of crisis is a moment of choice, it is a moment that places us before the decisions that we must make. All of us, in life, have had and will have moments of crisis: family crises, marriage crises, social crises, crises at work, many crises... This pandemic, too, is a moment of social crisis.

How does one react in a moment of crisis? "From this time many of His disciples turned back and no longer followed Him" (v. 66). Jesus makes the decision to question the apostles. "'You do not want to leave too, do you?' Jesus asked the Twelve" (*Jn* 6:67). Make a decision. And Peter makes the second confession: "Simon Peter answered

Him, 'Lord, to whom shall we go? You have the words of eternal life. We have come to believe and to know that You are the Holy One of God" (vv. 68-69). Peter confesses in the name of the Twelve that Jesus is the Holy One of God, the Son of God. The first confession, "You are the Christ, the son of the Living God" - and immediately afterwards, when Jesus began to explain the passion that was to come - Peter stops Him and says: "No, no Lord, not this", and Jesus reproaches him (see *Mt* 16:16-23). But Peter has matured a little and here he does not rebuke Jesus. He does not understand what Jesus is saying about eating His flesh and drinking His blood (see *Jn* 6:54-56), he does not understand, but he trusts the Master. He trusts Him. And he makes this second confession: "Lord, to whom shall we go? You have the message of eternal life" (see v. 68).

This helps us, all of us, to live through moments of crisis. In my land there is a saying: "When you're riding a horse and you have to cross a river, please, don't change horses in the middle of the river". In moments of crisis you need to be very steadfast in your convictions of faith. Those who left, changed horses, they sought another teacher who was not so "hard", as they said to Him. Moments of crisis demand perseverance, silence; staying where we are, steadfast. It is not the moment to make changes. It is the moment of fidelity, of faithfulness to God, of faithfulness to the things [decisions] we had made before. It is also the moment of conversion, because this faithfulness will inspire some kind of change for the better, not to distance us from good.

Moments of peace and moments of crisis. We Christians must learn to manage both. Both of them. A spiritual father said that going through a moment of crisis is like passing through fire so as to become strong. May the Lord send us the Holy Spirit so we may be able to resist the temptations of moments of crisis, to know how to be faithful to the first words, with the hope of living moments of peace later. Let us think of our crises: crises in the family, in our neighborhood, at work, social crises throughout the world, in our country… so many crises, many crises.

May the Lord give us the strength not to sell out our faith in moments of crisis.

Sunday, May 3, 2020

Fourth Sunday of Easter (A)

Holy Mass[56]

Introduction

Three weeks after the Resurrection of the Lord, the Church today in the fourth week of Easter celebrates Good Shepherd Sunday, Jesus the Good Shepherd. This makes me think of the many pastors throughout the world who give their lives for the faithful. Even in this pandemic, many of them, more than a hundred have died here in Italy. I also think of other pastors who are taking care of the good of others: doctors. We speak of doctors and what they do, but we must acknowledge that in Italy alone, 154 doctors have died in service. May the example of these pastors who are priests and doctors help us to take care of the holy people of God.

Homily – The meekness and tenderness of the Good Shepherd

The First Letter of the apostle Peter, which we have heard, is a passage of serenity (see 2:20-25). It talks about Jesus. It says, "He Himself bore our sins in His body upon the cross, so that, free from sin, we might live for righteousness. By His wounds you have been healed. For you had gone astray like sheep, but you have now returned to the shepherd and guardian of your souls" (vv. 24-25).

---

[56] Liturgy of the Word: *Acts* 2:14, 36-41; *Psalm* 22(23); *1 Pt* 2:20-25; *Jn* 10:1-10.

Jesus is the shepherd - this is how Peter sees Him - who comes to save, to save the sheep which had gone astray: they were us. And in Psalm 23, which we read after this Letter, we repeated: "The Lord is my shepherd, there is nothing I shall want" (v. 1). The presence of the Lord as a pastor, as a shepherd of the flock. And Jesus, in chapter 10 of John, which we have read, presents Himself as a shepherd. Moreover, not only as the shepherd, but the "door" through which the flock enters (see v. 8). All those who came before and did not enter through that door were thieves and brigands, or wanted to take advantage of the flock: false pastors. And in the history of the Church there have been many who have exploited the flock. They were interested not in the flock, but in advancing their careers, or politics, or money. But the flock recognizes them, has always recognized them, and has gone in search of God on their own path.

But then there is a good shepherd who leads them ahead, the flock advances. The good shepherd listens to the flock, guides the flock, takes care of the flock. And the flock knows how to distinguish between these shepherds, it makes no mistake. The flock entrusts itself to the good shepherd, it entrusts itself to Jesus. Only the pastor who resembles Jesus can earn the trust of the flock, because He is *the door*. Jesus's style must be the style of the shepherd, there is no other. But even Jesus the Good Shepherd, as Peter says in the First Letter, "Christ suffered for you and left an example for you to follow the way He took. He had not done anything wrong, and there had been no perjury in His mouth. He was insulted and did not retaliate with insults; when He was tortured He made no threats" (*1 Pt* 2:21-23). He was meek. One of the signs of the Good Shepherd is *meekness*. The Good Shepherd is meek. A pastor who is not meek is not a good pastor. He has something to hide, because meekness makes itself seen as it is, without defending itself. In addition, a good shepherd is tender; he has that *tenderness of closeness*, he knows the sheep one by one, by name, and he takes care of each one as if it were the only one, to the point that when he returns home tired after a day of work, and realizes that one is missing, he goes out to work again in search of that one, and carries it back home with him, on his shoulders (see *Lk* 15:4-5). This is a good shepherd, this is Jesus, this is the one who accompanies us all on the path of life. And this idea of the pastor, this idea of the flock and of the sheep, is a Paschal idea. The Church, in the first week of Easter, sings that beautiful hymn for the newly baptized. "These are the new lambs". Similar to what we heard at the beginning of the Mass. It is an idea of community, of tenderness, of goodness, of meekness. It is the Church that Jesus wants, and He guards this Church.

This Sunday is a beautiful Sunday, it is a Sunday of peace, it is a Sunday of tenderness, of meekness, because our Shepherd takes care of us. "The Lord is my shepherd, there is nothing I shall want" (*Ps* 23:1).

Regina Coeli

Dear Brothers and Sisters, good morning,

The Fourth Sunday of Easter, which we celebrate today, is dedicated to Jesus the Good Shepherd. The Gospel says that: "The sheep *hear His voice*, and He calls His own sheep by name and leads them out" (*Jn* 10:3). The Lord calls us by name, He calls us because He loves us. However, the Gospel says, there are *other voices*, that are not to be followed: those of strangers, thieves and brigands who mean harm to the sheep.

These different voices resonate within us. There is the voice of God, who speaks kindly to the conscience, and there is the tempting voice that leads to evil. How can we recognize the voice of the Good Shepherd from that of the thief, how can we distinguish the inspiration of God from the suggestion of the evil one? One can learn to discern these two voices: they speak two different languages, that is, they have opposite ways of knocking on [the door of] our hearts. They speak different languages. Just as we know how to distinguish one language from another, we can also distinguish the voice of God from the voice of the evil one.

The voice of God never forces us: God *proposes* himself, He does not *impose* himself. Instead, the evil voice seduces, assails, forces: it arouses dazzling illusions, emotions that are tempting but transient. At first it flatters, it makes us believe that we are all-powerful, but then it leaves us empty inside and accuses us: "You are worth nothing". The voice of God, instead, corrects us, with great patience, but always encourages us, consoles us: it always nourishes hope. God's voice is a voice that has a horizon, whereas the voice of the evil one leads you to a wall, it backs you into a corner.

Another difference: the voice of the enemy distracts us from the present and wants us to focus on fears of the future or sadness about the past – the enemy does not want the present – it brings to surface the bitterness, the memories of the wrongs suffered, of those who have hurt us, ... many bad memories. On the other hand, the voice of God speaks in the present: "Now you can do good, now you can exercise the creativity of love, now you can forego the regrets and remorse that hold your heart captive". It inspires us, it leads us ahead, but it speaks in the present: now.

Again: the two voices raise different questions in us. The one that comes from God will be: "What is good for me?". Instead the tempter will insist on another question: "What do I feel like doing?". What do I feel: the evil voice always revolves around the ego, its impulses, its needs, *everything straight away*. It is like a child's tantrums: everything, and now. The voice of God, however, never promises joy at a low price: it invites us to go beyond our ego in order to find the true, good peace. Let us remember: evil never brings peace. First it causes frenzy, and then it leaves bitterness. This is the style of evil.

Lastly, God's voice and that of the tempter, speak in different "environments": the enemy prefers darkness, falsehood, and gossip; the Lord loves sunlight, truth, and sincere transparency. The enemy will say to us: "Close yourself up in yourself, besides no one understands and listens to you, do not be trusting!" Goodness, on the contrary, invites us to open up, to be clear and trusting in God and in others. Dear brothers and sisters, during this time many thoughts and worries lead us to turn inwards into ourselves. Let us pay attention to the voices that reach our hearts. Let us ask ourselves where they come from. Let us ask for the grace to recognize and follow the voice of the Good Shepherd, who brings us out of the enclosures of selfishness and leads us to the pastures of true freedom. May Our Lady, Mother of Good Counsel, guide and accompany our discernment.

After the Regina Coeli

Dear Brothers and Sisters,

Today we celebrate World Day of Prayer for Vocations. Christian life is always a response to God's call, in any living condition. This Day reminds us of what Jesus said one day, that the field of the Kingdom of God requires much work, and we must pray the Father to send laborers to work in his harvest (see *Mt* 9:37-38). Priesthood and consecrated life require courage and perseverance; and one cannot continue along this path without prayer. I invite everyone to invoke the Lord for the gift of good workers for His Kingdom, with a heart and hands that are open to His love.

Once again I would like to express my closeness to those who are suffering from Covid-19, to those who are dedicated to their care and to all those who, in any way, are suffering from the pandemic. At the same time, I would like to support and encourage the international cooperation that is launching various initiatives aimed at responding adequately and effectively to the serious crisis we are experiencing. Indeed, it is important to bring together scientific capabilities, in a transparent and disinterested way, in order to find vaccines and treatments and to guarantee universal access to essential technologies that will enable every infected person, in every part of the world, to receive the necessary health care.

I offer a special thought to the "Meter" Association, promoter of the National Day for children victims of violence, exploitation and indifference. I encourage those in charge and the staff to continue their prevention and awareness raising work alongside the various educational agencies. And I thank the children from the Association who have sent me a collage with hundreds of daisies they colored. Thank you!

We have just started May, the quintessential Marian month, during which the faithful love to visit the Shrines dedicated to Our Lady. This year, because of the health situation, let us visit these places of faith and devotion spiritually, to place in the heart of the Blessed Virgin our worries, expectations and plans for the future.

And since prayer is a universal value, I have accepted the proposal of the Higher Committee for Human Fraternity for believers of all religions to unite spiritually this May 14, for a day of prayer, fasting, and works of charity, to implore God to help humanity overcome the coronavirus pandemic. Remember: May 14, all believers together, believers of different traditions, to pray, fast, and perform works of charity.

I wish everyone a good Sunday. Please do not forget to pray for me. Enjoy your lunch. *Arrivederci.*

Monday, May 4, 2020

Holy Mass[57]

Introduction

Let us pray today for families. In this time of quarantine, families, cooped up at home, are trying to do many new things; there is a lot of creativity with children, with everything, just to keep going. And there is also another thing: at times there is domestic violence. Let us pray for families, that they may continue in peace creatively and patiently, during this quarantine.

Homily – We all have one Shepherd: Jesus

When Peter goes up to Jerusalem, the faithful reproach him (see *Acts* 11:1-8). They reproach him because he had entered the house of uncircumcized men and had eaten with them, with the Gentiles: this was not allowed, it was a sin. The purity of the law did not permit it. But Peter had done it because it was the Spirit that led him there. There is always, in the Church - and often in the early Church, because matters were not clear - this spirit of "We are the righteous ones, the others are sinners". This "us" and "them", "us" and "them", divisions: "We have the correct position before God", whereas the others… Sometimes it is said that "they are already condemned". This is a *disorder* of the Church, a disorder that is born of ideolo-

---

[57] Liturgy of the Word: *Acts* 11:1-18; *Psalm* 41(42) and 42; *Jn* 10:11-18.

gies or out of different religious parties… To think that, in Jesus's time, there were at least four religious parties: the party of the Pharisees, and the parties of the Sadducees, the Zealots, and the Essenes, and each one interpreted the law according to their *idea* of it. And this idea is "beyond the law" when is becomes a way of thinking, a worldly spirit that then interprets the law. They even rebuked Jesus for entering the house of tax collectors - who were sinners in their opinion - and for eating with them, with the sinners, as the purity of the law did not permit it (see *Mt* 15:2, 20). Always that reproach that causes division: this is the important thing that I would like to emphasise.

There are ideas, positions that cause division, to the point that division becomes more important than unity. My idea is more important than the Holy Spirit that guides us. There is a cardinal "emeritus" who lives here in the Vatican, a good pastor, who used to say to his faithful: "The Church is like a river, you know? Some are closer to one bank, some closer to the other, but the important thing is that everyone is in the river". This is the unity of the Church. No one outside, everyone inside. With their peculiarities: this does not divide, it is not ideology, it is licit. But why does the Church have such a broad river? It is because the Lord wants it that way.

The Lord, in the Gospel, says: "There are other sheep I have that are not of this fold, and these I have to lead as well. They too will listen to my voice, and there will be only one flock, and one Shepherd" (*Jn* 10:16). The Lord says: "I have sheep everywhere and I am the shepherd of all of them". This "all of them" is very important. Let us think of the parable of the wedding feast (see *Mt* 22:1-10), when the guests did not want to go: one because he had bought a field, one had gotten married. Each one gave his own reason for not going. And the master became angry and said, "Go to the street corners and invite to the banquet anyone you find" (v. 9). Everyone. Old and young, rich and poor, good and bad. Everyone. This "everyone" has something of the view of the Lord who came for all and died for all. "But did He die even for that wretch who made my life impossible?" He died for him too. "And for that rascal?" He died for him. For everyone. And even for the people who do not believe in Him, or who are of other religions. He died for everyone. This does not mean that one must proselytize, no. But He died for everyone, He justified everyone.

Here in Rome there is a woman, a good woman, a professor, Professor [Maria Grazia] Mara, who when there were difficulties for various things, among the different parties, used to say, "But Christ died for everyone: let us go forward!". That constructive capacity. We have just one Redeemer, one unity: Christ died for everyone. Instead there is the temptation to say, and even Paul suffered from this: "I am Paul's, I am Apollo's, I belong to this one, I belong to the other..:" (see *1 Cor* 3:1-9). And think of us, fifty years ago, after the Council: the divisions that the Church suffered. "I am on this side, I think this way, you that way…". Yes, it is right to think in this way but *in the unity of the Church*, under the Shepherd, Jesus.

Two things. The apostles' rebuke to Peter because he had entered the house of the Gentiles. And Jesus who says: "I am everyone's shepherd", I am the shepherd to everyone, and who says, "There are other sheep I have that are not of this fold, and these I have to lead as well. They too will listen to my voice, and there will be only one flock, and one Shepherd" (see *Jn* 10:16). And the prayer for the unity of all humanity, so that everyone, men and women, we all have one Shepherd: Jesus.

May the Lord free us from that psychology of division, of dividing, and help us to see this aspect of Jesus, this great reality of Jesus: that in Him we are all brothers and sisters, and He is the Shepherd of *all*. That word, today: *everyone, everyone*. May it accompany us throughout the day.

Tuesday, May 5, 2020

Holy Mass[58]

Introduction

Today let us pray for the departed who have died due to the pandemic. They have died alone; they have died without the caress of their loved ones, many even without a funeral. May the Lord welcome them in glory.

Homily – Attitudes that prevent us from knowing Christ

Jesus was in the temple. It was close to the Feast of the Dedication (see *Jn* 10:22-30). During that time the Jews, too "gathered round him and said to him, 'How long will you keep us in suspense? If you are the Christ, tell us plainly'" (v. 24). They would make one lose patience, but quite meekly "Jesus answered them, 'I told you, and you do not believe'" (v. 25). They continued to say: "But is it you? Is it you?" "Yes, I said so, but you do not believe!" "But you do not believe, because you do not belong to my sheep" (v. 26). And this, perhaps, raises a doubt: I believe and I belong to Jesus's sheep; but if Jesus says to us: "You cannot believe because you do not belong", is there a faith prior to the encounter with Jesus? What is this *belonging* to Jesus's faith? What is it that stops me at the door which is Jesus?

There are attitudes prior to professing Jesus. For us too, who are in Jesus's flock. They are like "prior aver-

[58] Liturgy of the Word: *Acts* 11:19-26; *Psalm* 86(87); *Jn* 10:22-30.

sions", that do not allow us to go forward in knowledge of the Lord. The first of them is *wealth*. Many of us too, who have entered through the door of the Lord, stop and do not go forward because we are imprisoned in wealth. The Lord was harsh, about wealth, he was very harsh, very harsh. To the point of saying that it was easier for a camel to go through the eye of a needle than for a rich man to enter the Kingdom of Heaven (see *Mt* 19:24). This is harsh. Wealth is an obstacle to moving forward. But must we fall into poverty? No. But do not be slaves to wealth, do not live for wealth, because wealth is a lord, it is the lord of this world, and we cannot serve two lords (see *Lk* 16:13). And wealth stops us.

Another thing that prevents moving forward in knowledge of Jesus, in belonging to Jesus, is *rigidity*: rigidity of heart. Also rigidity in the interpretation of the Law. Jesus rebuked the Pharisees, the doctors of the Law for this rigidity (see *Mt* 23:1-36). Which is not faithfulness: faithfulness is always a gift to God; rigidity is a security for myself. I remember a time when I was entering a parish and a lady - a good lady - came up to me and said: "Father, a piece of advice..." - "Go on." - "Last week, Saturday, not yesterday, last Saturday, we went as a family to a wedding: it was with a Mass. It was Saturday afternoon, and we thought that with this Mass we had fulfilled the Sunday precept. But then, upon returning home, I thought that the readings for that Mass were not those for Sunday. And so I realized that I am in mortal sin, because I did not go on Sunday because I had gone on Saturday, but to a Mass *that was not real*, because the readings were not *real*". That rigidity.... And that lady belonged to an ecclesial movement. Rigidity. This distances us from the wisdom of Jesus, from the wisdom, beauty of Jesus: it takes away your freedom. And so many pastors cause this rigidity to grow in the souls of the faithful; and this rigidity does not help us enter through the door of Jesus (see *Jn* 10:7): observing the law as it is written or as I interpret it is more important than the freedom of moving forward following Jesus.

Another thing that does not allow us to move forward in the knowledge of Jesus is *sloth*. That weariness.... Let us think of that man at the pool: 38 years there (see *Jn* 5:1-9). Sloth. It takes away our will to go forward, and everything is "yes, but ... no, not now, no, but ...", which leads you to get cozy and makes you tepid. Sloth is another thing that prevents us from moving forward.

Another which is rather ugly is a *clericalist attitude*. Clericalism is put in Jesus's place: He says: "No, this must be like this, like this, like this..." - "But, the Teacher" - "Leave the Teacher be: this is like this, like this, like this, and if you do not do like this, like this, like this, you cannot enter". Clericalism takes away the freedom of believers. This is an ugly disease in the Church: the clericalist attitude.

Then, another thing that prevents us from going forward, from entering to know Jesus and profess Jesus, is *the worldly spirit*. When the observance of faith, the practice of faith ends up in worldliness. And everything is mundane. Let us consider the celebration of a few sacraments in some parishes: how much worldliness there is! And one does not really understand the grace of Jesus's presence.

These are the things that prevent us from belonging to Jesus's sheep. We are "sheep" [in pursuit] of all these things: wealth, sloth, rigidity, worldliness, clericalism, methods, ideologies, forms of life. Freedom is lacking. And you cannot follow Jesus without freedom. "But sometimes freedom goes beyond, and one slips". Yes, it's true. It is true. We can slip while moving. But it is worse to slip *before* moving, with these things that prevent us from beginning to move.

May the Lord enlighten us to see, within us, that there is freedom to pass through the door which is Jesus, and to go beyond Jesus in order to become a flock, to become sheep in his flock.

WEDNESDAY, MAY 6, 2020

Holy Mass[59]

Introduction

Let us pray today for the men and women who work in communications. In this time of pandemic they risk so much and there is a great deal of work. May the Lord help them in this work of transmitting the truth always.

Homily – Having the courage to see through our darkness, so the light of the Lord may enter and save us

This passage from the Gospel of John (see 12:44-50) shows us the intimacy there was between Jesus and the Father. Jesus did what the Father told Him to do. And therefore He says: "He who believes in me, believes not in me but in Him who sent me" (v. 44). He then explains His mission: "I have come as light into the world, that whoever believes in me may not remain in darkness" (v. 46). He presents himself as *light*. Jesus's mission is to enlighten: light. He himself said: "I am the light of the world" (*Jn* 8: 12). The Prophet Isaiah prophesied this light: "The people who walked in darkness have seen a great light" (9:1). The promise of the light that will enlighten the people. And the mission of the Apostles too was to bring light. Paul

---

[59] Liturgy of the Word: Acts 12:24—13:5; *Psalm* 66(67); *Jn* 12:44-50.

said to King Agrippa: "I was chosen to enlighten, to bring this light - which is not mine, but another's - but to bring light" (see *Acts* 26:18). It is Jesus's mission: to bring light. And the mission of the Apostles was to bring the light of Jesus. *To enlighten*. Because the world was in darkness.

But the tragedy of Jesus's light is that it was rejected. From the beginning of the Gospel, John said it clearly: "He came to His own home, and His own people did not welcome Him. They loved darkness more than light' (see *Jn* 1:9-11). Being accustomed to darkness, living in darkness: they did not know how to accept the light, they could not; they were slaves to darkness. And this would be Jesus's continuous battle: to enlighten, to bring the light that shows things as they are, as they exist; it shows freedom, it shows truth, it shows the path on which to go with the light of Jesus.

Paul had this experience of the passage from darkness to light, when the Lord encountered him on the road to Damascus. He was blinded. Blind. The Lord's light blinded him. And then, when a few days had passed, with baptism, he regained the light (see *Acts* 9:1-19). He had this experience of passing from darkness, in which he was, to the light. And our passage too, which we received sacramentally in Baptism: for this reason Baptism was called, in the first centuries, the *Illumination* (see Saint Justin, *Apology* I, 61, 12), because it gave you the light, it "let it enter" you. For this reason, in the ceremony of Baptism we give a lit blessed candle, a lit candle to the mother and father, because the little boy or the little girl is enlightened.

Jesus brings light. But the people, His people rejected it. They were so accustomed to the darkness that the light blinded them, they did not know where to go... (see *Jn* 1:1-

11). And this is the tragedy of our sin: sin blinds us and we cannot tolerate the light. Our eyes are sick. And Jesus clearly states it in the Gospel of Matthew: "If your eye is not sound, your whole body will be unsound. If your eye sees only darkness, how great is the darkness within you!" (see *Mt* 6:22-23). Darkness.... And conversion is passing from darkness to light.

But what are the things that sicken the eyes, the eyes of faith? Our eyes are ill: what are the things that "drag them down", that blind them? *Vices,* the *worldly spirit, pride*. The vices that "drag you down" and also these three things – vices, pride, the worldly spirit – lead you to associate with others in order to remain secure in the darkness. We often speak of "mafias": this is it. But there are "spiritual mafias"; there are "domestic mafias", always, seeking someone else so as to cover yourself and remain in darkness. It is not easy to live in the light. The light shows many ugly things within us that we do not want to see: vices, sins.... Let us think about our vices; let us think about our pride; let us think about our worldly spirit. These things blind us; they distance us from Jesus's light.

But if we start to think about these things, we will not find a wall, no. We will find a way out, because Jesus Himself says that He is the light, and also: "I have come into the world not to condemn the world, but to save the world" (see *Jn* 12:46-47). Jesus Himself, the light, says: "Take courage: let yourself be enlightened; let yourself see what you have within, because I have come to lead you forth, to save you. I do not condemn you. I save you" (see v. 47). The Lord saves us from the darkness we have within, from the darkness of daily life, of social life, of political life, of national, international life.... There is so much darkness within. And the Lord saves us. But He asks us to *see them*, first; to have the courage to see our darkness so that the Lord's light may enter and save us.

Let us not fear the Lord: He is very good; He is meek; He is close to us. He has come to save us. Let us not be afraid of the light of Jesus.

Thursday, May 7, 2020

Holy Mass[60]

Introduction

Yesterday I received a letter from a group of artists: they thanked us for praying for them. I would like to ask the Lord to bless them because artists enable us to understand and the Gospel cannot be understood without *beauty*. Let us pray once again for artists.

Homily – Being Christian means belonging to the People of God

When Paul was invited to speak in the Synagogue of Antioch [of Pisidia] to explain this new doctrine, that is, to explain Jesus, to proclaim Jesus, Paul began by speaking of salvation history (see *Acts* 13:13-21). Paul stood up and began: "The God of this people Israel chose our fathers and made the people great during their stay in the land of Egypt" (v. 17) … and [he recounted] all of salvation, the history of salvation. Stephen, the first martyr, did the same thing (see *Acts* 7:1-54) and Paul did too, another time. The author of the Letter to the Hebrews did the same thing, when he recounted the story of Abraham and "all our ancestors" (see *Heb* 11:1-39). We sang the same thing today "I will declare that your love stands firm forever, that you have established your faithfulness in heaven itself" (*Ps* 89:2). We sang the history of David: "I have found David

---

[60] Liturgy of the Word: *Acts* 13:13-25; *Psalm* 88(89); *Jn* 13:16-20.

my servant" (v. 20). Matthew and Luke did the same (see *Mt* 1:1-14, *Lk* 3:23-38): when they started speaking about Jesus, they began with Jesus's genealogy.

What is there behind Jesus? There is a history. A history of grace, a history of election, a history of promise. The Lord chose Abraham and went with His people. At the beginning of Mass, in the opening hymn, we said: "When you moved forth, Lord, before your people, and opened the path and walked beside your people, close to your people". There is a history of God with His people.

And this is why, when Paul was asked to explain the reason for faith in Jesus Christ, he did not begin with Jesus Christ: he began with the history. Christianity is a doctrine, but not only that. It is not only the things that we believe; it is a history that bears this doctrine which is God's promise, God's covenant, being chosen by God.

Christianity is not just an ethic. Yes, it is true, it has moral principles, but one is not Christian with only a vision of ethics. It is more. Christianity is not an elite of people chosen for truth. This sense of elitism that then goes ahead in the Church, right? For example, I am from that institute; I belong to this movement which is better than yours, than this or that other one.... It is an elitist sense. No, this is not Christianity: Christianity is *belonging* to a people, a people chosen by God, freely. If we do not have this consciousness of belonging to a people, we will be ideological Christians, with a tiny doctrine for affirming the truth, with an ethic, with a moral code - that's fine - or with an elite. We feel we are part of a group chosen by God - Christians - and the others will go to hell, or if they are saved it is by the mercy of God, but they are the discarded ones.... And so on. If we do not have a consciousness of belonging to a people, we are not true Christians.

For this reason Paul explained Jesus from the beginning, of his belonging to a people. And so often, so often we fall into these partialities, be they dogmatic, moral or elitist, do we not? The sense of being elite is what does us so much harm, and we lose that sense of belonging to the holy, faithful People of God, whom God chose in Abraham and promised, the great promise, Jesus, and He let them move with hope and made a covenant with them. Consciousness of being a people.

That passage from Deuteronomy always strikes me; I believe it is the 26th chapter, when it states: "Once a year when you go to present offerings to the Lord, the first harvest, and when your son asks you, 'Dad, why are you doing this?', you must not tell him: 'Because God commanded it', no. 'We were a people; we were this way and the Lord freed us...'" (see *Deut* 26:1-11). Recount the history, as Paul did here. Pass on the history of our salvation. In the same Deuteronomy the Lord advises: "When you come into the land that you did not conquer, that I conquered, and you eat of the fruits that you did not plant, and live in the houses that you did not build, in the moment to give the offering" (see *Deut* 26:1), recite the well-known creed of Deuteronomy: "A wandering Aramean was my father; and he went down into Egypt" (*Deut* 26:5) ... "He remained there for 400 years, then the Lord freed him, brought him forth...". It sings the history, *the memory of people*, of being a people.

And in this history of the People of God, up to arriving at Jesus Christ, there were saints, sinners, and many common, good people, with virtues and sins, but everyone. The well-known "crowd" that followed Jesus, that had *the sense* of belonging to a people. A self-styled Christian who does not have this sense is not a true Christian; he is a bit particular and feels justified without the people. Belonging to a people, having the memory of the People of God. And Paul, Stephen, Paul once again, the Apostles taught this.... And the advice of the author of the Letter to the Hebrews: "Remember your forebears" (see *Heb* 11:2), that is, those who came before us on this journey of salvation.

If someone were to ask me: "What do you think is the way Christians deviate today and always? What do you think is the most dangerous deviation Christians can make?", I would say without a doubt: the lack of memory of belonging to a people. When this is lacking, there is dogmatism, moralism, being moralistic, elitist movements. The people are missing. A sinful people, always, we all are, but one that generally does not make mistakes, that has the sense of being a chosen people, that journeys after a promise and has made a covenant that perhaps it may not fulfil, but knows.

We ask the Lord for this consciousness of being a people, which Our Lady sang beautifully in her Magnificat (see *Lk* 1:46-56), which Zacchariah sang so beautifully in his Benedictus (see *Lk* 1:67-79), canticles which we pray every day, in the morning and in the evening. Consciousness of being a people: we are the holy, faithful People of God who, as the First Vatican Council, then the Second, stated, in its totality has the sense of faith and is infallible in this way of believing.

FRIDAY, MAY 8, 2020

Holy Mass[61]

Introduction

Today is the World Red Cross and Red Crescent Day. Let us pray for those people who work in these meritorious institutions. May the Lord bless their work that does so much good.

Homily – His consolation is close, true and opens the doors of hope

This conversation between Jesus and the disciples again takes place at the table, during the Last Supper (see *Jn* 14:1-6). Jesus is sad, and all His followers are sad: Jesus said that He would be betrayed by one of them (see *Jn* 13:21) and they all perceive that something bad would happen. Jesus begins to console them, because one of the tasks, the "jobs" of the Lord is to console. The Lord consoles His disciples and here we see Jesus's way of consoling. We have many ways of consoling, from the most authentic, from the closest, to the most formal, such as telegrams of condolences: "Profoundly saddened by…". That does not console anyone, it is false, the consolation of formality. But how does the Lord console, because when we go through sad moments in our life, we too learn to perceive what is the true consolation of the Lord.

---

[61] Liturgy of the Word: Acts 13:26-33; *Psalm* 2; *Jn* 14:1-6.

And in this Gospel passage we see that the Lord always consoles with His closeness, through truth and hope. They are the three paths of the consolation of the Lord.

In closeness, never distant: "I am here". These beautiful words: "I am here". "I am here, with you". And very often, in silence. But we know that He is there. He is always there. That closeness that is God's style, even in the Incarnation, making Himself close to us. The Lord consoles in closeness. And He does not use empty words; on the contrary, He prefers silence. The strength of closeness, in presence. He speaks little, but He is close.

A second path of Jesus's closeness, of Jesus's way of consoling, is the truth: Jesus is truthful. He does not say formal things that are lies: "No, be calm, everything will pass, nothing will happen, it will pass, things come to an end…". No. He tells the truth. He does not hide the truth. Because He Himself in this passage says, "I am the truth" (see *Jn* 14:6). And the truth is, "I will go", that is, "I will die" (see vv. 2-3). We are faced with death. It is the truth. And He says it so simply and gently, without causing harm. But we are right before His death. He does not hide the truth.

And this is the third way. Jesus consoles with hope. Yes, this is a bad moment, but "do not let your hearts be troubled. … Have faith also in me" (v. 1). I will tell you something, Jesus says, "in my Father's house there are many dwelling places. If there were not, would I have told you that I am going to prepare a place for you?" (v. 2). He is the first to go and open the doors, the doors to that place, through which we will all pass, at least we hope. "I will come back again and take you to myself, so that where I am you also may be" (v. 3). The Lord returns every time that one of us is departing from this world. "I will come, I will take you with me": hope. He will come and take us by the hand, and bring us with Him. He does not say, "No, you will not suffer, it's nothing…". No. He tells the truth: "I am near you. This is the truth: it is a bad moment, of danger, of death. But do not let your heart be troubled, stay in that peace, that peace that is the basis of every consolation. Because I will come, I will and take you by the hand where I will be".

It is not easy to allow ourselves to be comforted by the Lord. Very often, in bad moments, we get angry with the Lord and we do not allow Him to come to speak to us like this, with this tenderness, with this closeness, with this gentleness, with this truth and with this hope.

Let us ask the grace to learn to let ourselves be comforted by the Lord. The consolation of the Lord is true, it does not deceive. It is not anaesthesia, no. But He is close, He is true, and He opens the doors to hope.

SATURDAY, MAY 9, 2020

Holy Mass[62]

Introduction

Today we commemorate Saint Louise de Marillac [the liturgical memorial is held on March 15, but since it fell within the Season of Lent, it has been moved to today]. Let us pray for the Vincentian sisters who have been managing this clinic, this "hospital" [the Santa Marta Paediatric Dispensary managed by the Sisters of the Congregation of the Daughters of Charity] for almost 100 years and who work here at Santa Marta, for this "hospital". May the Lord bless the sisters.

Homily – The Holy Spirit makes harmony in the Church, the evil spirit destroys it

We have recited in the Psalm: "Sing a new song to the Lord, for He has done marvellous deeds. His right hand and holy arm have won the victory. The Lord has made His victory known; has revealed His triumph in the sight of the nations" (*Ps* 98:1-2). This is true. The Lord has worked wonders. But how much effort! How much effort, for the Christian communities, to carry on these wonders of the Lord!

---

[62] Liturgy of the Word: *Acts* 13:44-52; *Psalm* 97(98); *Jn* 14:7-14.

We heard joy in the passage from the Acts of the Apostles (see 13:44-52): the entire city of Antioch gathered to heard the word of the Lord, because Paul and the apostles preached with power, and the Spirit helped them. But "when ... they saw the crowds, they were filled with jealousy and with violent abuse contradicted what Paul said" (v. 45). On the one hand, there is the Holy Spirit who makes the Church grow, and it grows ever more, this is true. But on the other hand there is the evil spirit that seeks to destroy the Church. It is always like that, always like that. Things go ahead, but then comes the enemy, trying to destroy. The balance is always positive in the long run, but how much difficulty, how much pain, how much martyrdom!

This happened here, in Antioch, and it happens everywhere in the Book of the Acts of the Apostles. Let us think, for example, of Lystra, when they arrived and they healed [a paralytic], and everyone believed that they were gods and wanted to make sacrifices to them, and all the people were with them (see *Acts* 14:8-18). Then the others came and they convinced them that it was not thus. And what happened to Paul and his companion? They ended up being stoned (*Acts* 14:19). There is always this battle. Think of the sorcerer Elymas, and how he tried to prevent the Gospel from reaching the proconsul (*Acts* 13:6-12). Think of the masters of that girl who was a soothsayer: they exploited the girl, because she "read palms" and received money that went into the pockets of her masters. And when Paul and the apostles showed that this was a lie, that it wasn't right, immediately there was a revolution against them (see *Acts* 16:16-24). Think of the artisans of the goddess Artemis [in Epheseus], who were losing business because they couldn't sell statuettes to the people, because they were being converted. In this way, one after another. On the one hand, the Word of God that summons, that makes one grow; and on the other, persecution, serious persecution, as they end up being driven out and beaten.

And what is the tool the devil uses to destroy the proclamation of the Gospel? *Envy.* The Book of Wisdom says clearly: "But through the devil's envy death entered the world" (*Wis* 2:24) - envy, jealousy, here. Always this bitter, bitter sentiment. These people saw how the Gospel was preached and they became angry, they were consumed by rage. And they were led on by this anger: it is the devil's anger, the anger that destroys, the anger of that "*Crucify Him! Crucify Him*!", of that torture of Jesus. It wants to destroy. Always. Always.

Seeing this struggle, that beautiful saying is valid for us too: "The Church has gone forward on pilgrimage amid the persecutions of the world and the consolations of God" (see Saint Augustine, *De Civitate Dei*, XVIII, 51:2). Something is missing from a Church that does not have any difficulties. The devil is too calm. And if the devil is calm, something is wrong. There are always difficulties, temptation, struggles... The jealousy that destroys. The Holy Spirit makes the harmony of the Church, and the evil spirit destroys. Even till today, till today. Always this battle. Temporal power is a tool of this jealousy, of this envy. Here it tells us that "the Jewish leaders incited the God-fearing women of high standing" (*Acts* 13:50). They went to these women and they said: "These are revolutionaries, drive them out". The women spoke with others and they banished them: it was the "God-fearing women" of the nobility and the leading men of the city (see v. 50). Those with temporal power, and temporal power can be good. People can be good, but power as such is always dangerous. The power of the world against the power of God moves all of this; and always, behind this, behind that power, there is money.

This is what happens in the early Church: the work of the Spirit to build up the Church, to harmonize the Church, and the work of the evil spirit to destroy it, and recourse to temporal powers to stop the Church, to destroy the Church. It is none other than a development of what happens on the morning of the Resurrection. The soldiers, seeing that triumph, went to the priests, and the priests "bought" the truth. And the truth was "silenced" (see *Mt* 28:11, 15). From the first morning of the Resurrection, the triumph of Christ, there is this betrayal, this silencing of the word of Christ, silencing the triumph of the Resurrection with temporal power: the chief priests and money.

Let us be careful, be careful with preaching the Gospel: never to give in to placing our trust in temporal powers and in money. Christians put their trust in Jesus Christ and in the Holy Spirit whom He sent! It is precisely the Holy Spirit that is the leaven, the force that makes the Church grow. Yes, the Church moves resignedly and joyfully forward: between the persecutions of the world and the consolations of God.

Sunday, May 10, 2020

Fifth Sunday of Easter (A)

Holy Mass[63]

Introduction

In these last two days, there have been two commemorations: the seventieth anniversary of the Robert Schuman Declaration, which gave rise to the European Union, and also the commemoration of the end of the war. Let us ask the Lord that Europe today might grow united, in that unity of brotherhood that makes all peoples grow in the unity of diversity.

Homily – Praying is going with Jesus to the Father who will give us everything

In this passage of the Gospel (see *Jn* 14:1-14), Jesus's farewell discourse, Jesus says that He is going to the Father. And He says that He will be with the Father, and that also those who believe in Him "will do the works I have been doing, and they will do even greater things than these, because I am going to the Father. And I will do whatever you ask in my name, so that the Father may be glorified in the Son. You may ask me anything in my name, and I will do it" (vv. 12-14). We can say that this

---

[63] Liturgy of the Word: *Acts* 2:36-41; *Psalm* 32(33); *1 Pt* 2:4-9; *Jn* 20:11-18.

passage of the Gospel of John is the declaration of ascent to the Father.

The Father was always present in Jesus's life, and Jesus spoke about Him. Jesus prayed to the Father. And many times, He spoke about the Father who cares for us, as He cares for the birds, the lilies of the field… the Father. And when the disciples asked to learn how to pray, Jesus taught them to pray to the Father: "Our Father" (*Mt* 6:9). He always addresses the Father. But in this passage it is very strong; it is also as if He opened the doors of the omnipotence of prayer. "Because I am with the Father: ask me and I will do anything. Because the Father will do it with me" (see *Jn* 14:11). This trust in the Father, trust in the Father who is capable of doing everything, This courage to pray, because it takes courage to pray! It takes the same courage, the same boldness it takes to preach: the same. Let us think of our father Abraham, when he – I think the right word is – "negotiated" with God to save Sodom (see *Gn* 18:20-33): "And if there were fewer? And fewer? And fewer…? He truly knew how to negotiate. But always with this courage: "Excuse me, Lord, but give me a discount: a bit less, a bit less…". Always the courage of struggling in prayer, because praying is struggling: struggling with God. And then, Moses: the two occasions that the Lord wanted to destroy the people (see *Ex* 32:1-35 and *Nm* 11:1-3), and to make him the leader of another people, Moses said "No!". And he said "No" to the Father! With *courage*! But if you go and pray like this [whispers a timid prayer] – this is a lack of respect! Praying is going with Jesus to the Father who will give you everything. Courage in prayer, boldness in prayer. The same that it takes to preach.

And we have heard in the first Reading about that conflict in the early times of the Church (see *Acts* 6:1-7), because the Christians of Greek origin were grumbling, complaining – they were already doing it back then: it is obvious that it is one of the Church's habits – they were complaining that their widows, their orphans were not well cared for; the apostles did not have the time to do many things. And Peter [with the apostles], enlightened by the Holy Spirit, "invented", let's put it that way, the deacons. "Let's do something: let's look for seven people who are good and these men can take care of the service" (see *Acts* 6:2-4). The deacon is the one who takes care of service, in the Church. "And so these people, who are right to complain, have their needs taken care and we," Peter says, we heard him, "and we can devote ourselves to prayer and the proclamation of the Word" (see v. 5). This is the bishop's task: praying and preaching. With this power that we heard in the Gospel: the bishop is the first who goes to the Father, with the trust that Jesus gave him, with courage, with *parrhesia,* to fight for his people. The first task of a bishop is to pray. Peter said so: "And to us, prayer and the proclamation of the Gospel".

I knew a priest, a holy parish priest, good, who when he found a bishop, greeted him well, very amiably, and always asked the question: "Your Excellency, how many hours a day do you pray?", and he always said, "Because your first task is to pray". Because it is the prayer of the head of the community, interceding to the Father so that He may safeguard the people.

The prayer of the bishop, the first task: *to pray.* And the people, seeing the bishop pray, learn to pray. Because the Holy Spirit teaches us that it is God who does things.

We do very little but it is He who "does things" in the Church, and prayer is what makes the Church progress. And therefore the heads of the Church, so to speak, the bishops, must persevere in prayer.

Peter's word in this case is prophetic: "May the deacons do all this, so that the people are taken care of well, their problems are solved and their needs met. But to us, bishops, prayer and the proclamation of the Word".

It is sad to see good bishops, good people, but busy with many things, the finances, with this, that and the other... Prayer must take first place. Then the other things. But when the other things take away space from prayer, then something is not right. And prayer is strong because of what we have heard in the Gospel of Jesus. It is "because I am going to the Father. And I will do whatever you ask in my name, so that the Father may be glorified in the Son" (*Jn* 14:12-13). Thus the Church progresses in prayer, in the courage of prayer because the Church knows that without this ascent to the Father, she cannot survive.

Regina Coeli

Dear Brothers and Sisters, good morning,

In today's Gospel passage (see *Jn* 14:1-12), we hear the beginning of Jesus's so-called "Farewell discourse". They are the words He addresses to the disciples at the end of the Last Supper, just before facing the Passion. In such a dramatic moment Jesus began by saying, "Do not let your hearts be troubled" (v. 1). He says it to us too, in life's troubles. But how can we ensure that our hearts are not troubled? Because the heart does become troubled.

The Lord indicates two remedies for being troubled. The first is: "Believe in me" (v. 1). It would seem to be rather theoretical, abstract advice. Instead, Jesus wants to tell us something precise. He knows that, in life, the worst anxiety, anguish, arises from the sensation of not being able to cope, of feeling alone and without points of reference when faced with events. We cannot overcome this anguish alone, when one difficulty is added to another. We need Jesus's help, and this is why Jesus asks us to have faith in him, that is, to lean not on ourselves but on him. Because liberation from being troubled depends upon entrusting ourselves. Entrusting ourselves to Jesus, taking the "leap". And this is liberation from feeling troubled. Jesus is risen and lives precisely to be always by our side. We can thus say to him, "Jesus, I believe that you rose again and are beside me. I believe that you listen to me. I bring to you what upsets me, my troubles; I have faith in you and I entrust myself to you".

There is then a second remedy for being troubled, which Jesus expresses with these words: "My Father's house has many rooms… I am going there to prepare a place for you" (v. 2). This is what Jesus did for us: He reserved a place in Heaven for us. He took our humanity upon Himself to carry it beyond death, to a new place, to Heaven, so that we might also be where he is. It is the certainty that comforts us: there is a place reserved for each of us.

There is a place for me too. Each of us can say: there is a place for me. We do not live aimlessly and without a destination. We are awaited. We are precious. God is in love with us, we are His children. And He has prepared for us the most worthy and beautiful place: Paradise. Let us not forget this: the dwelling place that awaits us is Paradise. We are in transit here. We are made for Heaven, for eternal life, to live forever. Forever: it is something we cannot even imagine now. But it is even more beautiful to think that this forever will be entirely in joy, in full communion with God and with others, without any more tears, without resentment, without division or turmoil.

But how can we reach heaven? What is the way? Here is Jesus's decisive phrase. He says to us today: "I am the Way" (v. 6). Jesus is the way to go up to Heaven: to have a living relationship with him, to imitate Him in love, to follow in his footsteps. And I, a Christian, you, a Christian, every one of us Christians, can ask ourselves: "Which way do I follow?". There are ways that do not lead to Heaven: the ways of worldliness, the ways of self-affirmation, the ways of selfish power. And there is Jesus's way, the way of humble love, of prayer, of meekness, of trust, of service to others. It is not the way of my self-centeredness. It is the way of Jesus, who is the protagonist of my life. It is to go forth every day, asking him: "Jesus, what do you think of the choice I made? What would you do in this situation, with these people?". It will do us good to ask Jesus, who is the way, for the directions to reach Heaven. May Our Lady, Queen of Heaven, help us to follow Jesus, who opened Heaven for us.

After the Regina Coeli

My thoughts today turn to Europe and Africa. To Europe, on the occasion of the 70th anniversary of the Schuman Declaration of May 9, 1950. It inspired the process of European integration, enabling the reconciliation of the peoples of the continent, after the Second World War and the long period of stability and peace from which we benefit today. May the spirit of the Schuman Declaration never fail to inspire those who hold responsibility in the

European Union, called to face the social and economic consequences caused by the pandemic in a spirit of harmony and collaboration.

And our gaze also turns to Africa, because on May 10, 1980, 40 years ago, during his first pastoral visit to the continent, Saint John Paul II gave voice to the cry of the people of the Sahel, who were harshly tested by drought. Today I congratulate the young people who are working for the initiative "Laudato Si' Alberi" (Laudato Si' Trees). The goal is to plant at least one million trees throughout the Sahel region, which will become part of the "Great Green Wall of Africa". I hope that many will follow the example of solidarity shown by these young people.

And today, Mother's Day is being celebrated in many countries. I would like to remember all mothers with gratitude and affection, entrusting them to the protection of Mary, our heavenly Mother. My thoughts also turn to mothers who have passed on to the other life, and who accompany us from Heaven. Let us be silent a moment so each one of us can remember our mother. [Silent pause].

MONDAY, MAY 11, 2020

Holy Mass[64]

Introduction

Today let us join with the faithful of Termoli, on the feast of the Discovery of the body of Saint Timothy. In these days many people have lost their jobs; they have not been re-employed, they work "under the table"... Let us pray for these brothers and sisters of ours who suffer as a result of this lack of work.

Homily – The Spirit teaches us everything, introduces us to mystery, makes us remember and discern

The passage from today's Gospel is from Jesus's farewell at the Last Supper (see *Jn* 14:21-26). The Lord ends with these verses: "I have told you this while I am with you. The Advocate, the Holy Spirit that the Father will send in my name - He will teach you everything and remind you of all that I told you" (vv. 25-26). It is the promise of the Holy Spirit; the Holy Spirit that dwells in us and whom the Father and the Son send. "The Father will send in my name", says Jesus, to accompany us in life. And they call Him Paraclete. This is the task of the Holy Spirit. In Greek, Paraclete is the one who supports, who accompanies you so you do not fall, who keeps you steadfast, who is near you to sustain you. And the Lord promised us this support, Who is God like Him: He is the Holy Spirit. What does the Holy Spirit do in us? The Lord tells us: "He

[64] Liturgy of the Word: *Acts* 14:5-18; *Psalm* 114(115); *Jn* 14:21-26.

will teach you everything and remind you of all that I told you" (v. 26). Teaching and remembering: this is the task of the Holy Spirit.

He *teaches* us: He teaches us the mystery of faith, He teaches us to enter into the mystery, to understand the mystery a bit more. He teaches us Jesus's doctrine and He teaches us how to develop our faith without making mistakes, so that the doctrine grows, but always in the same direction: it grows in comprehension. And the Spirit helps us to grow in the understanding of faith, to understand it more, to understand what faith says. Faith is not something static; doctrine is not something static, it grows. It grows like trees grow, always the same, but bigger, with fruit, but always the same, in the same direction. And the Holy Spirit prevents doctrinal error, He prevents it from remaining stuck there, without growing in us. He will teach us the things that Jesus taught us, He will develop our comprehension of what Jesus taught us, He will make the doctrine of the Lord grow in us until it reaches maturity.

And another thing that Jesus says the Holy Spirit does is to *remind:* "He will ... remind you of all that I told you" (v. 26). The Holy Spirit is like our memory, He rouses us: "Remember this, remember that". He keeps us awake, always awake in the things of the Lord, and He also makes us remember our life: "Think of that moment, think of when you encountered the Lord, think of when you left the Lord".

Once I heard it said that a person prayed before the Lord in this way: "Lord, I am the same person I was as a child. When I was little, I had these dreams. Then I set out on the wrong path. Now you have called me". I am the same: this is the memory of the Holy Spirit in one's own life. He leads us to the memory of salvation, to the memory of what Jesus taught, but also to the memory of one's own life. And what this man said made me think. It is a beautiful way to pray, to look at the Lord and say: "I am the same. I have journeyed a lot, I have made many mistakes, but I am the same, and you love me". The memory of the journey of life.

And in this memory, the Holy Spirit guides us; He leads us to discern, to discern what we must do now, which is the right path and which is the wrong one, even in small decisions. If we ask for the light of the Holy Spirit, He will help us to discern so as to make the right decisions, the little everyday ones and the big ones. He will accompany us and support us in this discernment.

Therefore, the Spirit teaches us: He will teach us everything, that is, He will make us grow in faith, He introduces us to the mystery. The Spirit reminds us: He reminds us of faith, He reminds us of our life; it is the Spirit who in this teaching and in this memory teaches us to discern the decisions we must make. And the Gospels give a name to this, to the Holy Spirit - yes, Paraclete, because He supports you, but another more beautiful name: the Gift of God. The Spirit is the Gift of God. The Spirit is indeed the gift. He will not leave you alone, He will send you a Paraclete who will sustain you and help you to progress, to remember, discern and grow. The Gift of God is the Holy Spirit.

May the Lord help us to keep this Gift that He has given us in Baptism, and which we all have within.

Tuesday, May 12, 2020

Holy Mass[65]

Introduction

Today is International Nurses Day. Yesterday I sent a message. Let us pray today for nurses: men, women, young men and women who exercise this profession, which is more than a profession, it is a vocation, a dedication. May the Lord bless them. In this time of the pandemic they have given an example of heroism and some have given their lives. Let us pray for nurses.

Homily – How does the world give peace, and how does the Lord give it?

Before leaving the Lord greets His followers and gives the gift of peace (see *Jn* 14:27-31), the Lord's peace: "Peace I leave with you; my peace I give to you. Not as the world gives do I give it to you. Do not let your hearts be troubled or afraid (v. 27). It is not universal peace, that peace without wars that we all want there to be forever, but the peace of the heart, the peace of the soul, the peace that each one of us has inside. And the Lord gives it, but, He emphasises, "not as the world gives" (v. 27). How does the world give peace and how does the Lord give it? Are they different forms of peace? Yes.

The world gives you "inner peace" - we are talking about this, peace in your life, living with your "heart at

---

[65] Liturgy of the Word: *Acts* 14:19-28; *Psalm* 144(145); *Jn* 14:27-31.

peace" – it gives you inner peace as if it were your own possession, like something that is yours and isolates you from others, that you keep for yourself, a personal acquisition: I am at peace. And without realizing it you close yourself up in that peace, it is a peace that is only for you, for each person; it is a solitary peace, it is a peace that makes you serene, even happy. And in this tranquillity, in this happiness, it can lull you to sleep, it anaesthetizes you and makes you stay within yourself in a certain tranquillity. It is a bit selfish: peace for me, closed up in myself. This is how the world gives it to you (see v. 27). It is a costly peace, because you must continually change the "instruments of peace": when you are enthusiastic about something, one thing gives you peace, then it ends and you have to find another. It is costly because it is *temporary and sterile.*

Instead, the peace that Jesus gives is another thing. It is a peace that puts you *in motion:* it does not isolate you, it puts you in motion, it makes you go towards others, it creates community, it creates communication. The world's peace is costly, whereas Jesus's is freely given, it is free; it is a gift from the Lord, the peace of the Lord. It is fruitful, it always leads you forward.

An example from the Gospel that makes me think of what the world's peace is like, is that man whose barns were full and whose harvest that year seemed to be very big, and thought: "I must build other warehouses, other barns to put this in, and then I will be fine... this is my tranquillity, this way I can live serenely". "You fool", says God, "this night your life will be demanded of you" (see *Lk* 12:13-21). It is a temporary peace, that does not open the door to the hereafter. Instead the Lord's peace opens to the place where He went, it is open to Heaven, it is open to Paradise. It is a fruitful peace that is open and brings others with you as well to Paradise.

I think that it would help us to think a bit: what kind of peace do I have, where do I find peace? In things, in well-being, in travel – but nowadays one cannot travel – in possessions, in many things, or do I find peace as a gift from the Lord? Must I *pay* for peace or do I receive it freely from the Lord? What kind of peace do I have? When I am missing something, do I get angry? This is not the Lord's peace. This is one of the tests. Am I calm in my peace, do I get "lulled to sleep"? It is not the Lord's. Am I in peace and do I want to communicate it to others, do I want to accomplish something? That is the Lord's peace! Even in bad or difficult moments, does that peace remain in me? It is the Lord's. And the Lord's peace is fruitful for me too, because it is full of hope, that is, it looks towards Heaven.

Yesterday – excuse me if I say these things, but they are things about life that are good for me – yesterday I received a letter from a priest, a good priest. And he said to me that I speak little about Heaven. I should speak about it more. And he is right, he is right. And because of this, I wanted to emphasize it today. That the peace Jesus gives us is a peace for today and for the future. It is beginning to live Heaven, with the fruitfulness of Heaven. It is not anaesthesia. The other peace is: you anaesthetize yourself with things of the world and when the dose of this anaesthetic wears off, you take another one, and another... This peace [of Jesus] is a *definitive* peace, fruitful and "contagious". It is not narcissistic, because it always looks to the

Lord. The other form of peace is about looking at yourself, it is a bit narcissistic.

May the Lord give us this peace, full of hope, that makes us fruitful, that makes us communicative with others, that creates community and that always looks to the definitive peace of Paradise.

Wednesday, May 13, 2020

Holy Mass[66]

Introduction

We pray today for students, the boys and girls who study, and for their teachers who need to find new ways to continue educating. May the Lord help them on this path and grant them courage and success.

Homily – The mutual remaining between the vine and the branches

The Lord returns to "remain in Him", and He tells us: "the Christian life is to remain in me". *Remain.* And here He uses the image of the vine, like the branches remain on a vine (see *Jn* 15:1-8). And this remaining is not a passive remaining, a falling asleep in the Lord. This might be a "beatific slumber", but that's not what it is. This *remain* is an active remaining, and it is also a mutual remaining. Why? Because He says: You remain in me and I in you" (v. 4). He also remains in us, it is not only we in Him. It is a *mutual* remaining. In another part He says: I and the Father "we will come to him and we will make our home in him" (*Jn* 14:23). This is a mystery, but it is a mystery of life, a beautiful mystery, this *mutual remaining*. Even with this example of the vine: it is true, the branches without the vine cannot do anything because the sap would not get to them. They need the sap to grow and bear fruit; but

---

66 Liturgy of the Word: *Acts* 15:1-6; *Psalm* 121(122); *Jn* 15:1-8.

even the tree, the vine needs the branches because the fruit is not attached to the tree, to the vine. There is a mutual need, a mutual remaining in order to bear fruit.

And this is the Christian life. It is true, the Christian life consists in fulfilling the commandments (see *Ex* 20:1-11), this must be done. The Christian life means following the path of the beatitudes (see *Mt* 5:1-13), this must be done. The Christian life is performing the works of mercy, as the Lord taught us in the Gospel (see *Mt* 25:35-36), this must be done . But even more, it is this *mutual remaining*. Without Jesus we can do nothing, like the branches without the vine. And He - may the Lord permit me to say so - without us it seems that He can do nothing, because the branches bear the fruit, not the tree, the vine. In this community, in this intimacy of "remaining", which bears fruit, the Father and Jesus remain me and I remain in Them.

What comes to my mind to say is: what does the vine "need" from the branches? It is to have fruit. What is the "need", let's say it that way, a bit daringly, what does Jesus "need" from us? *Witness.* When the Gospel says that we are the light, it says: "your light must shine before others, that they may see your good deeds and glorify your heavenly Father" (*Mt* 5:16). That is, it is witness that Jesus needs from us. To bear witness to His name because the faith, the Gospel grow because of witness. This is a mysterious way: Jesus, even though He is glorified in heaven, after having lived through the Passion, needs our witness for growth, for proclamation, so that the Church might grow. And this is the mutual mystery of this "remaining". He, the Father and the Spirit remain in us, and we remain in Jesus.

It is good for us to think, to reflect on this: to remain in Jesus, and Jesus remains in us. To remain in Jesus, to have the sap, the strength, to have justification, the gracious gift, to be fruitful. And He remains in us to give us the power to [bear] fruit (see *Jn* 5:15), to give us the strength to bear witness by which the Church grows.

And a question I ask myself: What is the relationship between Jesus who remains in me and I who remain in Him? It is a relationship of intimacy, a mystical relationship, a relationship without words. "But Father, but this is what mystics do!" No, this is for everyone one of us! Through small thoughts: "Lord, I know that You are here [in me]: grant me the strength and I will do what You will tell me". That intimate dialogue with the Lord. The Lord is *present*, the Lord is present in us, the Father is present in us, the Spirit is present in us, They remain and us. But I must remain in Them…

May the Lord help us to understand, to experience this *mysticism of remaining* on which Jesus insisted so, so, so much. Many times, when we speak of the vine and the branches, we stop at the image, the work of the vine grower, of the Father: who prunes the one [the branch] that bears fruit, and who cuts and throws out the one that does not (see *Jn* 15:1-2). It is true, He does this, but that is not everything, no. There is something else. And this is the help: the trials, the difficulties of life, even the corrections that the Lord gives us. But we should not stop here. Between the vine and the branches there is this intimate *remaining*. We the branches need the sap, and the vine needs the fruit of our witness.

Thursday, May 14, 2020

Holy Mass[67]

Introduction

Today, the Higher Committee for Human Fraternity has called for a day of prayer and fasting to ask the merciful God for an end to this tragic moment of the pandemic. We are all brothers and sisters. St Francis of Assisi used to say: "All brothers and sisters". And so, men and women of every religious confession are uniting themselves today in prayer and penance to ask for the grace of healing from this pandemic.

Homily – Day of fraternity, day of penance and prayer

In the first Reading, we heard the story of Jonah, in the style used at that time (see *Jon* 3:1-10). Since there was some type of pandemic, we do not know, in the city of Nineveh, a "moral pandemic" perhaps, it was about to be destroyed (see v. 4). And God sends Jonah to preach: prayer and penance, prayer and fasting (see vv. 7-8). Having to face that pandemic, Jonah [at first] got frightened and escaped (see 1:3). Then the Lord called him a second time and he agreed to go and preach this (see 3:1-3). And today, all of us, brothers and sisters of every religious tradition, are praying: a day of prayer and fasting and penance, organized by the Higher Committee for Human Fra-

---

[67] Liturgy of the Word: *Jon* 3:1-10; *Psalm* 112(113); *Jn* 15:9-17.

ternity. Each of us should pray, communities should pray, religious confessions should pray, pray to God: all of us *brothers and sisters*, united in the fraternity that unites us in this painful and tragic moment.

We were not expecting this pandemic, it came without us expecting it, but now it is here. And many people are dying. Many people are dying alone and many people are dying without being able to do anything. Often the thought can arise: 'Well, at least I haven't been affected. Thank God I'm safe". But think about others. Think about the tragedy and its consequences on the economy and education, the consequences ... that will come afterwards.

And it is for this that today, everyone, brothers and sisters, of whatever religious confession, are praying to God. Perhaps someone will say: "This is religious relativism and you cannot do that". But how can we not pray to the Father of all? Everyone prays as they know how, as they can, according to what they have received from their own culture. We are not praying against each other, this religious tradition against that one, no! We are all united as human beings, as *brothers and sisters*, praying to God according to each one's culture, according to each one's own tradition, according to each one's own beliefs, but brothers and sisters praying to God, this is what is important! Brothers and sisters, fasting, asking God to forgive our sins, so that the Lord might have mercy on us, so that the Lord will forgive us, so that the Lord may end this pandemic. Today is a day of fraternity, looking to the one Father: brothers and sisters and paternity. Day of prayer.

Last year, rather in November of last year, we did not know what a pandemic was: it came upon us like a flood, it came all of a sudden. Now we are waking up a bit. But there are many other pandemics that make people die and we are not even aware of it, we look the other way. We are a bit unaware before the tragedies that are happening in the world right now. I would like to tell you one official statistic from the first four months of this year that is not connected with the coronavirus pandemic, but about another one. During the first four months of this year, 3,700,000 people died of hunger. There is a *pandemic of hunger*. In four months, almost 4 million people. Today's prayer to ask that the Lord end this pandemic must make us think of other pandemics in the world. There are so many of them! The pandemic of war, of hunger and many others. What is important is that today - together, and thanks to the *courage* that this Higher Committee for Human Fraternity had - together, we are invited to pray, each one according to his or her own tradition and to observe a day *of penance, of fasting and also of charity*, of helping others. This is what is important. In the book of Jonah, we heard that the Lord, when He saw how the people responded - that they had converted - the Lord stopped, He refrained from doing what He had wanted to do.

May God put an end to this tragedy, may He stop this pandemic. May God have mercy on us and may He also put a stop to the other terrible pandemics of hunger, war, and uneducated children. This is what we ask as *brothers and sisters*, all together. May God bless us all, and have mercy on us.

Friday, May 15, 2020

Holy Mass[68]

Introduction

Today is the International Day of Families. Let us pray for families, that the Spirit of the Lord - the spirit of love, respect and freedom - may grow in families.

Homily – Our relationship with God is gratuitous, it is friendship

In the book of the Acts of the Apostles, we see that in the Church, in the beginning, there were times of peace. It says that many times: the Church was growing in peace and the Spirit of the Lord gave it growth (see *Acts* 9:31). Moments of peace. There were also moments of persecution, beginning with the persecution of Stephen (see *Acts* 6–7), then Paul the persecutor, converted, but even he persecuted... Moments of peace, moments of persecution; there were even moments of *turmoil*. And this is the theme of today's first Reading: a moment of turmoil (see 15:22-31). "We have heard that some from our number," the Apostles write to the Christians who have converted from paganism, "we have heard that some from our number who had no mandate from us have upset you," have disturbed you "with their teachings that have disturbed your peace of mind" (v. 24).

---

[68] Liturgy of the Word: *Acts* 15:22-31; *Psalm* 56(57); *Jn* 15:12-17.

What happened? These Christians, who had been pagans, believed in Jesus Christ and had received baptism. And they were happy: they had received the Holy Spirit. They went from paganism to Christianity without any intermediary stage. Instead, those People who were called "Judaizers" sustained that you could not do that, that if someone had been a pagan they had to become Jews first, a good Jew, and then become a Christian, so as to be in line with the election of the People of God. And these Christians did not understand this. "But why? Are we second-class Christians? We cannot go directly from paganism to Christianity? Didn't Christ's resurrection dissolve the ancient law and bring it to an even greater fullness?" They were disturbed and there were a lot of discussions among them. And those who wanted this were people who had pastoral arguments, even some moral ones. They sustained that no, you had to make the passage in this way! And this put into question the freedom of the Holy Spirit, and the free gift of Christ's resurrection and grace. They were methodical, and also rigid.

Jesus had said about these people, these teachers, these doctors of the Law: "Woe to you who traverse sea and land to make one convert, and when that happens you make him worse than before. You make him a child of Gehenna" Jesus more or less says that in the 23rd chapter of Matthew (see v. 15). These people who were "ideological" had reduced the Law, the doctrine, to an ideology: "you have to do this, and this, and this..." A religion of prescriptions, and thus they took away the Holy Spirit's freedom. And the people who followed them were rigid people, people who did not feel comfortable, they did not know the joy of the Gospel. The way of following Jesus to perfection was through *rigidity*. "You have to do this, this, this, and this". These people, these doctors, "manipulated" the consciences of the faithful, or they made them become rigid, or they would go away.

Because of this, I repeat this many times, and I say that rigidity is not from the good Spirit because it puts into question the *free gift* of the redemption, the free gift of Christ's resurrection. And this is something old: throughout the Church's history this has repeated itself. Let us think of the Pelagians, of those... those famously rigid people. And even in our own times we have seen some apostolic organizations that seem to be quite well organized, who work well..., but all of them are rigid, everyone is exactly the same, and then we have learned about the corruption that was inside, even in the founders.

The Spirit of God is not where there is rigidity, because the Spirit of God is *liberty*. And these people wanted to force these passages, taking away liberty from the Spirit of God and the *gratuitousness* of the redemption: "to be justified you have to do this, this, this, and this..". Justification is freely given. Jesus's death and resurrection are gratuitous. You do not pay for it, it cannot be purchased: it is a gift! And these people did not want to do it that way.

The path is beautiful [the way they proceeded]: the Apostles gathered together in this council and in the end they write a letter that says this: "It has been decided by the Holy Spirit and by ourselves not to saddle you with any burden" (*Acts* 15:28), and they put these obligations and a few common sense moral ones so as not to confuse Christianity with paganism, abstaining from meet offered to idols, etc. And in the end, these Christians who had been disturbed, gathered in an assembly, they received the letter, and "when they read it, they were delighted with the encouragement it gave them" (v. 31). From *turmoil* to *joy*. The spirit of rigidity always brings turmoil. "Did I do this all right?. Did I not do that all right? Scrupulosity. The Spirit of evangelical freedom brings you joy because that is exactly what Jesus did by His resurrection: He brought joy! Our relationship with God, our relationship with Jesus is not a relationship of "doing things": "I do this and You give me that". A relationship like that - forgive me, Lord - *commercial*. No! It is free, just like the relationship between Jesus and the disciples. "You are my friends" (*Jn* 15:14). "I do not call you slaves, I call you friends" (see v. 15). "You did not choose me, but I chose you" (v. 16). This is gratuitousness.

Let us ask the Lord to help us to discern the fruit of evangelical *gratuitousness* from the fruits of non-evangelical *rigidity*, and that He might free us from every turmoil caused by those who put the Faith, the life of Faith under detailed prescriptions, prescriptions that have no meaning. I refer to those prescriptions that have no meaning, not to the Commandments. May He free us from the spirit of rigidity that robs you of freedom.

Saturday, May 16, 2020

Holy Mass[69]

Introduction

Let us pray today for people who are burying the dead during the pandemic. To bury the dead is one of the works of mercy and, naturally, it is not something pleasant. Let us pray for them because they also risk their lives and risk being infected.

Homily – Christ died and rose for us: the only medicine against the worldly spirit

Especially while He was bidding farewell to the Apostles, Jesus, spoke of the world many times (see *Jn* 15:18-21). And here He says: "If the world hates you, know that it hated me before you" (v. 18). He speaks clearly of the hatred that the world had with Jesus and will have with us. And in the prayer that He says at table with the disciples during the Last Supper, He asks the Father not to take His disciples out of the world, but to defend them from the spirit of the world (see 17:15).

I think we can ask ourselves: What is *the spirit of the world*? What is this worldliness that is capable of hating, of destroying Jesus and His disciples, and more, of corrupting them and of corrupting the Church? What is this spirit of the world, what is this? It is good for us to think about it. It is a *style of life*, worldliness. But someone might think that worldliness is about partying, living life as a party…

---

[69] Liturgy of the Word: *Acts* 16:1-10; *Psalm* 99(100); *Jn* 15:18-21.

No, no. Worldliness may be this, but fundamentally this is not so.

Worldliness is a culture. It is a culture of the transitory, a culture of appearances, of *maquillage,* a culture of "today yes, tomorrow no; tomorrow yes and today no". It has superficial values. A culture that does not know fidelity, because it always changes according to circumstances, everything is negotiable. This is the worldly culture, the culture of worldliness. And Jesus insists on defending us from this and He prays that the Father might defend us from this culture of worldliness. It is a "use it and throw it away" culture according to whatever suits you. It is a culture without faithfulness, it has no roots. But it is a way of life, even a way of life for many who say that they are Christians. They are Christians, but they are worldly.

In the parable of the seed that falls to the earth, Jesus says that the preoccupations of the world - that is, of worldliness - suffocate the Word of God, they do not allow it to grow (see *Lk* 8:14). And Paul to the Galatians says: "You were slaves of the world, of worldliness" (see *Gal* 4:3). It always, always hits me when I read the last pages of Henri de Lubac's book *Splendor of the Church,* the last three pages, where he speaks specifically about a worldly spirituality. And he says it is the worst of evils that can befall the Church; and he is not exaggerating, because then he talks about some terrible evils. And this is the worst: worldly spirituality, because it is a *way of interpreting life,* it is a way of life, even a way of living Christianity. And to survive in the face of the preaching of the Gospel, the person hates, kills.

When we say that the martyrs are killed in hatred of the faith, yes, it is true for many, this hatred was over a theological problem; but this is not so for the majority. In the majority [of cases] it is worldliness that hates the faith and kills them, just as they did with Jesus.

It is curious: "But Father", someone might say to me, "worldliness is a superficial way of life..." Let us not deceive ourselves! Nothing about worldliness is superficial! It has deep roots, deep roots. It is like a *chameleon,* it changes, it comes and goes according to circumstances, but the substance is the same: a style of life that enters everywhere, including in the Church. Worldliness, the worldly hermeneutic, *maquillage*, everything can be made up to appear a certain way.

The Apostle Paul went to Athens, and he remained struck at seeing many monuments to the gods in the Areopagus. And he thought about speaking about this: "You are very religious people, I see this... That altar to the 'unknown god' has attracted my attention. I know Him and I have come to tell you who He is". And he began to preach the Gospel. But when he arrived at the cross and resurrection they were scandalized and they went away (see *Acts* 17:22-33). There is one thing that worldliness does not tolerate: the *scandal of the Cross*. It does not tolerate that. And the only medicine for worldliness is Christ who died and rose for us; scandal and foolishness (see *1 Cor* 1:23).

The apostle John in his First Letter picks up the theme of the world because of this. He says: "This is the victory that has overcome the world: our faith (*1 Jn* 5:4). The only thing: faith in Jesus Christ, who died and rose. This does not mean being fanatics. This does not mean neglecting to enter into dialogue with all people, no, but with the conviction of faith, beginning with the scandal of the Cross, of the foolishness of Christ and of Christ's victory. "This is our victory", John says, "our faith."

Let us ask the Holy Spirit in these last days, during the Novena to the Holy Spirit, in the last days of the Easter Season as well, for the grace of discerning what *worldliness* is, what the *Gospel* is, and that we not allow ourselves to be deceived, because the world hates us, the world hated Jesus and Jesus prayed so that the Father would defend us from the spirit of the world (see *Jn* 17:15).

Sunday, May 17, 2020

Sixth Sunday of Easter (A)

Holy Mass[70]

Introduction

Today our prayer is for the many persons who clean hospitals, streets, empty trash from the dumpsters, who go to each house to remove trash: work that no one sees, but it is a job that is necessary to survive. May the Lord bless them and help them.

Homily – The Holy Spirit reminds us how to access the Father

As He says farewell to His disciples (see *Jn* 14:15-21), Jesus gives them tranquility, He gives peace, with a promise: "I will not leave you orphans" (v. 18). He defends them from that pain, from that painful feeling of being orphans. In today's world, there is a great *sense of being orphaned*: many people have many things, but they lack the Father. And in the history of humanity, this has repeated itself: when the Father is missing, something is lacking and there is always the desire to meet, to rediscover the Father, even in the ancient myths. We can think of the myth of Oedipus, or Telemachus, and many others: always in search of the Father who is missing. Today we can say that we live

[70] Liturgy of the Word: Acts 8:5-8, 14-17; *Psalm* 64(65); *1 Pt* 3:15-18; *Jn* 14:15-21.

in a society where the Father is missing, a sense of being orphaned that specifically affects belonging and fraternity.

And so Jesus promises: "I will ask the Father and He will give you another Paraclete" (v. 16). Jesus says, "I am going away, but someone else will come who will teach you how to *access the Father*. He will remind you how to access the Father". The Holy Spirit does not come to "make us His clients"; He comes to point out how to access the Father, to remind us how to access the Father. That is what Jesus opened, what Jesus showed us. A spirituality of the Son alone or the Holy Spirit alone does not exist: the center is the Father. The Son is sent by the Father and returns to the Father. The Holy Spirit is sent by the Father to remind us and to teach us how to access the Father.

Only with this awareness of being children, that *we are not orphans,* can we live in peace among ourselves. Wars, either small ones or large ones, always have a dimension of being orphans: the Father who makes peace is missing. And so when Peter and the first community respond to the people regarding why they are Christians (see *1 Pt* 3:15-18), it says: "do it with gentleness and reverence, keeping your conscience clear" (v. 16), that is, the gentleness that the Holy Spirit gives. The Holy Spirit teaches us this gentleness, this tenderness of the Father's children. The Holy Spirit does not teach us to *insult.* And one of the consequences of this feeling like orphans is insulting, wars, because if there is no Father, there are no brothers, fraternity is lost. They are – this tenderness, reverence, gentleness – they are attitudes of belonging, of belonging to a family that is certain of having a Father.

"I will pray to the Father and He will send you another Paraclete" (*Jn* 14:16) who will remind you how to access the Father, He will remind you that we have a Father who is the center of everything, the origin of everything, the one who unites everyone, the salvation of everyone because He sent His Son to save everyone. And now He sends the Holy Spirit to remind us how to access Him, of the Father, of this paternity, of this fraternal attitude of gentleness, tenderness, and peace.

Let us ask the Holy Spirit to remind us always, always about this access to the Father, that He might remind us that we *have a Father*. And to this civilization, with this great feeling of being orphaned, may He grant the grace of rediscovering the Father, the Father who gives meaning to all of life, and that He might unite humanity into one family.

Regina Coeli

Dear Brothers and Sisters, good morning!

This Sunday's Gospel passage (see *Jn* 14:15-21) presents two messages: observance of the commandments and the promise of the Holy Spirit.

Jesus links love for Him to observance of the commandments, and He insists on this in His farewell discourse: "If you love me, then you will keep my commandments" (v. 15); "He who has my commandments and keeps them, he it is who loves me" (v. 21). Jesus asks us to love Him, but explains: this love does not end in a desire for Him, or in a feeling, no; it demands the willingness to follow His way, that is, the will of the Father. And this is summarized in the commandment of mutual love – the first love [in its fulfillment] – given by Jesus himself: "even as I have loved you, that you also love one another" (*Jn* 13:34). He did not say, "Love me as I have loved you", but "love one another as I have loved you". He loves us without asking us to do the same in return. Jesus's love is a gratuitous love; He never asks for the same in return. And He wants this gratuitous love of His to become the concrete form of life among us: this is His will.

To help the disciples walk this path, Jesus promises to pray for the Father to send "another Counselor" (v. 16), that is, a Consoler, a Defender, who will take His place and give them the intelligence to listen and the courage to observe His words. This is the Holy Spirit, who is the Gift of God's love that descends into the heart of the Christian. After Jesus has died and risen, His love is given to those who believe in Him and are baptized in the name of the Father and of the Son and of the Holy Spirit. The Spirit Himself guides them, enlightens them, strengthens them, so that everyone may walk in life, even through adversity and difficulty, in joys and sorrows, remaining on Jesus's path. This is possible precisely by remaining docile to the Holy Spirit, so that, through His presence at work in us, He may not only console but transform hearts, opening them up to truth and love.

Faced with the experience of error and sin - which we all do - the Holy Spirit helps us not to succumb and enables us to grasp and fully live the meaning of Jesus's words: "If you love me, you will keep my commandments" (v. 15). The commandments are not given to us as a kind of mirror in which to see the reflection of our miseries, our inconsistencies. No, they are not like that. The Word of God is given to us as the Word of life, which transforms the heart, life; which renews, which does not judge in order to condemn, but heals and has forgiveness as its aim. God's mercy is thus. A Word that is light for our steps. All this is the work of the Holy Spirit! He is the Gift of God; He is God Himself, who helps us to be free people, people who want and know how to love, people who understand that life is a mission to proclaim the wonders that the Lord accomplishes in those who trust in him.

May the Virgin Mary, model of the Church, who knows how to listen to the Word of God and to welcome the gift of the Holy Spirit, help us to live the Gospel with joy, knowing that we are sustained by the Spirit, the divine fire that warms our hearts and illuminates our steps.

After the Regina Coeli

Dear Brothers and Sisters, tomorrow is the centenary of the birth of Saint John Paul II, in Wadowice, Poland. Let us remember him with great affection and gratitude. Tomorrow morning, at 7 o'clock, I will celebrate Holy Mass, which will be broadcast throughout the world, at the altar where his mortal remains rest. From Heaven may he continue to intercede for the People of God and for peace in the world.

In some countries liturgical celebrations with the faithful have resumed; in others the possibility is being considered. In Italy, beginning tomorrow it will be possible to celebrate Holy Mass with the people; but please, let us proceed with the rules, the recommendations they give us, so as to protect the health of each person and of the people.

In the month of May, in many parishes it is traditional to celebrate Masses for First Communion. Clearly, due to the pandemic, this beautiful moment of faith and celebration has been postponed. Therefore I wish to send an affectionate thought to the boys and girls who should have received the Eucharist for the first time. Dear boys and girls, I invite you to experience this time of waiting as an opportunity to prepare yourselves better: by praying, reading your catechism book to deepen your knowledge of Jesus, and growing in goodness and in service to others. I wish you a good journey.

Today is the beginning of Laudato Si' Week, which will end next Sunday, in which we remember the fifth anniversary of the publication of the Encyclical. In these times of the pandemic, in which we are more aware of the importance of care for our common home, I hope that all the common reflection and commitment may help to create and strengthen constructive attitudes for the care of creation.

MONDAY, MAY 18, 2020

Holy Mass for the 100th anniversary of Saint John Paul II' s birth[71]

Homily – God has visited His people

"The Lord loves His people" (see *Ps* 149:4), we sang, was the refrain of the Responsorial Psalm. And was also a truth that the people of Israel would repeat; they liked to repeat: "The Lord loves His people". And in difficult moments, always "the Lord loves"; one must wait for how this love will manifest itself. When, out of this love, the Lord would send a prophet, a man of God, the people's reaction was: "The Lord *has visited his people*" (see *Ex* 4:31); because He loves them, He has visited them. And the multitude who followed Jesus, seeing the things that Jesus did, said the same: "The Lord has visited His people" (see *Lk* 7:16).

And here today we can say: 100 years ago the Lord *visited* His people. He sent a man; he prepared him to be a bishop and lead the Church. Remembering Saint John Paul II, we pick this up again: "The Lord loves His people"; "the Lord has visited His people"; He sent a pastor.

And what are the "traits", let us say, of a good pastor that we can find in Saint John Paul II? So many! But we shall only speak of three. Given that persons say Jesu-

---

[71] Liturgy of the Word: *Acts* 16:11-15; *Psalm* 148(149); *Jn* 15:26—16:4.

its always say things in threes, we shall say three: prayer, closeness to the people, and love of justice. Saint John Paul II was a man of God because he *prayed*, and he prayed a lot. But how did a man who had so much to do, so much work to lead the Church..., have so much time to pray? He was well aware that a bishop's first task is to pray. And Vatican II did not say this, Saint Peter said it. When they made the deacons they said: "And to us bishops, prayer and the proclamation of the Word" (see *Acts* 6:4). A bishop's first task is to pray, and he knew this, he did this. A model bishop who prays, the first task. And he taught us that when a bishop examines his conscience in the evening he must ask himself: how many hours did I pray today? A man of prayer.

The second trait: a man of *closeness*. He was not a man detached from people, but instead he went to find people; and he travelled the entire world, finding his people, seeking his people, drawing near. And closeness is one of the features of God with His people. Let us recall that the Lord said to the people of Israel: "For what people has its gods so near as I am to you?" (see *Deut* 4:7). A closeness of God with His people which then becomes even closer in Jesus, is strengthened in Jesus. A pastor is close to the people. If, on the contrary, he is not so, he is not a pastor, he is a hierarch, he is an administrator, perhaps a good one, but he is not a pastor. Closeness to the people. And Saint John Paul II gave us the example of this closeness. Close to those who were more important and less important, close to those who were near and far, always close. He made himself close.

The third trait, love of *justice*. But complete justice! A man who wanted justice, social justice, justice for all people, the justice that drives away wars. But total justice! For this reason Saint John Paul II was a man of mercy, because justice and mercy go together; they cannot be distinguished [separated], they go together: justice is justice, mercy is mercy, but one is not found without the other. And speaking of the man of justice and mercy, let us consider how much Saint John Paul II did so that people could understand God's mercy. Let us think about how he promoted devotion to Saint Faustina [Kowalska], whose liturgical memory *beginning today* will be extended to the entire Church. He had heard that God's justice had this face of mercy, this attitude of mercy. And this is a gift that he left us: *merciful justice* and *just mercy*.

Let us pray to him today, that he give to all of us, especially to the Church's pastors, but to everyone, the grace of prayer, the grace of closeness and the grace of justice-mercy, mercy-justice.

Appendix I

What if I can't participate in the sacraments?

How to receive the grace of the Lord when unable to participate physically in liturgical celebrations

Forgiveness without a priest? The Pope reminds us how to receive it[1]

People dying without chaplains, families confined to their homes and unable to reach a priest because of the Covid-19 emergency: in his homily at Santa Marta, Pope Francis mentions the *Catechism* and the "contrition" that obtains forgiveness from sins while one waits to go to confession.

The *salus animarum,* the salvation of souls, is the supreme law of the Church. This is the fundamental interpretative criterion for determining what is right. This is why the Church always seeks, in every way, to offer the possibility of reconciliation with God to all those who desire it, who seek it, who await it or who, in any case, become aware of their condition and feel the need to be welcomed, loved and forgiven. In these times of emergency due to the pandemic, with people seriously ill and isolated in intensive care wards, and families who are asked to stay at home to avoid the spread of the virus, it is useful to remind everyone of the richness of the Church's tradition. Pope Francis did this in his homily during Mass in Santa Marta on Friday, March 20:

"I know that many of you, for Easter, go to confession so you can be right with God again. But, many will say to me today: 'But, Father, where can I find a priest, a confessor, when I can't leave my house? And I want to make peace with the Lord, I want Him to embrace me, I want my Daddy to embrace me... What can I do if I can't find a priest?' You do what the Catechism says.

---

[1] *Vatican News,* March 20, 2020. Holy Mass presided over by Pope Francis at the Casa Santa Marta in the Vatican.

"It is very clear: if you cannot find a priest to whom you can confess," explained the Pontiff, "speak with God, He is your Father, and tell Him the truth: 'Lord, I have done this, this and this.... I am sorry', and ask Him for forgiveness with all your heart, with the Act of Contrition, and promise Him: 'Later I will go to confession, but forgive me now'. You will return immediately to God's grace. You yourself can approach God's forgiveness as the Catechism teaches us, without having a priest at hand. Think about it: this is the moment! And this is the right moment, the appropriate moment. An Act of Contrition, made well. In this way our souls will become as white as snow".

Pope Francis refers to **numbers 1451 and 1452 of the *Catechism of the Catholic Church*,** promulgated by Saint John Paul II and drafted under the guidance of the then-Prefect of the Congregation for the Doctrine of the Faith, Joseph Ratzinger. As far as "contrition" is concerned, the Catechism, citing the Council of Trent, teaches that among the acts of the penitent it "occupies first place. Contrition is sorrow of the soul and detestation for the sin committed, together with the resolution not to sin again".

"When it arises from a love by which God is loved above all else, contrition is called 'perfect' (contrition of charity)", continues the Catechism. "Such contrition remits venial sins; it also obtains forgiveness of mortal sins if it includes the firm resolution to have recourse to sacramental confession as soon as possible". Therefore, while waiting to receive absolution from a priest as soon as circumstances permit, it is possible with this act to be immediately forgiven. This too was already affirmed by the Council of Trent, in chapter 4 of the *Doctrina de sacramento Paenitentiae*, where it is stated that contrition accompanied by the intention of confession is able to "reconcile man with God, even before this sacrament is truly received".

This is a way to approach God's mercy, and is open to all. It belongs to the Church's tradition and can be useful to everyone, especially at this time to those who are near the sick in their homes and hospitals.

Numbers 1451 and 1452 of the *Catechism of the Catholic Church*

Contrition

1451. Among the penitent's acts contrition occupies first place. Contrition is "sorrow of the soul and detestation for the sin committed, together with the resolution not to sin again" (Council of Trent: Denz.-Schönm., 1676).

1452. When it arises from a love by which God is loved above all else, contrition is called "perfect" (contrition of charity). Such contrition remits venial sins; it also obtains forgiveness of mortal sins if it includes the firm resolution to have recourse to sacramental confession as soon as possible (see Council of Trent: Denz.-Schönm., 1677).

Decree of the Apostolic Penitentiary on the granting of special Indulgences to the faithful in the current pandemic

The gift of special Indulgences is granted to the faithful suffering from COVID19 disease, commonly known as Coronavirus, as well as to health care workers, family members and all those who in any capacity, including through prayer, care for them.

"Be joyful in hope, patient in affliction, faithful in prayer" (*Rom* 12:12). The words written by Saint Paul to the Church of Rome resonate throughout the entire history of the Church and guide the judgment of the faithful in the face of all suffering, sickness and calamity.

The present moment in which the whole of humanity, threatened by an invisible and insidious disease, which for some time now has become part of all our lives, is marked day after day by anguished fears, new uncertainties and above all widespread physical and moral suffering.

The Church, following the example of her Divine Master, has always had the care of the sick at heart. As Saint John Paul II points out, the value of human suffering is twofold: "It is *supernatural* because it is rooted in the divine mystery of the Redemption of the world, and it is likewise deeply human, because in it the person discovers himself, his own humanity, his own dignity, his own mission" (Apostolic Letter *Salvifici Doloris*, 31).

Pope Francis, too, in these recent days, has shown his paternal closeness and renewed his invitation to pray incessantly for those who are sick with the Coronavirus.

So that all those who suffer because of COVID-19, precisely in the mystery of this suffering, may rediscover "the same redemptive suffering of Christ" (*ibid.*, 30), this Apostolic

Penitentiary, *ex auctoritate Summi Pontificis,* trusting in the word of Christ the Lord and considering with a spirit of faith the epidemic currently underway, to be lived in a spirit of personal conversion, grants the gift of Indulgences in accordance with the following disposition.

The Plenary Indulgence is granted to the faithful suffering from Coronavirus, who are subject to quarantine by order of the health authority in hospitals or in their own homes if, with a spirit detached from any sin, they unite spiritually through the media to the celebration of Holy Mass, the recitation of the Holy Rosary, to the pious practice of the Way of the Cross or other forms of devotion, or if at least they will recite the Creed, the Lord's Prayer and a pious invocation to the Blessed Virgin Mary, offering this trial in a spirit of faith in God and charity towards their brothers and sisters, with the will to fulfil the usual conditions (sacramental confession, Eucharistic communion and prayer according to the Holy Father's intentions), as soon as possible.

Health care workers, family members and all those who, following the example of the Good Samaritan, exposing themselves to the risk of contagion, care for the sick of Coronavirus according to the words of the divine Redeemer: "Greater love has no one than this: to lay down one's life for one's friends" (*Jn* 15:13), will obtain the same gift of the Plenary Indulgence under the same conditions.

This Apostolic Penitentiary also willingly grants a *Plenary Indulgence* under the same conditions on the occasion of the current world epidemic, also to those faithful who offer a visit to the Blessed Sacrament, or Eucharistic adoration, or reading the Holy Scriptures for at least half an hour, or the recitation of the Holy Rosary, or the pious exercise of the Way of the Cross, or the recitation of the Chaplet of Divine Mercy, to implore from Almighty God the end of the epidemic, relief for those who are afflicted and eternal salvation for those whom the Lord has called to Himself.

The Church prays for those who find themselves unable to receive the Sacrament of the Anointing of the Sick and of the Viaticum, entrusting each and every one to divine Mercy by virtue of the communion of saints and granting the faithful a *Plenary Indulgence* on the point of death, provided that they are duly disposed and have recited a few prayers during their lifetime (in this case the Church makes up for the three usual conditions required). For the attainment of this indulgence the use of the crucifix or the cross is recommended (see *Enchiridion indulgentiarum*, no.12).

May the Blessed Virgin Mary, Mother of God and of the Church, Health of the Sick and Help of Christians, our Advocate, help suffering humanity, saving us from the evil of this pandemic and obtaining for us every good necessary for our salvation and sanctification.

The present Decree is valid notwithstanding any provision to the contrary.

Given in Rome, from the seat of the Apostolic Penitentiary, on March 19, 2020.

Mauro Cardinal Piacenza
Major Penitentiary

Krzysztof Nykiel
Regent

"I am with you always" (*Mt* 28: 20)

Note from the Apostolic Penitentiary on the Sacrament of Reconciliation in the current pandemic

The gravity of the present circumstances calls for reflection on the urgency and centrality of the Sacrament of Reconciliation, together with some necessary clarifications, both for the lay faithful and for ministers called to celebrate the Sacrament.

Even in the time of COVID-19, the Sacrament of Reconciliation is administered in accordance with universal canon law and with the provisions of the *Ordo Paenitentiae.*

Individual confession is the ordinary way of celebrating this sacrament (see can. 960 CIC), while collective absolution, without prior individual confession, cannot be imparted except where there is an imminent danger of death, since there is not enough time to hear the confessions of individual penitents (see can. 961, § 1 CIC), or a grave necessity (see can. 961, § 1 CIC). 961, § 1, 2 CIC), the consideration of which is the responsibility of the diocesan bishop, taking into account the criteria agreed upon with the other members of the Episcopal Conference (see can. 455, § 2 CIC) and without prejudice to the necessity, for valid absolution, of *votum sacramenti* on the part of the individual penitent, that is to say, the purpose of confessing serious sins in due time, which at the time could not be confessed (see can. 962, § 1 CIC).

This Apostolic Penitentiary believes that, especially in the places most affected by the pandemic contagion and until the phenomenon recedes, the cases of serious need mentioned in can. 961, § 2 CIC above mentioned, will occur.

Any further specification is delegated by law to diocesan bishops, always taking into account the supreme good of the salvation of souls (see can. 1752 CIC).

Should there arise a sudden need to impart sacramental absolution to several faithful together, the priest is obliged to warn the diocesan bishop as far as possible or, if he cannot, to inform him as soon as possible (see *Ordo Paenitentiae*, n. 32).

In the present pandemic emergency, it is therefore up to the diocesan bishop to indicate to priests and penitents the prudent attentions to be adopted in the individual celebration of sacramental reconciliation, such as the celebration in a ventilated place outside the confessional, the adoption of a suitable distance, the use of protective masks, without prejudice to absolute attention to the safeguarding of the sacramental seal and the necessary discretion.

Furthermore, it is always up to the diocesan bishop to determine, in the territory of his own ecclesiastical circumscription and with regard to the level of pandemic contagion, the cases of grave necessity in which it is lawful to impart collective absolution: for example, at the entrance to hospital wards, where the infected faithful in danger of death are hospitalized, using as far as possible and with the appropriate precautions the means of amplifying the voice so that absolution may be heard.

Consideration should be given to the need and advisability of setting up, where necessary, in agreement with the health authorities, groups of "extraordinary hospital chaplains", also on a voluntary basis and in compliance with the norms of protection from contagion, to guarantee the necessary spiritual assistance to the sick and dying.

Where the individual faithful find themselves in the painful impossibility of receiving sacramental absolution, it should be remembered that perfect contrition, coming from the love of God, beloved above all things, expressed by a sincere request for forgiveness (that which the penitent is at present able to express) and accompanied by *votum confessionis*, that is, by the firm resolution to have recourse, as soon as possible, to sacramental confession, obtains forgiveness of sins, even mortal ones (see CCC, no. 1452).

Never before has the Church experienced thus the power of the communion of saints, raising to her Crucified and Risen Lord her vows and prayers, especially the Sacrifice of Holy Mass, celebrated daily, even without the presence of the people, by priests.

Like a good mother, the Church implores the Lord that humanity may be freed from such a scourge, invoking the intercession of the Blessed Virgin Mary, Mother of Mercy and Health of the Sick, and of her Spouse Saint Joseph, under whose patronage the Church has always walked the world.

May Mary Most Holy and Saint Joseph obtain for us abundant graces of reconciliation and salvation, in attentive listening to the Word of the Lord, which he repeats to humanity today: "Be still and know that I am God" (*Ps* 46:10), "I am with you always" (*Mt* 28:20).

Given in Rome, from the seat of the Apostolic Penitentiary, on March 19, 2020, Solemnity of St. Joseph, Spouse of the Blessed Virgin Mary, Patron of the Universal Church.

Mauro Cardinal Piacenza
Major Penitentiary

Krzysztof Nykiel
Regent

Spiritual Communion

Those who are unable to make sacramental Communion with Christ by participating in the Eucharist, can express the desire to receive Him in their spirit with these words that help to make spiritual communion with him:

My Jesus, I believe that You are present
in the Most Blessed Sacrament.
I love You above all things,
and I desire to receive You into my soul.
Since I cannot now receive you sacramentally,
come at least spiritually into my heart.

I embrace You as if you were already there,
and I unite myself wholly to You.
Never permit me to be separated from You.

Saint Alphonsus Liguori

From the offices of the Congregation for Divine Worship and the Discipline of the Sacraments regarding the celebration of the Easter Triduum

Decree

In time of Covid-19 (II)

Considering the rapidly evolving situation of the Covid-19 pandemic and taking into account observations which have come from Episcopal Conferences, this Congregation now offers an update to the general indications and suggestions already given to Bishops in the preceding decree of March 19, 2020.

Given that the date of Easter cannot be transferred, in the countries which have been struck by the disease and where restrictions around the assembly and movement of people have been imposed, Bishops and priests may celebrate the rites of Holy Week without the presence of the people and in a suitable place, avoiding concelebration and omitting the sign of peace.

The faithful should be informed of the beginning times of the celebrations so that they can prayerfully unite themselves in their homes. Means of live (not recorded) telematic broadcasts can be of help. In any event it remains important to dedicate an adequate time to prayer, giving importance above all to the *Liturgia Horarum.*

The Episcopal Conferences and individual dioceses will see to it that resources are provided to support family and personal prayer.

1 - **Palm Sunday.** The Commemoration of the Lord's Entrance into Jerusalem is to be celebrated within sacred buildings; in Cathedral churches the second form given in the Roman Missal is to be adopted; in parish churches and in other places the third form is to be used.

2 - **The Chrism Mass.** Evaluating the concrete situation in different countries, the Episcopal Conferences will be able to give indications about a possible transfer to another date.

3 - **Holy Thursday.** The washing of feet, which is already optional, is to be omitted. At the end of the Mass of the Lord's Supper the procession is also omitted and the Blessed Sacrament is to be kept in the tabernacle. On this day the faculty to celebrate Mass in a suitable place, without the presence of the people, is exceptionally granted to all priests.

4 - **Good Friday.** In the Universal Prayer, Bishops will arrange to have a special intention prepared for those who find themselves in distress, the sick, the dead, (see *Missale Romanum*). The adoration of the Cross by kissing it shall be limited solely to the celebrant.

5 - **The Easter Vigil:** Is to be celebrated only in Cathedral and parish churches. For the "Baptismal Liturgy" only the "Renewal of Baptismal Promises" is maintained (see *Missale Romanum*).

Seminaries, houses of clergy, monasteries and religious communities shall follow the indications of this decree.

Expressions of popular piety and processions which enrich the days of Holy Week and the Paschal Triduum can be transferred to other suitable days in the year, for example September 14 and 15, according to the judgement of the Diocesan Bishop.

De mandato Summi Pontificis pro hoc tantum anno 2020.

From the offices of the Congregation for Divine Worship and the Discipline of the Sacraments, March 25, 2020, on the Solemnity of the Annunciation of the Lord.

Robert Card. Sarah
Prefect

✠ Arthur Roche
Archbishop Secretary

Appendix II

The prayer of the Church in difficult times*

The universality of intercession

* This appendix brings together various prayers and rituals through which the Church, in her different traditions, asks the Father for the grace, the strength and the gift of freedom from evil and from calamities.

Extraordinary moment of prayer before Saint Peter's Basilica[1]

The Holy Father:

In the name of the Father and of the Son and of the Holy Spirit.
R. Amen.

The Holy Father:

Let us pray.
Almighty and merciful God,
behold our sorrowful condition:
comfort your children and open our hearts to hope,
so that we might feel your Fatherly
presence in our midst.
Through our Lord Jesus Christ, your Son, Who lives and reigns
with You in the unity of the Holy Spirit, one God,
for ever and ever.
R. Amen.

---

[1] The following are the texts of the supplications during the prayer led by the Holy Father Pope Francis in front of Saint Peter's Basilica for the liberation of the world from the Covid-19 pandemic. The text of the homily delivered during the celebration can be found on page 78.

Litany of Supplication

We adore you, O Lord.
True God and true Man, truly present in this holy Sacrament,
R. We adore you, O Lord.
Our Savior, God with us, faithful and rich in mercy,
R. We adore you, O Lord.
King and Lord of creation and of history,
R. We adore you, O Lord.
Conqueror of sin and death,
R. We adore you, O Lord.
Friend of humankind, the Risen One, the Living One who sit at the right hand of the Father,
R. We adore you, O Lord.

We believe in you, O Lord.
Only begotten Son of the Father, descended from heaven for our salvation,
R. We believe in you, O Lord.
Heavenly physician, who bow down over our misery,
R. We believe in you, O Lord.
Lamb who was slain, who offer yourself to rescue us from evil,
R. We believe in you, O Lord.
Good Shepherd, who give your life for the flock which you love,
R. We believe in you, O Lord.
Living bread and medicine for immortality, who give us eternal life,
R. We believe in you, O Lord.

Deliver us, O Lord.
From the power of Satan and the seductions of the world,
R. Deliver us, O Lord.

From the pride and presumption of being able to do anything without you,

R. Deliver us, O Lord.
From the deceptions of fear and anxiety,
R. Deliver us, O Lord.
From unbelief and desperation,
R. Deliver us, O Lord.
From hardness of heart and the incapacity to love,
R. Deliver us, O Lord.

Save us, O Lord.
From every evil that afflicts humanity,
R. Save us, O Lord.
From hunger, from famine and from egoism,
R. Save us, O Lord.
From illnesses, epidemics and the fear of our brothers and sisters,
R. Save us, O Lord.
From devastating madness, from ruthless interests and from violence,
R. Save us, O Lord.
From being deceived, from false information and the manipulation of consciences,
R. Save us, O Lord.

Comfort us, O Lord.
Protect your Church which crosses the desert,
R. Comfort us, O Lord.
Protect humanity terrified by fear and anguish,
R. Comfort us, O Lord.
Protect the sick and the dying, oppressed by loneliness,
R. Comfort us, O Lord.

Protect doctors and healthcare providers exhausted by the difficulties they are facing,
R. Comfort us, O Lord.
Protect politicians and decision makers who bear the weight of

having to make decisions,
R. Comfort us, O Lord.

Grant us your Spirit, O Lord.
In the hour of trial and from confusion,
R. Grant us your Spirit, O Lord.
In temptation and in our fragility,
R. Grant us your Spirit, O Lord.
In the battle against evil and sin,
R. Grant us your Spirit, O Lord.
In the search for what is truly good and true joy,
R. Grant us your Spirit, O Lord.
in the decision to remain in you and in your friendship,
R. Grant us your Spirit, O Lord.

Open us to hope, O Lord.
Should sin oppress us,
R. Open us to hope, O Lord.
Should hatred close our hearts,
R. Open us to hope, O Lord.
Should sorrow visit us,
R. Open us to hope, O Lord.
Should indifference cause us anguish,
R. Open us to hope, O Lord.
Should death overwhelm us,
R. Open us to hope, O Lord.

Prayer for Liberation from the Epidemic to Our Lady of Divine Love[2]

O Mary,
You shine continuously on our journey
as a sign of salvation and hope.
We entrust ourselves to you, Health of the Sick,
who, at the foot of the cross, were united with Jesus's
suffering, and persevered in your faith.

"Protectress of the Roman people",
you know our needs,
and we know that you will provide,
so that, as at Cana in Galilee,
joy and celebration may return
after this time of trial.

Help us, Mother of Divine Love,
to conform ourselves to the will of the Father
and to do what Jesus tells us.
For He took upon Himself our suffering,
and burdened Himself with our sorrows
to bring us, through the cross,
to the joy of the Resurrection. Amen.

Sub tuum praesidium

We fly to your protection, O Holy Mother of God. Do not despise our petitions in our necessities, but deliver us always from every danger, O Glorious and Blessed Virgin.

---

[2] Pope Francis's video message for the day of prayer and fasting for liberation from the epidemic of March 11, 2020.

Letter of the Holy Father
to the faithful for the month of May 2020[3]

Dear Brothers and Sisters,

The month of May is approaching, a time when the People of God express with particular intensity their love and devotion for the Blessed Virgin Mary. It is traditional in this month to pray the Rosary at home within the family. The restrictions of the pandemic have made us come to appreciate all the more this "family" aspect, also from a spiritual point of view.

For this reason, I want to encourage everyone to rediscover the beauty of praying the Rosary at home in the month of May. This can be done either as a group or individually; you can decide according to your own situations, making the most of both opportunities. The key to doing this is always simplicity, and it is easy also on the internet to find good models of prayers to follow. I am also providing two prayers to Our Lady that you can recite at the end of the Rosary, and that I myself will pray in the month of May, in spiritual union with all of you. I include them with this letter so that they are available to everyone.

Dear Brothers and Sisters, contemplating the face of Christ with the heart of Mary our Mother will make us even more united as a spiritual family and will help us overcome this time of trial. I keep all of you in my prayers, especially those suffering most greatly, and I ask you, please, to pray for me. I thank you, and with great affection I send you my blessing.

---

[3] Rome, Saint John Lateran, April 25, 2020, Feast of Saint Mark the Evangelist.

Prayers to Virgin Mary

O Mary,
You shine continuously on our journey
as a sign of salvation and hope.
We entrust ourselves to you, Health of the Sick,
who, at the foot of the cross, were united with Jesus's
suffering, and persevered in your faith.

"Protectress of the Roman people",
you know our needs,
and we know that you will provide,
so that, as at Cana in Galilee,
joy and celebration may return
after this time of trial.

Help us, Mother of Divine Love,
to conform ourselves to the will of the Father
and to do what Jesus tells us.
For He took upon Himself our suffering,
and burdened Himself with our sorrows
to bring us, through the cross,
to the joy of the Resurrection. Amen.

We fly to your protection, O Holy Mother of God.
Do not despise our petitions in our necessities,
but deliver us always from every danger,
O Glorious and Blessed Virgin.

* * *

"We fly to your protection, O Holy Mother of God".

In the present tragic situation, when the whole world is prey to suffering and anxiety, we fly to you, Mother of God and our Mother, and seek refuge under your protection.

Virgin Mary, turn your merciful eyes towards us amid this coronavirus pandemic. Comfort those who are distraught and mourn their loved ones who have died, and at times are buried in a way that grieves them deeply. Be close to those who are concerned for their loved ones who are sick and who, in order to prevent the spread of the disease, cannot be close to them. Fill with hope those who are troubled by the uncertainty of the future and the consequences for the economy and employment.

Mother of God and our Mother, pray for us to God, the Father of mercies, that this great suffering may end and that hope and peace may dawn anew. Plead with your divine Son, as you did at Cana, so that the families of the sick and the victims be comforted, and their hearts be opened to confidence and trust.

Protect those doctors, nurses, health workers and volunteers who are on the front line of this emergency, and are risking their lives to save others. Support their heroic effort and grant them strength, generosity and continued health.

Be close to those who assist the sick night and day, and to priests who, in their pastoral concern and fidelity to the Gospel, are trying to help and support everyone.

Blessed Virgin, illumine the minds of men and women engaged in scientific research, that they may find effective solutions to overcome this virus.

Support national leaders, that with wisdom, solicitude and generosity they may come to the aid of those lacking the basic necessities of life and may devise social and economic solutions inspired by farsightedness and solidarity.

Mary Most Holy, stir our consciences, so that the enormous funds invested in developing and stockpiling arms will instead be spent on promoting effective research on how to prevent similar tragedies from occurring in the future.

Beloved Mother, help us realize that we are all members of one great family and to recognize the bond that unites us, so that, in a spirit of fraternity and solidarity, we can help to alleviate countless situations of poverty and need. Make us strong in faith, persevering in service, constant in prayer.

Mary, Consolation of the afflicted, embrace all your children in distress and pray that God will stretch out his all-powerful hand and free us from this terrible pandemic, so that life can serenely resume its normal course.

To you, who shine on our journey as a sign of salvation and hope, do we entrust ourselves, O Clement, O Loving, O Sweet Virgin Mary. Amen.

VARIOUS BLESSINGS[4]

Order for a blessing in Various Circumstances

When the community has gathered, the minister says:

In the name of the Father and of the Son, and of the Holy Spirit .

All make the sign of the cross and reply:
Amen.

A minister who is a priest or deacon greets those present with these or other suitable words, taken mainly from sacred Scripture.

May God, who is the fountain of all goodness, be with you all.

All make the following or some other suitable reply:
And also with you.

A lay minister greets those present in the following words.

Brothers and sisters, let us bless and praise the Lord, the fountain of all goodness. Blessed be God now and for ever.

All reply:

---

[4] The following *Blessings* are taken from the *Book of Blessings*, edited by the United States Conference of Catholic Bishops (1989), which collects prayers and rites of blessing for different circumstances in life. Here are available excepts from *The Order for a Blessing in Various Circumstances* (*Book of Blessings*, nn. 1987-2010) and excepts from *The Order for the Blessing of the Sick* (*Book of Blessings*, nn. 380-398. 406). The complete rites are available in *The Book of Blessings*, edited by The United States Conference of Catholic Bishops, 1989. The present order may be used by a priest or deacon. It may also be used by a layperson, who follows the rites and prayers designated for a lay minister (nn. 1245-1271).

Amen.

In the following or similar words, the minister prepares those present for the blessing.

All that God has created and sustains, all the events he guides, and all human works that are good and have a good purpose, prompt those who believe to praise and bless the Lord with hearts and voices. He is the source and origin of every blessing. By this celebration we proclaim our belief that all things work together for the good of those who fear and love God. We are sure that in all things we must seek the help of God, so that in complete reliance on his will we may in Christ do everything for his glory.

A reader, another person present, or the minister reads a text of sacred Scripture.

Brothers and sisters, listen to the words of the apostle Paul to the Colossians (1:9b-1 4)

We do not cease praying for you and asking that you may be filled with the knowledge of his will through all spiritual wisdom and understanding to live in a manner worthy of the Lord, so as to be fully pleasing, in every good work bearing fruit and growing in the knowledge of God, strengthened with every power, in accord with his glorious might, for all endurance and patience, with joy giving thanks to the Father, who has made you fit to share in the inheritance of the holy ones in light. He delivered us from the power of darkness and transferred us to the kingdom of his beloved Son, in whom we have redemption, the forgiveness of sins.

Or:

Brothers and sisters, listen to the words of the apostle Paul to the Romans (8:24-28):

For in hope we were saved. Now hope that sees for itself is not hope. For who hopes for what one sees? But if we hope for what we do not see, we wait with endurance.

In the same way, the Spirit too comes to the aid of our weakness; for we do not know how to pray as we ought, but the Spirit itself intercedes with inexpressible groanings. And the one who searches hearts knows what is the intention of the Spirit, because it intercedes for the holy ones according to God's will.

We know that all things work for good for those who love God, who are called according to his purpose.

Or:

Brothers and sisters, listen to the words of the first letter of Paul to Timothy (4:4-5):

For everything created by God is good, and nothing is to be rejected when received with thanksgiving, for it is made holy by the invocation of God in prayer.

Or:

Numbers 6:22-27; Deuteronomy 33:1, 13b-16a; Wisdom 13:1-7; Sirach 18:1 -9.

As circumstances suggest, one of the following responsorial psalms may be sung or said, or some other suitable song.

R. The Lord led his people out with rejoicing.

Psalm 105

Give thanks to the Lord, invoke his name;
make known among the nations his deed.
Sing to him, sing his praise,
proclaim all his wondrous deeds. **R.**

Glory in his holy name;
rejoice, O hearts that seek the Lord!
Look to the Lord in his strength;
seek to serve him constantly. **R.**

Recall the wondrous deeds that he has wrought
his portents, and the judgments he has uttered.
He, the Lord, is our God;
throughout the earth his judgments prevail. **R.**

He remembers forever his covenant
which he made binding for a thousand generations
Which he entered into with Abraham
and by his oath to Isaac. **R.**

Psalm 106:2-3, 4-5, 45-46, 47, 48

R. Give thanks to the Lord for he is good his love is everlasting.

Psalm 107:2-3, 8-9, 31-32, 42-43

R. They cried to the Lord in their troubles and he delivered them from their anguish.

Intercessions

As circumstances suggest, the prayer of blessing may be preceded by the intercessions. The minister introduces them and an assisting minister or one of those present announces the intentions. From the following intentions those best suited to the occasion may be used or adapted, or other intentions that apply to the particular circumstances may be composed.

The minister says:

God loves his creation and his goodness sustains the universe. Let us pray now that he will bestow his blessing upon us and that he will renew and support us with his strength.

R. Lord, send us your blessing.

Or:

R. Lord, hear our prayer.

Assisting minister:

Everlasting God, you give life a nobler meaning when we try wholeheartedly to do your will; fill us with the spirit of your own holiness. (For this we pray:) **R.**

Assisting minister:

You want us to increase your gifts and to return them to you and to our neighbor; accept the offering of our loving service. (For this we pray:) **R.**

Assisting minister:

You watch over us with fatherly care; hear the cries of those who trust in you. (For this we pray:) **R.**

Assisting minister:

You sent your Son into the world to remove the curse of sin and replace it with your blessing; in Christ fill us with every heavenly blessing. (For this we pray:) **R.**

Assisting minister:

You have poured forth into our hearts your Son's Spirit, in whom we cry out, Abba, Father; hear your children as they acclaim and praise your goodness (For this we pray:) **R.**

Assisting minister:

Through your Son's death and resurrection you have chosen us to be your people and your inheritance; remember us in our needs and bless your inheritance. (For this we pray:) **R.**

When there are no intercessions, the minister, before the prayer of blessing, says:

Let us pray.

As circumstances suggest all may they pray for a moment in silence before the prayer of blessing.

A minister who is a priest or deacon says the prayer of blessing with hands outstretched; a lay minister says the prayer with hands joined.

Lord,
let the effect of your blessing
remain with your faithful people
to give them new life and strength of spirit,
so that the power of your love
will enable them to accomplish what is right and good.
We ask this through Christ our Lord.

R. Amen.

Or:

Lord,
we, your people, pray for the gift of your holy blessing
to ward off every harm
and to bring to fulfillment every right desire.
We ask this through Christ our Lord.

R. Amen.

A minister who is a priest or deacon concludes the rite by saying:

May God, who is blessed above all, bless you in all things through Christ, so that whatever happens in your lives will work together for our good.

R. Amen

Then he blesses all present.

And may almighty God bless you,
the Father, and the Son, ✠ and the Holy Spirit.

R. Amen

A lay minister concludes the rite by signing himself or herself with the sign of the cross and saying:

May God, who is blessed above all, bless us in all things through Christ, so that whatever happens in our lives will work together for our good.

R. Amen.

Order for the Blessing of the Sick[5]

When the community has gathered, the minister says:

In the name of the Father, and of the Son, and of the Holy Spirit.

All make the sign of the cross and reply:
Amen.

A minister who is a priest or a deacon greets those present in the following or other suitable words, taken mainly from sacred Scripture.

Peace be with you (this house) and all who live here.

Or:

The peace of the Lord be with you always.

All make the following or some other suitable reply.

And also with you.

A lay minister greets those present in the following words.

Brothers and sisters, let us bless the Lord, who went about doing good and healing the sick. Blessed be God now and for ever.

R. Blessed be God now and for ever.

Or:

R. Amen.

In the following or similar words, the minister prepares the sick and all present for the blessing.

The Lord Jesus, who went about doing good works and healing sickness and infirmity of every kind, commanded his disciples

---

[5] The blessing of the sick by the ministers of the Church is a very ancient custom, having its origins in the practice of Christ himself and his apostles. The present order may be used by a priest or deacon. It may also be used by a layperson, who follows the rites and prayers designated for a lay minister. This blessing is proposed in both long and short forms.

to care for the sick, to pray for them, and to lay hands on them. In this celebration we shall entrust our sick brothers and sisters to the care of the Lord, asking that he will enable them to bear their pain and suffering in the knowledge that, if they accept their share in the pain of his own passion, they will also share in its power to give comfort and strength.

A reader, another person present, or the minister reads a text of sacred Scripture. The readings chosen should be those that best apply to the physical and spiritual condition of those who are sick.

Brothers and sisters, listen to the words of the second letter of Paul to the Corinthians: 1:3-7

Blessed be the God and Father of our Lord Jesus Christ, the Father of compassion and God of all encouragement, who encourages us in our every affliction, so that we may be able to encourage those who are in any affliction with the encouragement with which we ourselves are encouraged by God. For as Christ's sufferings overflow to us, so through Christ does our encouragement also overflow. If we are afflicted, it is for your encouragement and salvation; if we are encouraged, it is for your encouragement, which enables you to endure the same sufferings that we suffer. Our hope for you is firm, for we know that as you share in the sufferings, you also share in the encouragement.

Or:

Brothers and sisters, listen to the words of the holy gospel according to Matthew: 11:28-30

Jesus said to the crowds: "Come to me, all you who labor and are burdened, and I will give you rest. Take my yoke upon you and learn from me, for I am meek and humble of heart; and you will find rest for yourselves. For my yoke is easy, and my burden light."

Or:

Brothers and sisters, listen to the words of the holy gospel according to Mark: 6:53-56

After making the crossing, Jesus and his disciples came to land at Gennesaret and tied up there. As they were leaving the boat, people immediately recognized him. They scurried about the surrounding country and began to bring in the sick on mats to wherever they heard he was. Whatever villages or towns or countryside he entered, they laid the sick in the marketplaces and begged him that they might touch only the tassel on his cloak; and as many as touched it were healed.

As circumstances suggest, one of the following responsorial psalms may be sung or said, or some other suitable song.

R. Lord, you have preserved my life from destruction.

Isaiah 38

Once I said,
"In the noontime of life I must depart!
To the gates of the nether world I shall be consigned
for the rest of my years." **R.**

I said, "I shall see the Lord no more
in the land of the living.
No longer shall I behold my fellow men
among those who dwell in the world." **R.**

My dwelling, like a shepherd's tent,
is struck down and borne away from me;
You have folded up my life, like a weaver
who severs the last thread. **R.**

Those live whom the Lord protects;
yours . . . the life of my spirit.
You have given me health and life. **R.**

Psalm 102:2-3, 24-25

R. O Lord, hear my prayer, and let my cry come to you.

Intercessions

The intercessions are then said. The minister introduces them and an assisting minister or one of those present announces the intentions. From the following intentions those best suited to the occasion may be used or adapted, or other intentions that apply to those who are sick and to the particular circumstances may be composed.

The minister says:

The Lord Jesus loves our brothers and sisters who are ill. With trust let us pray to him that he will comfort them with his grace, saying:

R. Lord, give those who are sick the comfort of your presence.

Assisting minister:

Lord Jesus, you came as healer of body and of spirit, in order to cure all our ills. **R .**

Assisting minister:

You were a man of suffering, but it was our infirmities that you bore, our sufferings that you endured. **R.**

Assisting minister:

You chose to be like us in all things, in order to assure us of your compassion. **R.**

Assisting minister:

You experienced the weakness of the flesh in order to deliver us from evil. **R.**

Assisting minister:

At the foot of the cross your Mother stood as companion in your sufferings, and in your tender care you gave her to us as our Mother. **R.**

Assisting minister:

It is your wish that in our own flesh we should fill up what is wanting in your sufferings for the sake of your Body, the Church. **R.**

Instead of the intercessions or in addition to them, one of the following litanies taken from Pastoral Care of the Sick, nos. 245 and 138, may be used.

Minister:

You bore our weakness and carried our sorrows:
Lord, have mercy.

R. Lord, have mercy.

Minister:

You felt compassion for the crowd, and went about doing good and healing the sick: Christ, have mercy.

R. Christ, have mercy.

Minister:

You commanded your apostles to lay their hands on the sick in your name: Lord, have mercy.

R. Lord, have mercy.

Or:

The minister says:

Let us pray to God for our brothers and sisters and for all those who devote themselves to caring for them.

Assisting minister:

Bless N. and N: and fill them with new hope and strength: Lord, have mercy.

R. Lord, have mercy.

Assisting minister:

Relieve their pain: Lord, have mercy. **R.**

Assisting minister:

Free them from sin and do not let them give way to temptation: Lord, have mercy. **R.**

Assisting minister:

Sustain all the sick with your power: Lord, have mercy. **R.**

Assisting minister:

Assist all who care for the sick: Lord, have mercy. **R.**

Assisting minister:

Give life and health to our brothers and sisters on whom we lay our hands in your name: Lord, have mercy. **R.**

Prayer of Blessing

A minister who is a priest or deacon may, as circumstances suggest, lay his hands on the head of each sick person, and then say the prayer of blessing.

Lord, our God,
you sent your Son into the world
to bear our infirmities
and to endure our sufferings.
For N. and N., your servants who are sick,
we ask that your blessing will give them strength
to overcome their weakness
through the power of patience and the comfort of hope
and that with your aid they will soon be restored to health.

We ask this through Christ our Lord.

R. Amen.

Or, without the laying on of hands:

Lord Jesus,
who went about doing good and healing all,
we ask you to bless your friends who are sick.
Give them strength in body, courage in spirit, and patience with pain.
Let them recover their health,
so that, restored to the Christian community,
they may joyfully praise your name,
for you live and reign for ever and ever.

R. Amen.

A lay minister traces the sign of the cross on the forehead of each sick person and says the following prayer of blessing.

Lord, our God,
who watch over your creatures with unfailing care,
keep us in the safe embrace of your love.
With your strong right hand raise up your servants (N. and N.)
and give them the strength of your own power.
Minister to them and heal their illnesses,
so that they may have from you the help they long for.

We ask this through Christ our Lord.

R. Amen.

Or, for one sick person:

Lord and Father, almighty and eternal God,
by your blessing you give us strength and support in our frailty:
turn with kindness toward this your servant N.
Free him/her from all illness and restore him/her to health,
so that in the sure knowledge of your goodness
he/she will gratefully bless your holy name.

We ask this through Christ our Lord.

R. Amen.

After the prayer of blessing, the minister invites all present to pray for the protection of the Blessed Virgin. They may do so by singing or reciting a Marian antiphon, for example, We turn to you for protection (Sub tuum praesidium) *or Hail, Holy Queen.*

Concluding Rites

A minister who is a priest or a deacon concludes the rite by facing the sick and saying:

May God the Father bless you.

R. Amen.

May God the Son comfort you.

R. Amen.

May God the Holy Spirit enlighten you.

R. Amen.

Then he blesses all present.
And may almighty God bless you all,
the Father, and the Son, and the Holy Spirit.

R. Amen.

A lay minister invokes the Lord's blessing on the sick and all present by signing himself or herself with the sign of the cross and saying:
May the Lord Jesus Christ,
who went about doing good and healing the sick,
grant that we may have good health
and be enriched by his blessings.
R. Amen.

C. Shorter Rite

The minister says:

Our help is in the name of the Lord.

All reply:

Who made heaven and earth.

One of those present or the minister reads a text of sacred Scripture, for example:

2 Corinthians 1:3-4

Blessed be the God and Father of our Lord Jesus Christ, the Father of compassion and God of all encouragement, who encourages us in our every affliction, so that we may be able to encourage those who are in any affliction with the encouragement with which we ourselves are encouraged by God.

Matthew 11:28-29

Jesus said: "Come to me, all you who labor and are burdened, and I will give you rest. Take my yoke upon you and learn from me, for I am meek and humble of heart; and you will find rest for yourselves. For my yoke is easy, and my burden light."

As circumstances suggest, a minister who is a priest or deacon may lay hands on the sick person while saying the prayer of blessing; a lay minister may trace the sign of the cross on the sick person's forehead while saying the prayer.

Lord and Father, almighty and eternal God,
by your blessing you give us strength and support in our frailty:
turn with kindness toward your servant, N.
Free him/her from all illness and restore him/her to health, so that in the sure knowledge of your goodness
he/she will gratefully bless your holy name.

We ask this through Christ our Lord.

R. Amen.

Prayers from the tradition of local Churches

Akathistos hymn[6]

Biblical-liturgical section

1. The foremost of the Angels was sent down from Heaven to say "Hail!" to the Mother of God.
At his greeting of spirit, not earth,
when he saw you made flesh in her womb,
saving Lord,
your Angel was joyful,
proclaiming your Mother's great praise:

2. Since well Mary knew of her virginal calling,
with courage to th'Angel she spoke:
"Your singular word of announcement seems strange for my spirit to grasp and to know;
from the womb of a virgin a child you fortell,
as you cry: Alleluia!"

Rejoice: through you is our joy made resplendent;
Rejoice: through you is our curse now eclipsed.
Rejoice, the saving of Adam who fell;

---

[6] This is one of the most famous hymns of the Greek Church dedicated to the Theotokos (Mother of God). *Akathistos* in Greek means "not-seated", because it is sung or recited while standing as a sign of reverence for Mary, the Holy Mother of God. The structure is inspired by the description of the heavenly Jerusalem in chapters 21-22 of the Book of Revelation to Saint John. It sings of Mary in her identification with the Church, the Virgin Bride of the Lamb. The hymn comprises 24 stanzas which is the number of letters in the Greek alphabet. It is divided in two parts - narrative and dogmatic - in which the beauty of Mary, Mother of Christ and Believers, shines through.

Rejoice, annulment of tears of Eve.
Rejoice, inaccessible summit beyond understanding;
Rejoice, wondrous deepness of depth for the knowledge of angels.
Rejoice, holy place where the King did establish His Throne;
Rejoice, who gave birth to the Life and sustainer of all.
Rejoice, the Star who announces the Dawn;
Rejoice, the Womb wherein God is made Flesh.
Rejoice, for through you is Creation made new;
Rejoice, for its Maker is a Child born through you.
Rejoice, holy Virgin and Bride!

3. The Virgin then pondered
to enter the mystery
and asked of the Angel of God:
"How then can my virginal womb
ever bring forth a child to the world?
You must say!".
Then the Angel most reverently sang of her praises
and said:

4. The Power of the Highest
o'ershadowed and made Mother
the Virgin unknowing of man:
Her womb thus awakened by God,
did become a good field of rich life
unto all who are longing to welcome salvation
and sing forth in praise: Alleluia!

Rejoice, the guide to the planning of God:
Rejoice, the light of a mystery profound.
Rejoice, the first of the wonders of Christ;
Rejoice, in whom all His Truths are brought forth.
Rejoice, stair of Heaven, providing the pathway for God;
Rejoice, for you span the great gulf between Heaven
and Man.

Rejoice, splendid sign whom the choirs of angels proclaim;
Rejoice, fearful scourge of the legions and powers of ill.
Rejoice, o Bearer of ineffable Light;
Rejoice: sole keeper of the means of this sign.
Rejoice, ever greater than knowledge of sages;
Rejoice, in the hearts of the faithful you shine.
Rejoice, holy Virgin and Bride!

5. With the Lord in her womb,
holy Mary most caring,
paid visit and greeted her cousin.
The child whom Elizabeth bore heard
the words that the Virgin pronounced
and was glad,
and with dance for his song he gave praise
to the Mother of God:

6. With his heart in great turmoil,
his thoughts much opposed,
wise Joseph turned backwards and forth:
while seeing you still ever pure,
he feared that you may have been faithless,
o Virgin!
But once having heard of your Child
through the Spirit,
he exclaimed: Alleluia!

Rejoice, o branch of a root that is holy;
Rejoice, the tree with most perfect of Fruit.
Rejoice, you nurture the God of creation;
Rejoice, producing the Planter of life.
Rejoice, holy field bearing fruits of abundance of mercies;
Rejoice, too, the table o'erladen with heavenly gifts.
Rejoice, for you bring shoots of life to a land that was arid;
Rejoice, for you build for the faithful a refuge secure.
Rejoice, fine incense of all supplication;

Rejoice, sweet pardon for sorrowing World.
Rejoice, sign of mercy of God to our Race;
Rejoice, sign of hope of our Race before God.
Rejoice, holy Virgin and Bride!

7. The Shepherds had heard
the great chorus of angels
singing of Christ in our Flesh.
They ran to behold Him the Shepherd,
and looked on Him,
innocent Lamb of the Lord,
being nourished by Mary the Virgin,
to whom they sang praise:

8. In heaven a star pointing out
the Eternal was followed by Wise Men in light.
For them a sure lantern of guidance,
it helped them to seek You, o God,
the Most High.
On attaining the Lord unattainable great was their cry: Alleluia!

Rejoice, o Mother of Shepherd and Lamb;
Rejoice, the Fold for the Faithful of God.
Rejoice, o bolt barring evil assault;
Rejoice, the Key turning Heaven's own door.
Rejoice, for through you all the heavens exult with the earth;
Rejoice, for through you do the earth and the heav'n sing as one.
Rejoice, tireless voice of the chosen Apostles of God;
Rejoice, restless longing of Martyrs whose blood is for Christ.
Rejoice, o powerful foundation for Faith;
Rejoice, o wonderful ensign of Grace.
Rejoice, for through you evil Hell was laid bare;
Rejoice, for through you were we clothed in God's glory.
Rejoice, holy Virgin and Bride!

9. In the hands of His Mother
they saw Him at last, the great God,
whose own hand made us all.
Full well did they know He was Lord,
though hidden in form of a servant,
and gifts did they offer in kindness
and said to His Mother so blest:

10. The heralds of God did the Magi
become on the path back to Babylon bound.
Your prophecy, Lord, they fulfilled,
and your Name, saving Christ,
they announced to the world,
ever heedless of Herod, the foolish,
who never could sing: Alleluia!

Rejoice, o Mother of Sun without setting;
Rejoice, the dawning of spiritual Day.
Rejoice, extinguishing firebrands of falsehood;
Rejoice, o beacon to Trinity's Truth.
Rejoice, for you darken the throne of the Tyrant so hated;
Rejoice, for you show us the Christ of great mercy as Lord.
Rejoice: you absolve us from cruel and terrible rites;
Rejoice, for you save us from murk and the squalor of fate.
Rejoice: the worship of fire you destroy;
Rejoice: the burning of vice you extinguish.
Rejoice, clearest guide for the mind of believers;
Rejoice, purest joy of the world and its peoples.
Rejoice, holy Virgin and Bride!

11. Shining forth into Egypt the splendor of Truth, you drove out the darkness of error:
at your Power of God, blessed Lord,
the Idols fell down in their weakness made naught.
And men being saved to the Mother of God
sang in praise:

12. On the point of departing
this world so deceiving was Simeon,
the watchman, inspired.
As a baby presented, so small,
yet as Lord in perfection
he knew You, o Christ,
and moved by the Wisdom Eternal,
he cried out in praise: Alleluia!

Rejoice, raising up of humanity fallen;
Rejoice, tearing down of the Underworld's Reign.
Rejoice: the trampling of lies and of error;
Rejoice, unmasking idolatry's fraud.
Rejoice, blessed ocean engulfing the Pharaoh supreme;
Rejoice, blessed rock pouring forth the sound waters of Life.
Rejoice, fiery pillar, a light in the darkness for all;
Rejoice, never cloud of protection will shield us like you.
Rejoice: you give us the Manna of Heaven;
Rejoice: you serve us the holiest of Food.
Rejoice, ever spiritual Land of His Promise;
Rejoice, ever flowing with honey and milk.
Rejoice, holy Virgin and Bride!

13. The Maker of all made Creation
anew to appear amid us,
His dear children: the Lord blossomed forth
from the Virgin,
whose Womb He preserved
ever pure and unstained.
Thus thrilled by this wonder
we sing to the Virgin with joy:

14. Enthralled by His birth
we go forth from this world
to consider the wonders of heaven.
In humanity's lowliest likeness,

He came and was born in our midst,
the Most High,
to lead to the heavens all those who acclaim Him
with joy: Alleluia!

Rejoice, bright flower of a life uncorrupted;
Rejoice, chaste crown of possession of self.
Rejoice: awarding a glimpse of the Risen;
Rejoice, unveiling the life of the angels.
Rejoice, fairest plant bearing fruit to be food of the Faithful;
Rejoice, tree of beauty, whose shade is protection for all.
Rejoice: in your Womb you bore Him who would guide those who wander;
Rejoice: you brought forth to the light the Releaser of slaves.
Rejoice, People's plea to the righteous Judge;
Rejoice, forgiveness for all who are lost.
Rejoice, welcome garment for souls stripped of grace;
Rejoice, fullest love more than any desire.
Rejoice, holy Virgin and Bride!

15. He came to His earth
yet the heav'ns still
were filled by God's Word
in His infinite glory.
Our God, not by changing His place,
but inclining most humbly in love to our race,
was born of the Virgin, the Mother,
to whom we declare:

16. Amazed were the angels
to witness the awesome event
of your bless'd Incarnation:
inaccessible God above all they saw giving access to us in our Flesh, and dwelling with us,
so that each can acclaim You and cry: Alleluia!

Rejoice, o Throne of the infinite God;
Rejoice, the door of the Mystery sublime.
Rejoice, sure Truth which unsettles th'incredulous;
Rejoice, reliable boast for believers.
Rejoice, holy dwelling more holy than the throne of the Cherubim;
Rejoice, precious vessel more blessed than the throne of the Seraphim.
Rejoice: for in you are extremes of greatness united;
Rejoice: for together as one you are Virgin and Mother.
Rejoice: in you came forgiveness of sin;
Rejoice: in you Heaven's gates were flung wide.
Rejoice, blessed key of the Kingdom of Christ;
Rejoice, hopeful way to the treasure of God.
Rejoice, holy Virgin and Bride!

17. The finest of speakers
are silent as fish before you,
holy Mother of God.
Never word from their lips
will express how a Mother you are,
yet a Virgin remain.
But we, full of wonder can sing
of the Mystery in faith:

18. To save the creation the Lord
of the universe freely
came down to the earth.
The God, who was always our Shepherd,
now chose to appear in our midst as the Lamb;
in our image He called us whose image we are,
thus we pray: Alleluia!

Rejoice, o vessel of Wisdom Eternal;
Rejoice, the treasure of God's loving care.
Rejoice: you show how the clever are foolish;

Rejoice: you send into silence the wise.
Rejoice: before you subtle schemes of disputors are stupid;
Rejoice: before you mortal myths and their makers are empty.
Rejoice: all the sophists are snared in confusion by you;
Rejoice: simple fishermen catch their fulfillment in you.
Rejoice: you draw us from depths of dark error;
Rejoice, great lighthouse to lead us to Truth.
Rejoice, saving vessel for those who seek Rescue;
Rejoice, port and haven on seaways of life.
Rejoice, holy Virgin and Bride!

19. Defender of virgins
who follow your way,
are you, blessed Virgin and Mother:
for thus, Purest Creature,
He made you,
the Lord who holds sway over Heaven and Earth,
as He dwelt in your Womb
while inviting us all to proclaim:

20. No song has been written
that ever could equal your numberless graces, o Lord.
Indeed, were we offering canticles countless
as grains in the sand of the sea,
we never could compass your gifts
to your servants,
who sing: Alleluia!

Rejoice, blest column of holy virginity;
Rejoice, o passage and portal to Rescue.
Rejoice, beginning of birth for the spirit;
Rejoice: bringing forth all the bounty of God.
Rejoice: you have given back Life to those born in disgrace;
Rejoice, for in you have the foolish found fulness of wisdom.
Rejoice: the Seducer of Hearts was made pow'rless by You;
Rejoice: the Begetter of Chastity touched us through you.

Rejoice: where Heaven and Earth are encoupled;
Rejoice: where Faithful and Lord are made one.
Rejoice, loving Woman: you nourish all virgins;
Rejoice, holy Maid: you lead brides to the Groom.
Rejoice, holy Virgin and Bride!

21. We look to the Virgin most holy,
the beacon who brightens the camp of our darkness.
In her shines the light of God's presence:
she shows us the way to the knowledge of God.
A splendour is she for our minds
as all praise her with song:

22. His wish to redeem
that most ancient of Debts
brought the Savior to dwell in our midst.
In His person was payment for all,
who had lost every title to gift of God's Grace.
He cancelled Sin's charter and therefore
we chant in His praise: Alleluia!

Rejoice, bright ray of the Sunlight of Heaven;
Rejoice, the beam of a Light never setting.
Rejoice, clear lightning to flash in our minds;
Rejoice, o thunder of fear for our foes.
Rejoice, for from you comes the Light who illumines the world;
Rejoice, blessed spring giving manifold waters of Life.
Rejoice, Pool of Healing where people were bathed as of old;
Rejoice, for in you comes the One who now washes our sins.
Rejoice, bless'd Font where our souls are made pure;
Rejoice, the cup overflowing with joy:
Rejoice, pleasant fragrance of Christ who anoints us;
Rejoice, from whose life comes the Mystical Banquet.
Rejoice, holy Virgin and Bride!

23. At the birth of your Son
all His creatures rejoice,

Living Temple, o Bearer of God.
Your Womb was the worthiest dwelling of Him
who holds all in His hand as the Lord.
Most holy and glorious
He made you and taught us to sing:

24. O merciful Mother:
who bear us the greatest of Saints,
God's own Word ever holy:
accept, in your kindness, our song!
From every misfortune and malice preserve us!
From threatening punishment free us,
your children who call: Alleluia!

Rejoice, o Tent where God's Word finds repose;
Rejoice, excelling the "Holy of Holies".
Rejoice, the Ark that the Spirit has burnished;
Rejoice, unfailing rich treasure of Life.
Rejoice, precious crown: saintly Rulers acclaim you their glory;
Rejoice, noble banner: good priests all proclaim you their boast.
Rejoice, mighty fortress defending the Church of the Lord;
Rejoice, wall of strength for protecting the Nations of God.
Rejoice: through you spoils of vict'ry are raised;
Rejoice: through you the great enemies fall.
Rejoice, healing remedy, curing my weakness;
Rejoice, for my soul finds salvation with you.
Rejoice, holy Virgin and Bride!

The *Stella Caeli Extirpavit* Chant in Time of Pestilence[7]

The Star of Heaven that nourished the Lord
drove away the plague of death
which the first parents of man brought into the world.
May this bright Star now vouchsafe to extinguish
that foul constellation whose battles have
slain the people with the wound of death.
O Glorious Star of the Sea,
preserve us from pestilence;
hear us, O Lady, for Thy Son honors
Thee by denying Thee nothing.
Save us, O Jesus,
for whom Thy Virgin Mother supplicates Thee.
O most pious Star of the Sea, preserve us from pestilence;
hear us, O Lady,
for Thy Son honors Thee by denying Thee nothing.
Save us, O Jesus,
for whom Thy Virgin Mother supplicates Thee

---

[7] Ancient hymn asking for an end to pestilence, within the Franciscan tradition. The source of the chant can be traced back to the seraphic tradition of the Franciscans: See https://sspx.org/en/news-events/news/stella-coeli-extirpavit-prayer-our-lady-times-pestilence-56625.

Saint Patrick's Breastplate[8]

I arise today through
God's strength to pilot me,
God's might to uphold me,
God's wisdom to guide me,
God's eye to see before me,
God's ear to hear me,
God's word to speak for me,
God's hand to guard me,
God's way to lie before me,
God's shield to protect me,
God's host to secure me –
against snares of devils,
against temptations and vices,
against inclinations of nature,
against everyone who shall wish me ill,
afar and anear,
alone and in a crowd...

Christ, be with me, Christ before me, Christ behind me,
Christ in me, Christ beneath me, Christ above me,
Christ on my right, Christ on my left,
Christ where I lie, Christ where I sit,
Christ where I arise,

---

[8] *St Patrick's Breastplate* is a prayer beseeching protection. It is also known as "*The Deer's Cry*", the "*Lorica of St Patrick*", or "*St Patrick's Hymn*". Tradition attributes it's authorship to St Patrick who composed it during his ministry to the people of Ireland in the 5th century.

Christ in the heart of every man who thinks of me,
Christ in the mouth of every man who speaks of me,
Christ in every eye that sees me,
Christ in every ear that hears me.
May your salvation, O Lord, be ever with us.

Act of offering[9]

Lord, what You will let it be so
Where You will there we will go
What is Your will help us to know.

Lord, when You will the time is right
In You there's joy in strife
For Your will I'll give my life.

To ease Your burden brings no pain
To forego all for You is gain
As long as I in You remain.

Because You will it, it is best
Because You will it, we are blest
Till in Your hands our hearts find rest
Till in Your hands our hearts find rest.

---

[9] Blessed Rupert Mayer, SJ (1876-1945), Jesuit priest: dedicated to fighting injustice, great preacher, who, beginning in the 1920s demonstrated the irreconcilable differences between the Christian Faith and National Socialism. He was arrested and interned in various concentration camps to the point that his health was seriously compromised. This is one of his prayers of trusting abandonment to the Lord in a time of difficulty.

Thematic Index *

---

* This thematic index indicates the themes, rather than specific words, that appear most frequently in the homilies, messages, *Angelus* and *Regina Coeli* discourses collected in this volume. The numbers, therefore, refer to the initial page of the Pope's address and not to the precise page on which the word appears: This is intended to help the reader to contextualize the theme within the Pontiff's arguments, to grasp all its richness and depth.

CPSIA information can be obtained
at www.ICGtesting.com
Printed in the USA
BVHW032237020820
585292BV00064B/24